MASKS OF CONQUEST

GAURI VISWANATHAN

MASKS OF CONQUEST

Literary Study and British Rule in India

OXFORD
UNIVERSITY PRESS

Oxford University Press is a department of the University of Oxford.
It furthers the University's objective of excellence in research, scholarship,
and education by publishing worldwide. Oxford is a registered trademark of
Oxford University Press in the UK and in certain other countries

Published in India by
Oxford University Press
YMCA Library Building, 1 Jai Singh Road, New Delhi 110001, India

© Columbia University Press 1989

The moral rights of the author have been asserted

This reprint edition is a complete reproduction of the
US edition of 'Masks of Conquest', especially authorized by
the original publisher, Columbia University
Oxford India Paperbacks 1998
Sixth impression 2012

ISBN-13: 978-0-19-564640-5
ISBN-10: 0-19-564640-1

Printed in India by Ram Printograph, Delhi 110 051

FOR MY PARENTS

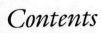

Contents

Acknowledgments

THIS BOOK began as a doctoral dissertation at Columbia University under the astute guidance of Ainslie Embree, Robert Bone, Trygve Tholfsen, and Edward Said. I am very grateful for their intellectual generosity and constructive advice. A Mellon Fellowship at Columbia's Society of Fellows in the Humanities enabled the completion of the book manuscript. The Society provided a warm, supportive environment for writing and research; I owe special thanks to Barbara Stoler Miller for her personal interest and encouragement. Stimulating discussions with Mary Campbell, Richard Andrews, and Peter Sahlins helped sharpen main arguments. I want to thank Gayatri Chakravorty Spivak for her instructive reading of the manuscript and for the many helpful suggestions and comments she took the time to make. I am particularly thankful to my editor, Jennifer Crewe, whose cheerfulness and patient understanding made preparation of the manuscript much less painful. I have benefited from the support of many institutions. The library staffs of Columbia University, the Union Theological Seminary, Teachers College, and the New York Public Library were always resourceful in tracking down elusive material. The National Archives of India, the National Library in Calcutta, and the Madras Literary Society were responsive to many queries. I am grateful to the Executive Council of the University of Delhi for approving a generous leave of absence that permitted me to begin work on this project. I thank Robert Bagg and Murray Schwartz for many courtesies extended by the University of Massachusetts at Amherst. Portions of the book were published in the *Oxford Literary Review* (1987), vol. 9, and *Social Text* (Fall 1988), vol. 7. I am grateful to Robert Young, Aijaz Ahmad, and Bruce Robbins for their encouraging response.

For their continued friendship and sympathetic understanding I am very thankful to Anne McClintock and Rob Nixon. Tim Kelly and Timothy Cabot taught me more about ideology and education than they could ever learn from me. Philip and Veena Oldenburg never failed to rush to my assistance in untangling problems related to computers and Indian history, respectively. Roger Blumberg is much appreciated for his resourcefulness in inventing titles.

The project was sustained in great measure by the reassuring constancy and friendship of Una Chaudhuri, Rupen Guha Majumdar, Lynn Mulkey, Tanusree Raha, Rubina Saigol, and Rachel Trubowitz. My parents were supportive in many ways too.

Finally, to Edward Said, who inspired me to write this book in the first place, I offer my warmest appreciation. The most encouraging of teachers, he deepened the excitement of intellectual inquiry. His friendship, kindness, generosity, and enthusiasm hold these pages together.

MASKS OF CONQUEST

Now we are to behold a literature so full of all qualities of loveliness and purity, such new regions of high thought and feeling . . . that to the dwellers in past days it should have seemed rather the production of angels than of men.
— *Madras Christian Instructor and Missionary Record* (1844), 2(4):195.

We are not afraid of what we do see of the British power, but of what we do not see.
— Tipu Sultan's minister, quoted in *Parliamentary Papers, 1852–53*, 29:42.

Introduction

THIS BOOK is about the institution, practice, and ideology of English studies introduced in India under British colonial rule. It does not seek to be a comprehensive record of the history of English, nor does it even attempt to catalog, in minute historical fashion, the various educational decisions, acts, and resolutions that led to the institutionalization of English. The work draws upon the illuminating insight of Antonio Gramsci, writing on the relations of culture and power, that cultural domination works by consent and can (and often does) precede conquest by force. Power, operating concurrently at two clearly distinguishable levels, produces a situation where, Gramsci writes, "the supremacy of a social group manifests itself in two ways, as 'domination' and as 'intellectual and moral leadership'. . . . It seems clear . . . that there can, and indeed must be hegemonic activity even before the rise to power, and that one should not count only on the material force which power gives in order to exercise an effective leadership."[1]

The importance of moral and intellectual suasion in matters of governance is readily conceded on theoretical grounds as an implicit tactical maneuver in the consolidation of power. There is an almost bland consensus in post-Arnoldian cultural criticism that the age of ideology begins when force gives way to ideas. But the precise mode and process by which cultural domination is ensured is less open to scrutiny. The general approach is to treat "ideology" as a form of masking, and the license given to speculative analyses as a result is sometimes great enough to suspend, at least temporarily, the search for actual intentions.

Admittedly, detailed records of self-incrimination are not routinely preserved in state archives. But where such records do exist the evidence is often compelling enough to suggest that the Gramscian notion is not merely a theoretical construct, but an uncannily accurate description of historical process, subject to the vagaries of particular circumstances. A case in point is British India, whose checkered history of cultural confrontation conferred a sense of urgency to voluntary cultural assimilation as the most effective form of political action. The political choices are spelled out in the most chilling terms by J. Farish in a minute issued in the Bombay Presidency: "The Natives must either be kept down by a sense of our power, or they must willingly submit from a conviction that we are more wise, more just, more humane, and more anxious to improve their condition than any other rulers they could possibly have."[2]

This book sets out to demonstrate in part that the discipline of English came into its own in an age of colonialism, as well as to argue that no serious account of its growth and development can afford to ignore the imperial mission of educating and civilizing colonial subjects in the literature and thought of England, a mission that in the long run served to strengthen Western cultural hegemony in enormously complex ways. It is not enough, as D. J. Palmer, Terry Eagleton, Chris Baldick, Peter Widdowson, and Brian Doyle, among others, seem to believe, to provide token acknowledgment of the role of empire by linking the Indian Civil Service examinations, in which English literature was a major subject, to the promotion of English studies in British schools and universities.[3] Important as these examinations were, they do not indicate the full extent of imperialism's involvement with literary culture. The amazingly young history of English literature as a subject of study (it is less than a hundred and fifty years old) is frequently noted, but less appreciated is the irony that English literature appeared as a subject in the curriculum of the colonies long before it was institutionalized in the home country.[4] As early as the 1820s, when the classical curriculum still reigned supreme in England despite the strenuous efforts of some concerned critics to loosen its hold, English as the study of culture and not simply the study of language had already found a secure place in the British Indian curriculum. The circumstances of its ascendancy are what this book is immediately concerned with, though it also seeks simultaneously to draw attention to the subsequent institutionalization and ideological content of the discipline in England as it developed in the colonial context.

I have two general aims in writing this book: the first is to study the adaptation of the content of English literary education to the administrative and political imperatives of British rule; and the other is to examine the ways in which these imperatives in turn charged that content with a radically altered significance, enabling the humanistic ideals of enlightenment to coexist with and indeed even support education for social and political control. As a description of process, this study is specifically directed at elucidating the relationship between the institutionalization of English in India and the exercise of colonial power, between the processes of curricular selection and the impulse to dominate and control. The curriculum is conceived here not in the perennialist sense of an objective, essentialized entity but rather as discourse, activity, process— as one of the mechanisms through which knowledge is socially distributed and culturally validated.

The history of education in British India shows that certain humanistic functions traditionally associated with literature—for example, the shaping of character or the development of the aesthetic sense or the disciplines of ethical thinking—were considered essential to the processes of sociopolitical control by the guardians of the same tradition. Despite occasional murmurs to the contrary, the notion that these functions are unique to English literature still persists in modern curricular pronouncements, with a consequent blurring of the distinction between "English literature" and "English studies"—a blurring that Richard Poirier noted as a by now more general characteristic of contemporary culture. "English studies," he argues in an essay that still remains timely, has been allowed to appropriate literature in ways "not unarguably belonging to it."[5] The distinction proposed in Poirier's title—"What Is English Studies, and If You Know What That Is, What Is English

Literature?"—is a useful one to bear in mind in connection with British Indian educational history, insofar as it draws attention to literary *education*, as opposed to *literature*, as a major institutional support system of colonial administration. The transformation of literature from its ambivalent "original" state into an instrument of ideology is elsewhere described by another critic, Terry Eagleton, as

> a vital instrument for the insertion of individuals into the perceptual and symbolic forms of the dominant ideological formation. . . . What is finally at stake is not literary texts but Literature—the ideological significance of that process whereby certain historical texts are severed from their social formations, defined as "literature," and bound and ranked together to constitute a series of "literary traditions" and interrogated to yield a set of ideological presupposed responses.[6]

Indeed, once such importance is conceded to the educational function, it is easier to see that values assigned to literature—such as the proper development of character or the shaping of critical thought or the formation of aesthetic judgment—are only problematically located there and are more obviously serviceable to the dynamic of power relations between the educator and those who are to be educated. A vital if subtle connection exists between a discourse in which those who are to be educated are represented as morally and intellectually deficient and the attribution of moral and intellectual values to the literary works they are assigned to read.

Critical consciousness in matters of education is entirely dependent on perceiving and illuminating the unique role of such representations in producing and sustaining structures of domination. In specific terms, it involves determining the degree to which representation of moral and intellectual ideals forms the substratum of educational discourse and then linking such representation to the changing structure of relationships between those for whom educational prescriptions are made and those who arrogate to themselves the status of "prescriber." Unfortunately histories of modern Indian education abound in a mass of detail of event and place that often obscures the expressive context within which those events occurred.

Of course, it will be argued that any verbal act is a representation and that no analysis of reality can ever be devoid of ideological content as long as it is encoded in language. Therefore, the suggestion that modern Indian education grew out of a body of utterances that embodied the collective attitudes of a hegemonic class will not appear to many to merit further examination to the degree that it is suggested here as necessary. But the point of my argument is that language functions at different *levels* of mediation and the language of educational discourse is itself part of a larger representational system that provides the superstructure for what Edward Said has called "methodological attitudes." It is hoped illumination of the embedding of educational discourse in that system will check the propensity of formerly colonized societies to employ upon themselves the structures of cultural domination inherent in the language of educational discourse.

AMONG THE several broad areas of emphases in this book the first and perhaps most important is that the history of English and that of Indian developments in the same areas are related but at the same time quite separate. I stress the word *separate* to indicate the gap between functions and uses of literary education in England and in India, despite the comparability of content at various points. I refer specifically to such instances as differing uses of the same curricula, the different status of various literary genres like romantic narrative, lyric poetry, and pastoral drama, and different conceptions of mind and character that marginalized the work of such Orientalist scholars as William Jones in the context of Indian educational policy while simultaneously elevating to a new status in British literary and educational culture those same "Oriental" tales denounced for their deleterious effects on Indian morals and character.

One of the great contradictions in early nineteenth-century developments is uncovered at the level of comparison of the educational histories of England and India. With the educational context, one runs head-on into the central paradox of British deliberations on the curriculum as prescribed for both England and India: while Englishmen of all ages could enjoy and appreciate exotic tales, romantic narrative, adventure stories, and mythological literature for their charm and even derive instruction from them,[7] their colonial subjects were believed incapable of doing so because they lacked the prior mental and moral cultivation required for literature—especially their own—to have any instructive value for them.[8] A play like Kalidas' *Shakuntala*, which delighted Europeans for its pastoral beauty and lyric charm and led Horace Wilson, a major nineteenth-century Sanskrit scholar, to call it the jewel of Indian literature, was disapproved of as a text for study in Indian schools and colleges, and the judgment that "the more popular forms of [Oriental literature] are marked with the greatest immorality and impurity" held sway.[9] The inability to discriminate between decency and indecency was deemed to be a fixed characteristic of the native mind, a symptom of the "dulness of their comprehension."[10] Clearly such a statement suggests that it is not the morality of literature that is at issue, but the mental capabilities of the reader. Raising Indians to the intellectual level of their Western counterparts constituted a necessary prerequisite to literary instruction, especially in texts from the native culture, and consequently to forestalling the danger of having unfortified minds falsely seduced by the "impurities" of the traditional literature of the East.

But far from resulting in a markedly different curriculum from the English, this view of Indian character produced almost an identical one, though qualified by stipulated prerequisites. The claim that literature can be read meaningfully only when a high degree of morality and understanding is present in the reader implied that certain controlled measures were necessary to bring the reader up to the desired level. But paradoxically, those measures took the form of instruction in that same literature for which preparation was deemed necessary. To raise the reader to a level of morality that would better prepare him to read literature effectively, the method that was struck on was instruction in Western aesthetic principles; by giving young Indians a taste for the arts and literature of England, "we might insensibly wean their affections from the Persian muse, teach them to despise the barbarous splendour of their ancient princes, and, totally supplanting the tastes which flourished under the Mogul reign, make them look to this country with that veneration, which the youthful student feels for the classical soil of Greece."[11] At the same time the self-justification of the literature curriculum—its use as both method and object of moral and intellectual study—remained the central problematic of British ideology, its authority necessarily requiring external support and validation to be more than merely self-confirming.

Clearly the relatedness of the two histories is no less real than their separateness, but I do not find it particularly useful to argue in behalf of a common pattern of development if the chief intent is to indicate simultaneity, identity of purpose, and parallelism of design. Suggesting that the educational histories of England and India constitute a common history invariably communicates the erroneous impression that the functions of education remain constant regardless of context. The view that a humanistic education holds the same meaning and purpose for both colonizer and colonized quickly crumbles under the weight of even the most casual scrutiny. On the other hand, tightening what appears in the above construction to be an arbitrarily conceived relation by alternatively proposing a cause-effect paradigm veers toward quite the other extreme, imputing an overly reductive determinism to the colonialist project and proposing equivalences between the composition of the various groups, including both rulers and ruled, that grossly oversimplify a complex, heterogeneous formation. As tempting as it is to read, say, Matthew Arnold's *Culture and Anarchy* and British Parliamentary Papers on Indian education as parallel cultural texts outlining a common strategy of social and political control, there are great dangers in reading the history of the education of Indians exclusively in terms of the education of the English lower classes. There are obvious differences, the two most important being, first, a well-entrenched learned class in India that was recognized by the British themselves as continuing to exert power and influence over the people, and second, a policy of religious neutrality that paralyzed British officials in administering a religious curriculum to the Indians comparable to the one taught in English parish schools and charity schools. Under the circumstances, the educational model of the West was inadequate to deal with the learned classes of India, possessing as the latter did their own deeply rooted systems of learning and institutions of specialized studies in philology, theology, and ancient science. In what must be described as a wryly ironic commentary on literary history, the inadequacy of the English model resulted in fresh pressure being applied to a seemingly innocuous and not yet fully formed discipline, English literature, to perform the functions of those social institutions (such as the church) that, in England, served as the chief disseminators of value, tradition, and authority. The surrogate functions that English literature acquired in India offer a powerful explanation for the more rapid institutionalization of the discipline in the Indian colony than in the country where it originated.

The heterogeneity of the colonial population and its quite different relation to institutional structures as understood and practiced in England prompted a series of experiments that could not readily be tried out in England because of well-defined church-state relations and firmly entrenched orthodoxies and traditions prevailing there. Well before any other group, missionaries perceived the East India Company's secularist policy to be a calculated response to a cultural situation in England in which the secular practice of education had virtually been driven underground by the aristocratic and clerical orders. Protesting what they saw as governmental arrogance in severing Indian education from the influence of religious culture, missionaries were led to suspect that the official policy of secularism in India had been instituted in a spirit of experimentation and that India was merely being used as a "fair and open field for testing the non-religion theory of education."[12] On the evidence of communications between the Court of Directors and the governor-general-in-council in Calcutta, there is strong support for the view that India had become an experimental laboratory for testing educational ideas that had either been abandoned in England or fallen victim to insuperable opposition from entrenched traditions and orthodoxies. Because the East India Company perceived the colonized culture as lacking in counteractive influences (by which was meant direct church control) it considered India fertile ground for experimentation with untested ideas and observing and recording their effects under controlled conditions. The classical study of English as language, without the cultural, social, and religious associations it had in England, was enabled by a secular approach to fields of knowledge that were considered objects of study in and for themselves. If secularism in the British control of India eventually faced the kind of opposition it experienced in England and English studies abandoned its secular character to acquire overtly religious and cultural functions, it was largely due to the fierce resistance put up by missionaries who unequivocally denounced secular education as an expression of British middle-class, laissez-faire interests.

The relation between the educational histories of England and India is best understood as structured on the principle of complementarity. By complementarity I mean a dynamic interaction of interests whose resolution is not necessarily confined to the context in which any given concern originates but extends actively to those contexts that provide the soil for such resolution. Practically speaking, the point of reference for a dilemma encountered in India may conceivably be a comparable situation in England that demonstrably yielded effective solutions, and vice versa. Complementarity does not imply that one precedes or causes the other, nor that both are parallel, arbitrarily related developments with few or no points of contact. Its defining characteristic is the capacity for transference, in criss-cross fashion, of any one or more of these factors—subject, agent, event, intention, purpose—not in the sense of wholesale borrowing, but of readaptation. The degree to which transference is enabled or alternatively thwarted by elements in the society for which solution is sought provides the outlines for demarcation of each new block of history.[13]

The interactive dynamism, the fluidity of movement between social contexts, at once promoting and resisting change, is effectively captured in the model proposed by Raymond Williams in his brief critique of Lukács in "Base and Superstructure in Marxist Cultural Analysis." Williams persuasively argues that while it is accurate to define society as a set of practices that allow it to function as a society, such an exercise cannot be undertaken without also showing that it has a specific organization and structure directly related to certain social intentions, "intentions by which we define the society, intentions which have been the rule of a particular class."[14]

As Williams goes on to argue, to subscribe to a notion of totality that presents society monolithically as "composed of a large number of social practices which form a concrete social whole that interact, relate, and combine in very complicated ways" is to advance a static model that systematically closes off the possibility of an inner dynamics at work, both in the thrust toward and the resistance to historical change. Williams quite clearly wishes to see culture and society studied in terms of process and has therefore little use for a static or highly determined, rule-governed model in which the rules of society are highlighted to the exclusion of the processual and the historical.

But though intentionality as Williams uses it may seem merely another term for determination, it would be a mistake to infer that by this he means unmediated control. Rather, he sees the determinative principle in intention as more closely allied with the notion of "setting of limits" and "exertion of pressure." Williams' reading of intention as a "setting of limits" allows for the possibility of conflict, for the crucial nodes where constraints are placed are more readily identifiable as the places where resistance may occur against the gross "exertion of pressure." Indeed, Williams' main contribution is in offering a dynamic model that will permit one to study culture and society in terms of how social will or intention (the terms are interchangeable) is engaged in an unceasing activity of circumscribing human behavior on the one hand and diluting resistance to the authority it represents on the other. To know the "social intentions" by which a society is defined is thus to identify not only the potential places where the collective will seeks to assert itself, but also where it is most subject to the fracturing and dissipation caused by extreme pressure.

THE FACT that English literary study had its beginnings as a strategy of containment raises the question, Why literature? If indeed the British were the unchallenged military power of India, why was the exercise of direct force discarded as a means of maintaining social control? What accounts for the British readiness to turn to a disciplinary branch of knowledge to perform the task of administering their colonial subjects? What was the assurance that a disguised form of authority would be more successful in quelling potential rebellion among the natives than a direct show of force? By what reasoning did literary texts come to signify religious faith, empirically verifiable truth, and social duty? Why introduce English in the first place only to work at strategies to balance its secular tendencies with moral and religious ones?

These questions suggest a vulnerability in the British position that is most sharply felt when the history of British rule is read in light of the construction of ideology. There is little doubt that a great deal of strategic maneuvering went into the creation of a blueprint for social control in the guise of a humanistic program of enlightenment. But merely acknowledging this fact is not enough, for there is yet a further need to distinguish between strategy as unmediated assertion of authority and strategy as mediated response to situational imperatives. That is to say, it is important to determine whether British educational measures were elaborated from an uncontested position of superiority and strength and as such are to be read as unalloyed expressions of ethnocentric sentiment or whether that position itself was a fragile one that it was the role of educational decisions to fortify, given the challenge posed by historical contingency and confrontation.

The argument of this book leans toward the second proposition, specifically, that the introduction of English represented an embattled response to historical and political pressures: to tensions between the East India Company and the English Parliament, between Parliament and missionaries, between the East India Company and the Indian elite classes. The vulnerability of the British, the sense of beleaguerment and paranoid dread, is reflected in defensive mechanisms of control that were devised in anticipation of what British administrators considered almost certain rebellion by natives against actions and decisions taken by the

British themselves. The inordinate attention paid by parliamentary discussions and debates and correspondence between the Court of Directors and the governor-general to *anticipated* reactions by the native population to, for example, the teaching of the Bible or the termination of funds for the support of Oriental learning is often in excess of accounts of *actual* response.

This leads one to surmise that a scenario unfolded in British policy-making that did not necessarily correspond with what was in reality occurring in the subjugated population. At one level, representation of Indians as morally and intellectually deficient provided the ameliorative motive and self-righteous justification for colonial intervention. But at another level that same system of representation, depicting the natives as irrational, inscrutable, unstable, and volatile, doomed British rulers to inhabiting an imagined, dreaded world of imminent rebellion and resistance. British disorientation and disengagement from an immediate Indian social and political reality can be dated back to the Cornwallis period (1786–1793). The reorganization of administrative machinery set in motion by Lord Cornwallis, whose ambition was to achieve an impersonal government of law, produced greater distance between rulers and ruled as a result of the gradual removal of Indians from offices of responsibility. In the absence of the direct interaction with the indigenous population that characterized earlier administrations, the colonial subject was reduced to a conceptual category, an object emptied of all personal identity to accommodate the knowledge already established and being circulated about the "native Indian." The strategies of British administrators, the reversals, the disavowals, the imagined successes, and the imagined failures are all part of an unstable foundation of knowledge, and the experiment in control that was born of it—the introduction of English education—was as much an effort, however feeble, at strengthening that foundation as an instrument of discipline and management.

For this reason it is entirely possible to study the ideology of British education quite independently of an account of how Indians actually received, reacted to, imbibed, manipulated, reinterpreted, or resisted the ideological content of British literary education. In the first place, the question of the success or efficacy of the British ideology is better reserved for studies employing a mode of analysis that is not restricted to the literary, textual analysis with which this book is mainly concerned. But methodological considerations aside, not only is an account of why

Indians might want to believe the British ideology given their own intentions and of how they manipulated it and selectively reinterpreted it for their own purposes outside the scope of this book; it is in fact irrelevant to it. To be sure, the charge of conspiring to erase the voice of the colonized and blot out his identity will remain to some extent and must be contended with at the outset. Yet it is not generally realized how infinitely more binding the tyranny of representation can be on the colonizer than it is on the colonized, for if the colonial subject is a construct emanating from the colonizer's head, and therefore removed from history, the history to which the British administrator responds— the impending "event" to which his measures are so crucially attached— is real only to the extent that it provides the rationale for his actions. How the native *actually* responds is so removed from the colonizer's representational system, his understanding of the meaning of events, that it enters into the realm of another history of which the latter has no comprehension or even awareness. That history can, and perhaps must, be told separately for its immensely rich and complex quality to be fully revealed.

Indeed, to record the Indian response to ideology is no more an act of restoring the native's voice as not recording it is to render him mute. As Benita Parry points out in a penetrating essay, neither the critical positions against universalizing narratives nor the "self-righteous rhetoric of resistance" that is limited to "devices circumventing and interrogating colonial authority" sufficiently recognizes the colonized as possessor of another knowledge and history and as producer of alternative traditions.[15] Edward Said illuminatingly describes the process of negation initiated in the mind of the colonizer thus:

> The journey, the history, the fable, the stereotype, the polemical confrontation . . . are the lenses through which the Orient is experienced, and they shape the language, perception, and form of the encounter between East and West. . . . Something patently foreign and distant acquires, for one reason or another, a status more rather than less familiar. One tends to stop judging things either as completely novel or as completely well-known; a new median category emerges, a category that allows one to see new things, things seen for the first time, as versions of a previously known thing. In essence such a category is not so much a way of receiving new information as it is a method of controlling what seems to be a threat to some established view of things. . . . The threat is muted, familiar values impose themselves, and in the end the mind reduces the pressure upon it by accommodating things to itself as either "original" or "repetitious."[16]

To illustrate with a relevant episode from British Indian history, out of deference to Indian religious sentiment the Bible was proscribed in Indian schools and colleges. But teaching of the Bible was a sensitive issue more from the point of view of the British than the Indians. It was often remarked that fear of the Bible was really an English, not a Hindu one and had its origins in the objections of Roman Catholics. Those objections, which came out of a bitter European religious history of acrimony and dissent, were transposed onto a contrived, culturally homogenized Indian situation, strengthening the conviction that instruction in the Bible was sure to meet with violent hostility from Hindus and Muslims. The fact that reports to the contrary ("The Hindus despise our Bible; they do not believe it is the power of God to upset their whole system. . . . They care as little for the Bible in its religious character as we do for Homer")[17] were little heeded indicates the degree to which the heterogeneity of Indian tradition, society, and culture was glided over in the rush to appropriate it to the pattern of European religious history.

But that heterogeneity remained to enable the writing of an altogether different history of response from the one being fashioned by the rulers. Autobiographies, journals, and memoirs of nineteenth-century Indians reveal quite a different perspective on the issue of Bible instruction: far from attaching the absolutist values to it that their rulers thought was the case, they were indisputably guided more by instrumental motives. Lal Behari Day, biographer and former student of the Scottish missionary Alexander Duff, records that his father had worked out an elaborate plan to give his son a good English education without exposing him to the dangers of proselytism in a mission school: he would wait for the moment when his son had learned enough English to obtain a decent situation outside, but was not yet intellectually advanced to understand lectures on Christianity—as soon as that moment arrived, he would instantly be withdrawn from school and placed in an office.

YET ANOTHER reason for not establishing the effects of English education as a point of reference for studying British ideology is the methodological tyranny that such an orientation is heir to. Histories of Indian education, particularly of the British period, typically fall into a fairly predictable pattern. They are in quite a number of instances written as a history of acts and resolutions whose interest lies in their presumed effect on the existing social and cultural system. The broad questions addressed are frequently not dissimilar to these: What political and social relationships are altered, modified, redefined, or at the other extreme perhaps maintained or perpetuated? What new behaviors or modes of thought are promoted? What institutions are brought into existence, and what impression do they leave upon the social fabric? From this sample of questions it is apparent that such histories tend to be written in terms of the transformative influence of educational decisions on the pattern of behavior and action in that society. Therefore, though the starting point may be a specific resolution, educational historians have chosen to concern themselves less with what goes into its making—the discourse that led to its formulation, the expressive context in which the event occurred—than with the outcome it had with regard to the targeted population.

The consequence of this methodological choice is that the changes wrought upon the society and its individual members then become the basis for qualitative descriptions of the historical function of any given educational decision. On the surface Bruce McCully's *English Education and the Origins of Indian Nationalism* does not seem particularly insidious in that it takes as its subject the reversal of colonialism through the very agency of its dissemination. The book is a documentation of the thesis that the growth of Indian nationalism was spurred by the formal training of Indians in the liberal doctrines of Western thought. That thesis is supported by descriptions of the educated Indian class—their backgrounds, their reading, their engagement in political and literary activities, their involvement in matters relating to social reform. By focusing so minutely on the activities of this class of Indians, McCully's ostensible purpose is to show how the education they received provided them with the tools for questioning colonial authority and eventually subverting it. But on the subject of precisely how English education worked toward this end or how it was so specially constituted as to produce the reaction that it did McCully is remarkably silent. He is equally taciturn about what British administrators set out to do by introducing an education based on English principles or what changes that purpose underwent in the course of its institutional development— changes that, I shall contend here, were more in the nature of attempts to mediate the secularized, dehistoricized, and therefore potentially disruptive brand of literary instruction that the British themselves had introduced to Indians.

The other study that I single out for contributing to the same sort of tacit valorization of British educational policies is David Kopf's *British Orientalism and the Bengal Renaissance*. Kopf's thesis, put quite simply, is that the dynamics of Indian modernization were set in motion by British Orientalism, or the cultural policy of promoting Oriental learning in India. Like McCully, Kopf proceeds from an observation that there developed during the late eighteenth century an Indian national consciousness vigorously directed to a renaissance of the arts and sciences. From this observation he infers that Orientalism, far from being the moribund policy that it was thought to be, was in fact the instrument for achieving a transformation of Indian society along modern lines. His message is substantially not very different from McCully's: were it not for British mediation, the Indians would have never been acquainted with their own culture or recognized the possibilities of national growth on indigenous foundations. Though Kopf claims to use this understanding to show that modernization need not necessarily mean Westernization, the terms of his descriptions indicate otherwise:

> The Orientalists served as avenues linking the regional elite with the dynamic civilization of contemporary Europe. They contributed to the formation of a new Indian middle class and assisted in the professionalization of the Bengali intelligentsia. They started schools, systematized languages, brought printing and publishing to India, and encouraged the proliferation of books, journals, newspapers, and other media of communication. Their impact was urban and secular. They built the first modern scientific labs in India, and taught European medicine. They were neither static classicists nor averse to the idea of progress; and they both historicized the Indian past and stimulated a consciousness of history in the Indian intellectual. It was they who transmitted a new sense of identity to Bengalis that enlarged what Robert Bellah has called "the capacity for rational goal setting," an instrumental process in the development of a modern outlook.[18]

What clearly makes it possible for Kopf to credit the Orientalists with the appearance of a cohesive native population is the unquestioned assumption that the latter had neither a sense of national history nor a historical consciousness from which a distinct identity could be shaped. If a heightened national consciousness emerged in the late eighteenth century among the Bengali elite, the only possible explanation for it in Kopf's analysis is the introduction of institutions and ideas developed in the West. It is a premise that encourages him to focus almost exclusively on these institutions as the cause of an enlightened Bengali intelligentsia.

By reading Indian educational history in terms of the impact of policy on individuals and on the native society at large, both McCully and Kopf leave unresolved the relationship of effect and intention, with the result that motive is either subordinated to effect or effect made an arbitrary outcome of intention. In both cases, effect takes on a separate existence of its own, empirically distinct and historically independent of its generating principle. For the same reason, a quasi-innocence is imputed to intention: by perceiving effect as an incidental rather than willed outcome, McCully frees himself from the obligation of having to determine the motive force of English education, as does Kopf from that of British Orientalism. What lies beneath the event—the shaping discourse or informing idea—is either treated as too indeterminate for analysis or made synonymous with cause. In studying Indian nationalism as a by-product of English education, McCully implicitly draws upon a causal model to suggest that the only grounds on which it can be meaningfully understood are those that demand our submitting to a sense of randomness and unpredictability of event—in other words, to see Indian nationalism as a complete and unexpected reversal of the aims of British education by virtue of being an all too faithful application of its lessons.

This mode of explanation compels an ironic reading of the history of Indian nationalism, instilling an exaggerated sense of contrast between the assimilation into the rulers' culture that Western education could be expected to ensure and the subversion it instead helped to promote. Far from allowing the ideological contradictions of the situation to emerge, a forced antithesis of this kind causes the phenomenon of Indian nationalism to be interpreted as the product of an unmediated form of English thought, with the ideas of the Western liberal tradition seeming to seep into the Indian mind in a benignly osmotic fashion. Implicit in this model of incidental causality is a certain political innocence in the British decision to introduce English education of the kind best exemplified in Macaulay's speech before the House of Commons:

> What is power worth if it is founded on vice, on ignorance, and on misery; if we can hold it only by violating the most sacred duties which as governors we owe to the governed and which, as a people blessed with far more than ordinary measure of political liberty and of intellectual light, we owe to a race debased by three thousand years of despotism and priest-

craft. We are free, we are civilized to little purpose, if we grudge to any portion of the human race an equal measure of freedom and civilization.[19]

The view represented in this passage is that British colonialism knowingly put the tools of enlightenment into the hands of the subjects at the risk of endangering its own position. From it further springs the general historical judgment that the Western commitment to the ideals of liberal thought was so unqualified that it took complete precedence over whatever political apprehensions were bound to prevail.

This sort of description demands that we subscribe to two notions: first, that the functions of education remain constant regardless of context or circumstance, so that a humanistic education would have the same meanings and serve the same purposes for both colonizer and colonized, the ruling class and the class it rules; and second, that the curricular elaboration of a given body of knowledge or thought is a faithful representation of that content as it occurs in its free, unbounded, non-institutional form. Both notions construe the reading experience as a direct and open source of attitudes, beliefs, and ideas whose transmission is entirely unmediated by the political and historical realities that in fact affect and influence the processes of education. Indeed, to take account of these realities is inevitably to see reading as a situated activity whose ideas undergo some degree of transformation when filtered through the educational apparatus. In this connection it is well to recall Pierre Bourdieu's admonition that it would be "naive to disregard the fact that the school modifies the content and the spirit of the culture it transmits and above all, that its express function is to transform the collective heritage into a common individual unconscious."[20]

These two notions work together to reinforce the idea that English education had a salutary, emancipatory influence because it released Indians from false consciousness and replaced outmoded styles of thought with enlightened concepts of justice and liberty. If that enlightenment extended to an awareness of British rule as unjust, then it was all the more to be taken as a measure of the success of English education, not its failure.

When converted into methodological axioms, these assumptions contribute to a distinctly colonialist bias in the literature on British Indian education, producing the kinds of formulations seen earlier in the work of McCully and Kopf. If these formulations have persisted over time, it is largely because the curriculum has been perceived as a given and the selection of content understood to be based on well-established canonical principles transcending the immediate realities of time, place, and circumstance. Presumably, the principles of curricular selection are drawn from the principles by which literary knowledge itself is organized—for example, according to genres, periods, and movements. No discrimination is apparently made here between the curriculum and its content; an education in literature is unreservedly identified with the program of perception, thought, and action that is culture.

The effect of such identification is an exclusion of extraliterary considerations, such as the exigencies of the political and historical situation, the power relations between educator and educated, and the relations of curricular content to social structure and modes of social organization. Recent work in educational sociology, particularly that of Pierre Bourdieu, Basil Bernstein, Michael Young, Michael Apple, and Ioann Davies, has attempted to correct this imbalance by reorienting the task of historical inquiry to treating the received categories of the curriculum not as absolutes, but as constructed realities realized in particular institutional contexts. With reference to the literature curriculum the argument can be extended to the dogmas of reason and morality, their problematization being a necessary preliminary to conceiving of non-manipulative, non-coercive alternatives.

A FINAL area of emphasis in this book is concerned with a set of assumptions about human nature that emerges from British parliamentary debates on the political uses of literature in India. These are specifically related on one hand to a transcendental ideal and on the other to a tangible political and social order. An approach to civilization as the humanization of man through various influences, including literature and the arts, raises questions about whether it is at all possible to respond to literature at the level of who we are, in all our "naturalness" and "ordinariness,"[21] or whether the ameliorative project is so indelibly built into the nature of literary instruction as to endorse an implicit dualism of actual and ideal selves. Lionel Gossman points to early British arguments for literary instruction, intensely Calvinist in their formulation, that assumed a condition of innate depravity; the rhetoric of dualism ensuing from that assumption demarcated a "cultivated" self formed by learning, language, and literature, from a "natural" self still burdened by sin, willful pride, and vileness of temperament. The religious import of the dualism persists into the Arnoldian notion of culture as man's "better self," offering him the promise of perfection. In *Culture and Anarchy* Arnold writes:

> The aim of culture [is to set] ourselves to ascertain what perfection is and to make it prevail; but also, in determining generally, in what perfection consists, religion comes to a conclusion identical with that which culture —culture seeking the determination of this question through all the voices of human experience which have been heard upon it, of art, science, poetry, philosophy, history, as well as of religion, in order to give a greater fullness and certainty to its solution—likewise reaches. Religion says: The Kingdom of God is within you; and culture, in like manner, places human perfection in an internal condition, in the growth and predominance of our humanity proper, as distinguished from our animality. . . . Not a having and a resting, but a growing and a becoming, is the character of perfection as culture conceives it; and here, too, it coincides with religion.[22]

Though Arnold does not dismiss the improvement of material conditions as part of the work of culture, there is no question in his mind that social or political amelioration can only follow upon moral reformation. Indeed, Arnold opens himself up to considerable criticism in his accommodation of existing material conditions to a religious interpretation of culture. Elsewhere, in an essay on the French poet Maurice de Guérin, Arnold defines poetry as a form of art that "reconciles him with himself and his universe,"[23] carefully excluding criticism of society from poetry's "criticism of life." Therefore, though culture may be concerned with making the individual better, that is not necessarily to say that it is concerned with the restructuring of society.

If, in the context of nineteenth-century Evangelicalism, an innately depraved self could hope for regeneration through the transformative, moral action of literary instruction, Utilitarian formulations attached a different value to Western literary education as providing the means for the exercise of reason, moral will, and critical understanding. The secular revision of the notion of innate depravity reconceives moral law as part of the innate knowledge from which man has been led astray as a result of tyranny, despotism, and false rule and to which he is to be restored through a fortified intellect. From the viewpoint of Utilitarian philosophy, the action of bad government was responsible for the corruption of individuals, thwarting their capacity for good. But before that process could be reversed, the individual had to have sufficient critical understanding of the causes of his abasement and be adequately detached from his immediate situation to be able to analyze both its logic and its contradictions. A sharpened critical sense therefore was held to be an absolutely essential prerequisite to the restoration of the individual to his original condition of moral virtue and, by extension, of a well-ordered political society. In secular formulations literature is less a branch of religion than a department of knowledge that includes, among other disciplines, science, history, and philosophy.

But the assumptions of human nature that allow literature to usurp functions not necessarily intrinsic to it, such as those of religion in one instance or of empirical disciplines like history in another, also enable the suppression of material relations. The affirmation of an ideal self and an ideal political state through a specific national literature—English literature—is in essence an affirmation of English identity. But that identity is equally split along the lines of actual and ideal selves, and the Englishman actively participating in the cruder realities of conquest, commercial aggrandizement, and disciplinary management of natives blends into the rarefied, more exalted image of the Englishman as *producer* of the knowledge that empowers him to conquer, appropriate, and manage in the first place. The self-presentation of the Englishman to native Indians through the products of his mental labor removes him from the place of ongoing colonialist activity—of commercial operations, military expansion, and administration of territories—and de-actualizes and diffuses his material reality in the process. In a parodic reworking of the Cartesian axiom, the Englishman's true essence is defined by the thought he produces, overriding all other aspects of his identity—his personality, actions, and behavior. His material reality as subjugator and alien ruler is dissolved in his mental output; the blurring of the man and his works effectively removes him from history.

The introduction of English literature marks the effacement of a sordid history of colonialist expropriation, material exploitation, and class and race oppression behind European world dominance. The English literary text, functioning as a surrogate Englishman in his highest and most perfect state, becomes a mask for economic exploitation, so successfully camouflaging the material activities of the colonizer that one unusually self-conscious British colonial official, Charles Trevelyan, was prompted to remark, "[The Indians] daily converse with the best and wisest Englishmen through the medium of their works, and form ideas, perhaps higher ideas of our nation than if their intercourse with it were of a more personal kind."[24] The split between the material and the cultural practices of colonialism is nowhere sharper than in the progressive refinement of the rapacious, exploitative, and ruthless actor of history into the reflective subject of literature.

THIS BOOK does not attempt to be a "definitive" study of English studies in India. It leaves aside many questions apart from those concerning the effects of literary instruction on individual Indians and the readings that educated Indians gave to the English texts they were taught. The book is necessarily selective and partial, concentrating on major themes and developments rather than aiming to show the available material in all its variety. Still less does it aim to provide a chronological narrative of British Indian educational history. I have taken considerable license with Edward Said's formulation of "beginnings" as a moment that "includes everything that develops out of it, no matter how eccentric the development or inconsistent the result,"[25] to write a history of English studies as if it were entirely contained by its political and historical beginnings.

This book is simple in conception and design. The first chapter, outlining the early history of British involvement in Indian education, locates the beginnings of English literary studies in the Charter Act of 1813, an act born of the tensions between Parliament and the East India Company and between Company officials and missionaries and whose wording was so ambiguous as to encourage an unexpected prominence to English studies. The two chapters that follow describe the missionary influence in precipitating a new role and function for literary study, infusing English studies with cultural and religious meanings: chapter 2 outlines the efforts of one missionary, Alexander Duff, to adapt the existing English curriculum to religious ends; chapter 3 examines the British government's appropriation of the religious uses of literature to appease the missionaries on the one hand and to quell native insubordination on the other.

The second half of the book details the reverse movement away from religious functions toward a return to secular uses of literature, but now with a strengthened cultural base to give literature a new political authority: chapter 4 describes the dramatic disavowal of English literature's association with Christianity, signaling a shift from universal Christian truths to the legitimacy of British authority—from forms of religious to intellectual control; chapter 5 examines the gradual emphasis on literary study as a branch of historical analysis in its relation to the consolidation of British cultural hegemony; chapter 6 analyzes the gradual breakdown of the success of English literary education, tracing native disenchantment with colonial rule to erratic, unstable changes in the functions of English education, exposing the growing disjunction between the seemingly unlimited possibilities for self-elevation promised by literary training and the restrictive conditions of British rule under which "moral and intellectual" growth was actually promoted.

The Beginnings of English
Literary Study

As soon as [the Indians] become first-rate European scholars, they must cease to be
Hindoos.
— Edward Thornton. *Parliamentary Papers,* 1852–53. 32:36.

ENGLISH LITERATURE made its appearance in India, albeit indirectly,
with a crucial act in Indian educational history: the passing of the
Charter Act in 1813. This act, renewing the East India Company's charter
for a twenty-year period, produced two major changes in Britain's relationship with her colony: one was the assumption of a new responsibility toward native education, and the other was a relaxation of controls
over missionary activity in India.

Without minimizing the historical importance of the renewal of the
Company's charter, it would be safe to say that the more far-reaching
significance of the Charter Act lay in the commitment enjoined upon
England to undertake the education of the native subjects, a responsibility which it did not officially bear even toward its own people. Hitherto,
measures to educate the Indians were entirely at the discretion of the

governor-general at Calcutta and the Company was in no way obligated to attend to their instruction. Indeed, reluctant as it was to spend any more money on the natives than necessary, the East India Company was all too willing to abide by the practice in England, where education was not a state responsibility. The Charter Act, however, radically altered the prevailing state of laissez-faire in Indian educational matters. The 13th Resolution categorically stated that England was obligated to promote the "interests and happiness" of the natives and that measures ought to be adopted "as may tend to the introduction among them of useful knowledge, and of religious and moral improvement."[1]

The pressure to assume a more direct responsibility for the welfare of the subjects came from several sources. The earlier and perhaps more significant one, decisively affecting the future course of British administrative rule in India, was the English Parliament. Significantly, the goal of "civilizing the natives" was far from being the central motivation in these first official efforts at educational activity. Parliamentary involvement with Indian education had a rather uncommon origin in that it began with the excesses of their own countrymen in India. The extravagant and demoralized life-styles of the East India Company servants, combined with their ruthless exploitation of native material resources, had began to raise serious and alarming questions in England about the morality of the British presence in India. Henry Montgomery, a speaker in the House debate, relentlessly exposed the hypocrisy of the English people in daring to reform Indians when their own behavior was not beyond reproach: "If we wished to convert the natives of India, we ought first to reform our own people there, who at present only gave them an example of lying, swearing, drunkenness, and other vices."[2] Montgomery's disenchantment with British behavior led him to see the customary British association of Hindu practice with Hindu religion as a device to forestall introspection and self-scrutiny. The practice of "women burning themselves on the death of their husbands," he pointed out, "[was not] any more a religious rite than suicide was a part of Christianity."[3] British greed was a reality of the Company's presence in India that was too embarrassing for Parliament to ignore without appearing to endorse Company excesses. But unable to check the activities of these highly placed "Nabobs," or wealthy Europeans whose huge fortunes were amassed in India, it sought instead to remedy the wrongs committed against the Indians by attending to their welfare and improvement.[4]

The English interest in Indian improvement was informed from the earliest period with the need to come to terms with its own depredations in India. Even when religious sentiment later overtook the educational enterprise, no British administrator ever lost sight of the original, compensatory reasons for intervention in Indian education. Charles Grant, who made perhaps one of the most impassioned pleas for missionary activity, was amazingly candid in spelling out the two most important motives. The first was abuse of power by the Nabobs, who not only acquired illicit fortunes but showed a shameful dereliction of responsibility by delegating authority loosely to sycophantic local leaders. Challenging the complacency of those who believed that "British genius and principles" simply radiated from the center, Grant urged British penetration into all sectors of Indian society, provinces and towns alike, to diffuse central authority. In this way he hoped to correct the self-centeredness of a pampered Company that had become insulated from the rest of Indian society, causing it to place power in the wrong hands.

The other factor Grant cited for necessitating British action in the education of Indians was the damage done to India following early British conquests.

> Certainly a great deal was due from us to the people in compensation of the evils which the establishment of our power had introduced among them; and in return for the vast advantages which we reaped from the change, it was but fit that what the country had suffered, or was subjected unavoidably to lose by being dependent upon us, should be repaid by all the benefits which good government, in consistency at least with that dependence, could bestow.[5]

In a brashly manipulative explanation that was basically a thinly disguised appeal for increased territorial control, Grant attributed the irresponsible behavior of early English administrators to British uncertainty about the durability of colonial rule. Britain's anxiety about the permanence of its rule was so intense, he suggested, that India had meaning only as an object of appropriation. The land had not yet acquired a value that develops through an activity akin to aesthetic contemplation of the colonial experience: "Those provinces which we professedly held in perpetuity cease to be regarded here as permanently our own. A secret idea of their insecurity prevailed, and our conduct towards them was perhaps influenced by this apprehension. We were eager to acquire, but slow to cherish."[6] In the same way that aesthetic appreciation involves the valuing of experience embodied in a work of art, through which that work becomes one's own, so the act of conquest too involves valuing as a result of which the ambiguity of the colonial situation begins to find resolution. It is the moment at which self-interest fuses with and becomes indistinguishable from a sense of discharging one's duty toward the other. Grant's intense disenchantment with British avarice left room for a commingling of altruism and paternalism, as in the following passage:

> The primary object of Great Britain, let it be acknowledged, was rather to discover what could be obtained from her Asiatic subjects, than how they could be benefited. In process of time it was found expedient to examine how they might be benefited in order that we might continue to hold the advantages which we at first derived from them. . . . [Their] happiness is committed to our care.[7]

But at the same time valuing is a process that selects what is useful or meaningful and rejects everything else. As a selective process it detaches the portion that is valued from the totality of which it is a part. By valuing the happiness of the people, Grant performs a similar operation of disengagement from the whole, objectifying a subjective state that is exclusive to and inseparable from the individual into a separate, autonomous entity also to be appropriated and made one's own.

Thus in the course of the argument the question of how England can serve the people of India blends indistinguishably with the question of how power can best be consolidated. The shift has far-reaching consequences. Duty toward the people is seen less as a motive for involving the government than as the end point of a process of consolidation of territorial control. To the question, "What are the best means of perpetuating our empire there?" Grant provides two answers. One is "by securing to the people their religion and laws."[8] But Grant rejects this solution, speculating: "What if the religion should be less favourable to our dominion than another system, and the people were induced voluntarily to make that other religion their own; would not the change be for our interest?"[9] There is no suggestion in this statement that Christianity is intrinsically more meritorious than the native religions; the issue is simply one of taking action favorable to British rule.

However much parliamentary discussions of the British presence in India may have been couched in moral terms, there was no obscuring the real issue, which remained political, not moral. The English Parliament's conflict with the East India Company was a long-standing one, going back to the early years of trading activity in the East Indies, when rival companies clashed repeatedly in a bid to gain exclusive rights to trade in the region. The East India Company, formed from two rival companies, eventually became the only group of English merchants entitled to carry on English trade. But the clamor for a broadening of commercial privileges in India never died down, and Parliament found itself besieged by Free Trade groups, lobbying to break the Company's hold. In 1813 it had no choice but to concede them greater trading privileges.

Moreover, the English Parliament itself was becoming alarmed by the danger of having a commercial company constituting an independent political power in India. By 1757 the East India Company had already become virtual master of Bengal and its territorial influence was growing steadily despite numerous financial problems besetting it. But in the absence of any cause for interference in the activities of the Company, the British Crown could conceivably do little to reorganize the Company's system of administration and win control of its affairs. Pitt's India Bill of 1784 had earlier rejected an outright subordination of the political conduct of the Company to the Crown. Not until the last quarter of the eighteenth century, when reports of immorality and depravity among Company servants started pouring in, did Parliament find an excuse to intervene, at which point, in the name of undertaking responsibility for the improvement of the natives, it began to take a serious and active interest in Indian political affairs. It was a move that was to result in a gradual erosion of the unchallenged supremacy of the Company in India.

It is impossible not to be struck by the peculiar irony of a history in which England's initial involvement with the education of the natives derived less from a conviction of native immorality, as the later discourse might lead one to believe, than from the depravity of their own administrators and merchants. In Edmund Burke's words, steps had to be taken to "form a strong and solid security for the natives against the wrongs and oppressions of British subjects resident in Bengal."[10] While the protectiveness contained in this remark may seem dangerously close to an attitude of paternalism, its immediate effect was beneficial, as it led to a strengthening of existing native institutions and traditions to act as a bulwark against the forces of violent change unleashed by the British presence.

This mission to revitalize Indian culture and learning and protect it from the oblivion to which foreign rule might doom it merged with the then current literary vogue of "Orientalism" and formed the mainstay of

that phase of British rule known as the "Orientalist" phase. Orientalism
was adopted as an official policy partly out of expediency and caution
and partly out of an emergent political sense that an efficient Indian
administration rested on an understanding of "Indian culture." It grew
out of the concern of Warren Hastings, governor-general from 1774 to
1785, that British administrators and merchants in India were not sufficiently responsive to Indian languages and Indian traditions. The distance between ruler and ruled was perceived to be so vast as to evoke
the sentiment that "we rule over them and traffic with them, but they
do not understand our character, and we do not penetrate theirs. The
consequence is that we have no hold on their sympathies, no seat in
their affections."[11] Hastings' own administration was distinguished by a
tolerance for the native customs and by a cultural empathy unusual for
its time. Underlying Orientalism was a tacit policy of what one may call
reverse acculturation, whose goal was to train British administrators and
civil servants to fit into the culture of the ruled and to assimilate them
thoroughly into the native way of life. The great scholars produced by
eighteenth-century Orientalism—William Jones, Henry T. Colebrooke,
Nathaniel Halhed, and Charles Wilkins—entirely owed their reputa-
tions to a happy coincidence of pioneering achievement and official
patronage. Their exhaustive research had ambitious goals, ranging from
the initiation of the West to the vast literary treasures of the East to the
reintroduction of the natives to their own cultural heritage, represented
by the Orientalists as being buried under the debris of foreign conquests
and depredations.

Yet no matter how benign and productive its general influence might
appear, as David Kopf among other historians has insisted to the point
of urging it as fact, there is no denying that behind Orientalism's exhaustive inquiries, its immense scholarly achievements and discoveries, lay
interests that were far from scholarly. Whether later Orientalists were
willing to acknowledge it or not, Warren Hastings clearly understood
the driving force of Orientalism to be the doctrine that "every accumu-
lation of knowledge, and especially such as is obtained by social communication with people over whom we exercise a dominion founded on
the right of conquest, is useful to the state: it is the gain of humanity."[12]
Hastings' argument of course is an overt and unabashed rationalization
of "the dialectic of information and control" that Edward Said has
characterized as the basis of academic Orientalism, though even Said's
by now well-known argument does not quite prepare one for the pro-

grammatic assurance with which Hastings promotes his cultural ideology. Aside from his obviously questionable assumptions about the "right of conquest," what is most striking about this statement is the intellectual leap it makes from knowledge that is useful to the state to knowledge that becomes the gain of humanity. The relationship of power existing between England and India is certainly one condition allowing for such a leap, but more to the point is the role of the state in mediating between the worlds of scholarship and politics. For Hastings, it was not merely that the state had a vital interest in the production of knowledge about those whom it ruled; more important, it also had a role in actively processing and then selectively delivering that knowledge up to mankind in the guise of "objective knowledge."

A peculiar logic runs through the argument, and it has to be monitored closely if one is to appreciate Hastings' keen understanding of the powerful reinforcing effect of Orientalist scholarship upon state authority. The acquisition of knowledge about those whom it governs is clearly perceived to be of vital importance to the state for purposes of domination and control. But the fact that this knowledge eventually passes into the realm of "humanistic" scholarship (again through the agency of the state) confers a certain legitimacy upon the quest and, by extension, upon the state that promotes it. In other words, even though "social communication" may have its roots in the impulse to enforce dominion over the natives, as Hastings had no hesitation in acknowledging, its political motivation is nullified by virtue of the fixed body of knowledge it produces and makes available to the rest of mankind. The disinterestedess and objectivity that this now shared and therefore "true" knowledge purports to represent help to confirm the state's "right of conquest," which duly acquires the status of the sine qua non of knowledge production. What therefore appears on the surface as a rhetorical leap is in fact the carefully controlled effect of a self-fortifying dialectic.

As a candid acknowledgment of the implicit political goals of Orientalism, Hastings' argument belies some of the arbitrary distinctions that are at times made between Orientalism and Anglicism, the countermovement that gained ascendancy in the 1830s. Briefly, Anglicism grew as an expression of discontent with the policy of promoting the Oriental languages and literatures in native education. In its vigorous advocacy of Western instead of Eastern learning it came into sharp conflict with the proponents of Orientalism, who vehemently insisted that such a move would have disastrous consequences, the most serious being the alienation of the natives from British rule. However, while it is true that the two movements appear to represent diametrically opposed positions, what is not adequately stressed in the educational literature is the degree to which Anglicism was dependent upon Orientalism for its ideological program. Through its government-supported research and scholarly investigations Orientalism had produced a vast body of knowledge about the native subjects that the Anglicists subsequently drew upon to mount their attack on the culture as a whole. In short, Orientalist scholarship undertaken in the name of "gains for humanity" gave the Anglicists precisely the material evidence they needed for drawing up a system of comparative evaluations in which one culture could be set off and measured against the other. For a variety of reasons that will be outlined shortly, it would be more accurate to describe Orientalism and Anglicism not as polar opposites but as points along a continuum of attitudes toward the manner and form of native governance, the necessity and justification for which remained by and large an issue of remarkably little disagreement.

WARREN HASTINGS was succeeded in the governor-generalship by Lord Cornwallis (1786- 1793), who found himself at the helm of a government seriously compromised by financial scandals and deteriorating standards. For this state of affairs the new governor-general squarely laid the blame on the earlier policy of accommodation to the native culture. In his view the official indulgence toward Oriental forms of social organization, especially government, was directly responsible for the lax morals of the Company servants. If the Company had sorely abused its power, what better explanation was there than the fact that the model of Oriental despotism was constantly before its eyes? To Cornwallis, the abuse of power was the most serious of evils afflicting the East India Company, not only jeopardizing the British hold over India but, worse still, dividing the English nation on the legitimacy of the colonial enterprise.

The most pressing task therefore was to ensure that no further abuse would occur. In the process of working toward this end Cornwallis evolved a political philosophy that he believed would be consistent with British commercial aims. His theoretical position was that a good government was held together not by men but by political principles and laws, and in these alone rested absolute power. The Oriental system lacking a strong political tradition (and in this belief Cornwallis was doing no more than echoing a view that was common currency), he turned to English principles of government and jurisprudence for setting the norms of public behavior and responsibility by which administrators were to function. Determined to run a government that would remain free of corrupting influences from the native society, Cornwallis concentrated his entire energies on the improvement of European morals on English lines. The colonial subjects engaged his attention only minimally; for the most part, he appeared wholly content to leave them in their "base" state, in the belief that their reform was well beyond his purview.

Clearly, the first steps toward Anglicization were aimed at tackling the problem of corruption within the ranks. To this extent, as Eric Stokes has rightly pointed out in *The English Utilitarians and India,* Anglicism began as an entirely defensive movement. But even in this form it was not without elements of aggression toward the native culture, as is apparent in certain measures that Cornwallis adopted to streamline the government. Convinced that contact with natives was the root cause of declining European morals, he resolved to exclude all Indians from appointment to responsible posts, hoping by this means to restore the Englishman to his pristine self and rid him once and for all of decadent influences.

Predictably, the exclusion of Indians from public office had serious repercussions on Anglo-Indian relations. The personal contact that Englishmen and Indians had enjoyed during Hastings' administration vanished with Cornwallis, and the result was that a more rigidified master-subject relationship set in. One historian, Percival Spear, has gone so far as to suggest that this event marks the point at which there developed "that contempt for things and persons Indian . . . and which produced the views of a Mill or a Macaulay."[13] Denied all opportunities for expression as a result of the harsh measure, public ability declined steadily. But curiously, when this occurred it was taken to mean that civic responsibility had never existed in India, thus giving rise to one of the most durable legends of British rule: that the Indian mind was best suited to minor pursuits of trade, but not to government or administration.

With Cornwallis charting an apparently serious course for administrative rule on English principles, one would expect Anglicism as a cultural movement to have triumphed much earlier than it actually did (i.e., the

1830s). Its momentum was badly shattered, however, by the cultural policy of his immediate successors, a group of skilled and politically astute administrators who had all at one time served under Lord Welles-ley, a governor-general (1798–1805) noted for his caution and reserve, and later under the Marquess of Hastings, under whose governor-gen-eralship (1812–1823) British rule was more firmly consolidated. Conserva-tive in their outlook and fiercely Romantic in their disposition, these accomplished officers—John Malcolm, Thomas Munro, Charles Met-calf, and Mountstuart Elphinstone—had no use for the impersonal, bureaucratic system of government carved out for India by Cornwallis. It is important to know that these officers assumed power at a time when England's wars both abroad and within India had come to an end and the task of consolidating the empire lay before them. Under such altered circumstances the earlier Company policy of expediency and caution was clearly outmoded.

But for reasons pertaining to their aristocratic backgrounds, feudal beliefs, and romantic temperament, this new generation of administra-tors was fiercely resistant to replacing the rule of men with the rule of law. It is true that in certain respects the form of government they favored was no different from their predecessor's particularly in its commitment to the liberal doctrine of protection of property rights. But the kind of relationship they envisaged between ruler and ruled was an outright rejection of the abstract and impersonal one of the Cornwallis system in which the mechanistic operations of law had ultimate author-ity. Distrusting the power of law to effect changes either in individuals or in society, they belonged to an older tradition, which, as Eric Stokes points out, "saw the division of society into ruler and ruled as a natural ordering, and which envisaged submission to authority as necessary to the anarchic nature of man."[14] With its strong feudal overtones, the form of government they wanted for India was a frankly paternalistic one, firm, yet benevolent, and open to the native traditions of law, government, and religion.

While Cornwallis had no particular interest in either promoting or discouraging Oriental learning, as long as Englishmen were not com-pelled to go through its studies, his successors decidedly did not share his indifference. Indeed, they were shrewd enough to see that it was entirely in their interest to support Orientalism if it meant the preserva-tion of the feudal character of British rule. Their espousal of Orientalism might lead one to suspect a return to the earlier Company policy of

Warren Hastings. But to do so is to ignore the changed political circumstances under which the Orientalist policy now received patronage.
Hastings' wholehearted enthusiasm for Orientalism was in large part a
response to the volatile and uncertain political position of Britain in
India. A touch of ad hocism was unmistakable in his approach, as is
evident in an educational policy that failed to show any signs of being
informed by a clear conception of government or a distinct political
philosophy. Gaining the affection of the people was his primary goal. If
that meant British patronage of the native traditions and systems of
learning, he could conceive of no better tactic than to allow the immediate situation to guide and shape policy.

But Wellesley's officers were too conscious of England's by. then
strengthened position in India to resort to the promotion of native
culture as a purely defensive measure. Rather, Orientalism represented
for them the logical corollary of a precise and meticulously defined
scheme of administration. In that scheme, as was noted earlier, the
British government was to function as a paternal protectorate governing
India not by direct rule (that is, through the force of British law) but
through various local functionaries. In other words, the Cornwallis
system of centralized administration was spurned in favor of one that
was more diffuse and operated through a network of hierarchical relationships between British officers at one level and between the British
and the Indians on the other. In order to draw the Indians into this
bureaucratic structure it was imperative for the British administration to
maintain an alliance with those who formed the traditional ruling class.
This was essential partly to conciliate the indigenous elite for their
displaced status, but partly also to secure a buffer zone for absorbing the
effects of foreign rule, which, if experienced directly by the masses,
might have an entirely disastrous impact.

This scheme of administration, at once more personal and more
rigidly stratified in its conception, was further bolstered by the philosophy that no political tradition could be created anew or superimposed
on another without a violent rejection of it by the preexisting society.
For a new political society to emerge the native tradition and culture
were increasingly viewed as vital in providing the soil for its growth.
The imagery of grafting that permeated the discourse around this time
pointed to an emerging theory of organicism that conceived of political
formation as part of a process of cultural synthesis.[15]

These theoretical and practical considerations made Orientalism a highly appealing cultural program to Wellesley's subordinates. In it may be seen the first seeds of what came to be known as the Filtration Theory, which was predicated on the notion that cultural values percolate downward from a position of power and by enlisting the cooperation of intermediate classes representing the native elite. The Filtration Theory is conventionally associated with Macaulay's Anglicism, and it is in his famous 1835 minute that it is advanced most forcefully as a theory of culture. But its unacknowledged forebear is the Orientalism of Wellesley's administration. The differences between an intermediate class of native elite educated in the vernaculars and one in English are of course by no means inconsequential, nor is it the intention here to minimize them in any way. But all the same it is essential to recognize that despite the conflict over language, the Orientalist and Anglicist programs assumed a common method of governance; in both, an influential class was to be coopted as the conduit of Western thought and ideas.

The policy in the years immediately following the Charter Act was to establish institutions devoted to the teaching of Oriental languages and literature, "freed as much as possible from its lumber."[16] From the beginnings of British involvement with Indian education the effort was toward pruning Oriental literatures of their undesirable elements, with a view to reviving the indigenous learning in its practical, useful aspects. Colleges were set up from the money that came in from endowment of lands and funds, sometimes yielding an annual income of more than twenty thousand rupees.[17] The argument given at the time was that the money came from the people and that some attempt therefore should be made to give the people something in return. This education was open to all classes of the native population and was directed to those branches of instruction of most use to Indian society. The introduction of European science and English as a medium of instruction was deferred on the grounds that the people were not yet ready for it.

Roughly spanning the first two and a half decades of the nineteenth century, the phase of British rule dominated by the group around Wellesley appears as a period of relative inactivity in education. But it nonetheless acquires a special significance in this narrative for marking the historical moment when political philosophy and cultural policy converged to work toward clearly discernible common ends. The promotion of Orientalism no less than Anglicism became irrevocably tied from this point onwards to questions of administrative structure and governance. For example, how were Indian subjects to be imbued with a sense of public responsibility and honor, and by what means could the concept of a Western-style government be impressed on their minds to facilitate the business of state?

Such questions also implied that, with the reversal of the Cornwallis policy of isolationism from Indian society and the hierarchical reordering of the Indian subjects for administrative purposes, the problem of reform was no longer confined to the British side, but extended more actively to the Indian side as well. The more specialized functions devolving upon a government now settling down to prospective long-term rule brought the Indians as a body of subjects more directly into the conceptual management of the country than was the case in either Hastings' or Cornwallis' time. As a result, the "Indian character" suddenly became a subject of immense importance, as was the question of how it could best be molded to suit British administrative needs.

But curiously, it was on this last point that Orientalism began to lose ground to Anglicism, for even though it appeared to be the most favorable cultural policy for an administration that resembled feudalism, its theoretical premises were seriously undermined by the gathering tide of reform that accompanied the restructuring of government. This was a government that had grown acutely aware of both its capacity for generating change (thus far internally) and its own vested authority over the natives. The Orientalist position was that a Western political tradition could be successfully grafted upon Indian society without having to direct itself toward the transformation of that society along Western lines. But as a theory it found itself at odds with the direction of internal consolidation along which British rule was moving. The strengthening of England's position in India, as exemplified by a recently coordinated and efficient administrative structure, put the rulers under less compulsion to direct change inward than to carry over the reformist impulse to those over whom they had dominion.

That tendency was reinforced by two outside developments. One was the opening of India to free trade in 1813, which resulted in the Private Trade and City interests steadily exerting stronger influence on the Crown at the expense of the Indian interest. The "Private Traders" had no tradition of familiarity with India behind them and, according to the historian C. H. Philips, "could hardly expect to retain the good opinion of either the Board of Control or of their governments in India."[18] Removed from direct knowledge of the country they were ruling, these new political groups were more prone to taking decisions that reflected their own biases and assumptions about what was good for their subjects than what the current situation demanded.

A second and more important influence in the thrust toward reform was exerted by a group of missionaries called the Clapham Evangelicals, who played a key role in the drama of consolidation of British interests in India. Among them were Zachary Macaulay, William Wilberforce, Samuel Thornton, and Charles Grant, and to these men must be given credit for supplying British expansionism with an ethics of concern for reform and conversion. Insisting that British domination was robbed of all justification if no efforts were made to reform native morals, the missionaries repeatedly petitioned Parliament to permit them to engage in the urgent business of enlightening the heathen. Unsuccessful with the earlier Act of 1793 that renewed the Company's charter for a twenty-year period, the missionaries were more triumphant by the time of the 1813 resolution, which brought about the other major event associated with the Charter Act: the opening of India to missionary activity.

ALTHOUGH CHAPLAINS had hitherto been appointed by the East India Company to serve the needs of the European population residing in India, the English Parliament had consistently refused to modify the Company charter to allow missionary work in India. The main reason for government resistance was an apprehension that the inhabitants would feel threatened and eventually cause trouble for England's commercial ventures. The insurrection at Vellore, near Madras, in 1806 was blamed on proselytizing activity in the area. The fear of further acts of hostility on religious grounds grew so great that it prompted a temporary suspension of the Christianizing mission. Despite assurances by influential parliamentary figures like Lord Castlereagh that the Indians would be as little alarmed by the appearance of Christian ministers as "by an intercourse with the professors of Mahometanism, or of the various sects into which the country was divided,"[19] the British government remained unconvinced that the Indians would not be provoked by interference with their religious beliefs. In keeping with the government policy of religious neutrality, the Bible was proscribed and scriptural teaching forbidden.

The opening of India to missionaries, along with the commitment of the British to native improvement, might appear to suggest a victory for the missionaries, encouraging them perhaps to anticipate official support for their Evangelizing mission. But if they had such hopes, they were to be dismayed by the continuing checks on their activities, which grew impossibly stringent. Publicly, the English Parliament demanded a guarantee that large-scale proselytizing would not be carried out in India. Privately, though, it needed little persuasion about the distinct advantages that would flow from missionary contact with the Indians and their "many immoral and disgusting habits."

Though representing a convergence of interests, these two events— British involvement in Indian education and the entry of missionaries— were far from being complementary or mutually supportive. On the contrary, they were entirely opposed to each other both in principle and in fact. The inherent constraints operating on British educational policy are apparent in the central contradiction of a government committed to the improvement of the people while being restrained from imparting any direct instruction in the religious principles of the English nation. The encouragement of Oriental learning, seen initially as a way of fulfilling the ruler's obligations to the subjects, seemed to accentuate rather than diminish the contradiction. For as the British swiftly learned, to their dismay, it was impossible to promote Orientalism without exposing the Hindus and Muslims to the religious and moral tenets of their respective faiths—a situation that was clearly not tenable with the stated goal of "moral and intellectual improvement."

Apart from the effect of thwarting the diffusion of Christian principles, the conflict of interests between commitment to Indian education on one hand and to religious neutrality on the other rendered the communication of modern knowledge virtually impossible. The impasse was created by what was perceived to be the sustaining structure of error embedded in Hinduism, blocking instruction in modern science, history, and other empirical disciplines. Because the knowledge of the West could not be imparted directly without seeming to tamper with the fabric of indigenous religions, British administrators were virtually paralyzed from moving in either direction. Since it was believed that knowledge could not be separated from religion in the Indian tradition, there was widespread fear among Council of Education members that Western scientific propositions opposed to the tenets of Hinduism would not merely be denounced as false, but would also be interpreted by overly suspicious Indians as deliberately hostile to the foundation of that religion. The more unambiguous, direct, singularly fixed the stance of a discipline toward objects of inquiry, the greater the likelihood that learned Indians steeped in the indigenous tradition would perceive lines of opposition. On the other hand, a discipline with a double stance toward knowledge and belief, empiricism and intuition, reason and faith, suppressing at once its affiliation with Christianity on one side and with modern science on the other, was believed to be ideally suited to mediating the conflict of British interests.

THE TENSION between increasing involvement in Indian education and enforced noninterference in religion was productively resolved through the introduction of English literature. Significantly, the direction to this solution was present in the Charter Act itself, whose 43d section empowered the governor-general-in-council to direct that "a sum of not less than one lac of rupees shall be annually applied to the revival and improvement of literature, and the encouragement of the learned natives of India."[20] As subsequent debate made only too obvious, there is deliberate ambiguity in this clause regarding which literature was to be promoted, leaving it wide open for misinterpretations and conflicts to arise on the issue. While the use of the word *revival* may weight the interpretation on the side of Oriental literature, the almost deliberate imprecision suggests a more fluid government position in conflict with the official espousal of Orientalism. Over twenty years later Macaulay was to seize on this ambiguity to argue that the phrase clearly meant Western literature and denounce in no uncertain terms all attempts to interpret the clause as a reference to Oriental literature.

> It is argued, or rather taken for granted, that by literature, the Parliament can have meant only Arabic and Sanskrit literature, that they never would have given the honourable appellation of a learned native to a native who was familiar with the poetry of Milton, the Metaphysics of Locke, the Physics of Newton; but that they meant to designate by that name only such persons as might have studied in the sacred books of the Hindoos all the uses of cusa-grass, and all the mysteries of absorption into the Deity.[21]

The first rumblings of discontent with the policy of supporting Oriental seminaries came well before the time of James Mill, but from his official position with the East India Company as examiner of correspondence he succeeded more than anyone else in stirring up debate on the wisdom of encouraging an apparently nonutilitarian system of learning. In a dispatch to the governor-general-in-council of Bengal dated February 18, 1824, he called attention to the state of the Madrassa (Mohammedan College) in Calcutta and the Hindu College in Benares set up during the tenure of Warren Hastings. Recalling the ends proposed at the time, "to make a favourable impression, by our encouragement of their literature, upon the minds of the natives,"[22] he charged the government with failure to reach the intended objectives, particularly that of utility. Mill questioned whether Oriental poetry was a worthwhile objective for establishing colleges in the first place, for "it has never been thought necessary to establish colleges for the cultivation of poetry, nor is it certain that this would be the effectual expedient for the attainment of the end [of utility]."[23] While Mill's dispatch commended the government for making all possible attempts to achieve the desired goals, its central thrust was that the original aim of imparting Oriental learning was fundamentally erroneous and that the great end should have been "useful learning."

At the same time Mill made a careful distinction between imparting useful learning through the Sanskrit and Arabic languages, which he was willing to tolerate, and establishing institutions for the purpose of teaching only Hindu or Muslim literature, "where you bound yourselves to teach a great deal of what was frivolous, not a little of what was purely mischievous, and a small remainder indeed in which utility was in any way concerned."[24] But at the same time he conceded that if that small remainder contained enough that was useful, it had to be preserved at all costs. Undoubtedly Mill was cautious in pressing for any type of educational program that would offend native sentiments. Moreover, his main concern was to see India well governed in order to implement social reforms effectively and speedily. To that purpose English was not essential. Indeed, as Eric Stokes has pointed out, Mill was skeptical about any type of formal education, whether in English or the vernaculars, and this cynicism marked his isolation from the mainstream of English liberal thought.[25] Yet, though he vested far greater faith in the power of law and government to produce social change, on the point of social utility he was inflexible, and it remained the criterion in his mind for mediating between existing interests and feelings of the Indians and the "pernicious" elements of Oriental learning.

Responding to Mill's dispatch, the Committee of General Instruction agreed that the legitimate object was the introduction of European knowledge. But it expressed reluctance about debarring Indians, particularly the Muslims, from cultivating a native literature held in pious veneration—a literature that was deeply interwoven with the habits and religion of the people and comprised valuable records of their culture. As a branch of study in all colleges, poetry was an integral part of the literary seminaries founded for Muslims and Hindus. To an administration officially committed to respecting the integrity of a proud civilization it was obvious that denying the Indians their poetry would in effect amount to cutting them off from a significant source of their cultural pride.

A group of Orientalists on the Committee (including Horace Wilson, Holt Mackenzie, and Henry Prinsep) responded in much sharper terms to Mill's dispatch. They had no quarrel with Mill's view that the Indians required a superior form of instruction than the one dispensed under their own system. But they were more pessimistic about the likelihood of Western knowledge taking root in India as long as European literature and science continued to be held in low esteem. As Horace Wilson observed: "A mere English scholar is not respected for his learning by the natives; they have no notion of English as learning, but they have a high respect for a man who knows Sanskrit or who knows Arabic."[26] This contempt for English was partly created by the *maulvis* and the *pundits* (men learned in Arabic and Sanskrit respectively) who viewed this new language and literature as a threat to their own power and influence over the people. "As long as this is the case," Wilson continued, "and we cannot anticipate the very near extinction of such prejudice, any attempt to enforce an acknowledgement of the superiority of intellectual produce amongst the natives of the West [can] only create dissatisfaction."[27] The import of his argument was somber: in the absence of prior steps to persuade Indians of the need for moral and intellectual improvement, European literature would continue to exert a culturally marginal influence. The Orientalists in sum urged that until such educational strategies were carefully worked out, a policy of deference be adopted to the political, cultural, and spiritual hold of the learned classes of India.

But increasingly there was less patience with a policy of conciliation. The initial wave of euphoria over the literary treasures of India, rapturously described as "so new, so fresh, so original, so unlike all the antiquated types and models of the West, that the mind was at once aroused and enraptured,"[28] had by the 1820s given way to caustic criticisms of its systems of learning. Minto's minute of 1813, favoring the revival of Oriental learning, was harshly criticized for not making the slightest effort to introduce "in whole or in part, by implantation or

engraftment, the improved Literature and Science of Europe, embodying, as these do, all that is magnificent in discovery, ennobling in truth,
and elevating in sentiment. No! Orientalism—the whole of Orientalism,
and nothing but Orientalism—is the sole burden of the Christian viceroy of British India."[29] Intent on unsettling Orientalism's hold, Macaulay, joined by his brother-in-law, C. E. Trevelyan, directed his energies
at reviving the links between Hindu religion and Hindu social practice
that had been severed in the heyday of Orientalist enthusiasm.

> These are the systems under the influence of which the people of India
> have become what they are. They have been weighed in the balance, and
> have been found wanting. To perpetuate them, is to perpetuate the deg-
> radation and misery of the people. Our duty is not to teach, but to unteach
> them—not to rivet the shackles which have for ages bound down the
> minds of our subjects, but to allow them to drop off by the lapse of time
> and the progress of events.[30]

By the time of the 1835 English Education Act of Governor-General
William Bentinck, which swiftly followed Macaulay's famous minute of
that same year,[31] the teaching of English was taken out of the Sanskrit
College and the Madrassa and confined to institutions devoted to studies
entirely conducted in English. The grounds for doing so was the charge
that the young men learned nothing in the native seminaries and failed
to speak English fluently because they had to divide their time between
the three languages.

The Orientalist Horace Wilson objected strongly to this move as an
attempt to create a different kind of caste hierarchy in Indian education,
claiming that these two native colleges produced many excellent English
scholars who showed a mastery of the language for all useful purposes.
Presenting the government with works translated into English by some
of the boys who were Sanskrit scholars, he made a vain attempt to show
that they learned the construction of the language much more rapidly
and efficiently than the boys of the English college.

A more serious charge that Wilson and other Orientalists leveled
against Bentinck's Anglicist resolution was that in diverting funds from
the Oriental seminaries to the institutions where English was taught
exclusively they were promoting a scheme for the total extinction of
native classical literature.

> By annihilating native literature, by sweeping away all sources of pride
> and pleasure in their own mental efforts, by rendering a whole people

dependent upon a remote and unknown country for all their ideas and for the very words in which to clothe them, we should degrade their character, depress their energies and render them incapable of aspiring to any intellectual distinction.[32]

Wilson's argument was not mere polemics. If the Sanskrit College and the Calcutta Madrassa had become mere vehicles of superstition, "temples of darkness which were falling of themselves into decay,"[33] the Anglicists had to share responsibility for it, even at the moment they declared there was no point in supporting a learning that had sunk Indians in a deeper gulf of degradation. By denying learned men any honor or reward or marks of distinction and achievement, British policy virtually doomed these institutions to decay. The erosion of the traditional Indian respect for learning seriously affected its status in Indian society and progressively reduced native learning to an archaic institution. Yet though the British policy of withdrawing funds contributed distinctly to this situation, Anglicist explanations of the degradation of indigenous institutions curiously refrained from any mention of Anglicist accountability, instead preferring to interpret such decline as an effect of the fallacious content of Oriental learning.

For Wilson the preservation of the "national imagery" of a people was the key to their creative, moral, and intellectual development. But the Anglicist faction, denying the validity of such links for subject peoples, refused to acknowledge any connection between expenditures on English education and the annihilation of native literature. In a letter to the governor-general, Lord Auckland, the Scottish missionary Alexander Duff, himself an Anglicist sympathizer, chafed at suggestions of impropriety: "As well, surely, might we assert that endowments for encouraging the study of Latin and Greek in this island were destined to exterminate the language which Shakespeare and Milton and Addison had rendered classical, with all its provincial dialects."[34] Duff attempted to persuade his opponents that two distinct but not incompatible issues were involved in the debate, one being the patronage of native literature and the other the education of the native youth. Drawing analogies with the British situation, he argued that though ancient Scottish literature may have had claims on the patronage of the government to confer awards on those who rescued it from decay (after all, Walter Scott had collected and published border songs and ballads and MacPherson volumes of Celtic poetry), no government in its right senses would use money from revenues to "endow seminaries on the Tweed or on the

Tay, for the purpose of furnishing education to hundreds of youth, exclusively on border legends and Ossianic tales."[35]

But however strong the Orientalists' condemnation of the policy of disbursing government funds for the exclusive study of English, the intensity of their feelings was not always shared by upper-caste Bengalis. The most striking example of differences between the Orientalists' objectives and Indian needs is that of the founding in 1816 of Hindu College, a college that sprang up entirely from the demands of a group of Calcutta citizens who wanted instruction not only in their own languages and sciences but also in the language and literature of England. Initially, the movement for English education, spearheaded by Calcutta's foremost citizen, Rammohun Roy, and the English watchmaker David Hare, was sparked by a need for translations of English literature into the vernaculars and not for a wholesale transfusion of Western thought. It is highly probable that no one expected to see introduced the full range of purely secular English literature and science through the medium of English. Sir Edward Hyde, chief justice of the Supreme Court, was not unappreciative of the irony of a situation where he found himself visited by a group of Calcutta citizens deploring the "national deficiency in morals" and requesting him for a college offering European education and imparting an English system of morals. Hyde reports that they were particularly insistent on receiving a classical knowledge of the English language and literature.

> When they were told that the Government was advised to suspend any declaration in favour of their undertaking, from tender regard to their peculiar opinions, which a classical education after the English manner might tread upon, they answered very shrewdly, by stating their surprise that they had any objection to a liberal education, that if they found anything in the course of it which they could not reconcile to their religious opinions, they were not bound to receive it; but still they should wish to be informed of everything that the English gentlemen learnt, and they would take that which they found good and liked best.[36]

The instrumental motives of the Bengali Brahmins, unambiguously seeking out the English language over the literature of England, were all too apparent to Hyde, as they surely must be to the modern reader. Bentinck's English Education Act of 1835 made note of the great rush for English places by Indians and offered the explanation that the study of English was accepted as a necessary part of polite education.[37] The Calcutta Hindus seemed on the whole more eager for English than the

Muslims and, some Englishmen believed, were also much easier to instruct. A less flattering explanation was that they were fonder of gain and other lucrative employments that required knowledge of English.[38] But British interpretations failed to take account of the extraordinary complacency the Bengali upper classes felt toward their educational futures, to the extent that the introduction of English was not cause for fear. A relationship of symbiosis between Oriental literature and English studies was much more easily conceivable for them (as the above passage indicates) than for their English patrons, for whom instrumental motives were less significant than motives of assimilation, acculturation, and amelioration.

The English Education Act of 1835, proposed by Governor-General William Bentinck on Macaulay's advice, made English the medium of instruction in Indian education. With the formal institutionalization of English as the language of instruction, the stage was set for a new direction to Indian education. But as the next chapter will elaborate, Bentinck's resolution was not as revolutionary in the introduction of a new language (the English language was already being taught in India even before 1835) as in endorsing a new function and purpose for English instruction in the dissemination of moral and religious values. In withdrawing funds from support of Oriental studies in favor of English, the act dramatically reversed England's commitment to a non-partisan, eclectic policy. Administrators preceding Bentinck, including Minto, Mountstuart Elphinstone, Charles Metcalf, Thomas Munro, and John Malcolm, had instinctively advocated a classical approach to the study of language and literature as an end in itself, resisting both Utilitarian and missionary pressures to enlist literary study as a medium of modern knowledge and as a source of religious instruction, respectively. With the Charter Act, the conflict between commitments to active intervention and neutrality pressed into existence a new discipline—English literature.

2
Praeparatio Evangelica

> The ample teaching of our improved European literature, philosophy and science, we knew, would shelter the huge fabric of popular Hindooism, and crumble it into fragments. But as it is certainly not good simply to destroy and then leave men idly to gaze over the ruins, nor wise to continue building on the walls of a tottering edifice, it has ever formed the grand and distinguishing glory of our institution, through the introduction and zealous pursuit of Christian evidence and doctrine, to strive to supply the noblest substitute in place of that which has been demolished, in the form of sound general knowledge and pure evangelical truth.
> —Alexander Duff, *Parliamentary Papers, 1852–53,* 32:57.

THE 1835 English Education Act of William Bentinck, which swiftly followed Macaulay's minute of that same year, officially required the natives of India to submit to the study of English literature, irrevocably altering the direction of Indian education. But the momentous significance of Bentinck's resolution ought not obscure the fact that English was in existence in India even before that time, for rudimentary instruction in the language had been introduced more than two decades earlier. Though based on literary material, the early British Indian curriculum in English was primarily devoted to language studies. Initially, English did not supersede Oriental studies but was taught alongside it. Yet it was clear that it enjoyed a different status, for there was a scrupulous attempt to establish separate colleges for its study. Even when English was taught within the same college, the English course of studies was kept separate from the course of Oriental study and was attended by a different set of students. The rationale was that if the English department drew students who were attached only to its department and to no other (that is, the Persian or the Arabic or the Sanskrit), the language might then be taught "classically," in much the same way that Latin and Greek were taught in England.

From an administrative point of view, the demands of secularism dictated an educational policy that required a strictly disciplinary approach to fields of knowledge understood as objects of study in and for themselves. The pattern of studies in rhetoric and logic then current in England provided a convenient model for adaptation in India. As a legacy of the medieval school curriculum, the cultivation of classical languages for their own sake suited the prevailing temper of conservatism. Grammar was not taught separately but alongside the reading of texts, which consisted of parsing, memorization, and recitation. That this happened also to be a parallel mode of instruction in the Indian classical languages explains in part the alacrity with which the European model of classical humanism was taken up and refined for formal use in India. Unaffected by Baconian ideas of educational reform and indifferent to the "words" versus "things" controversy raging in England, the British administrators preceding Bentinck, specifically Minto, Holt Mackenzie, A. D. Campbell, Mountstuart Elphinstone, Thomas Munro, and John Malcolm, gravitated intuitively toward a classical approach to the study of language and literature as an end in itself, resisting implicitly utilitarian pressures to enlist literary study as a medium of modern knowledge.

The model was not without distinct political advantages. Translated into secular terms, classical humanism assured protection of the integrity of native learning, defusing potential protest by Indians against overtures of cultural domination, for quite independently of the actual sentiment of officials toward the native culture, the classical model in delineating disciplinary boundaries around subjects as independent areas of study permitted the assertion of the respective claims of both Oriental and Western learning to the status of true knowledge without necessarily invoking normative criteria.

The entry of missionaries into India, however, precipitated a new role for English literary study. By the 1820s the atmosphere of secularism in which English studies were conducted became a major cause for concern to the growing numbers of missionaries who had gained fresh access to

India after 1813. Within England itself, there was a strong feeling that literary texts read as a form of secular knowledge were "a sea in which the voyager has to expect shipwreck"[1] and that they could not be relied on to exert a beneficial effect upon the moral condition of society in general. This sentiment was complemented by an equally strong one that for English works to be studied even for language purposes a high degree of mental and moral cultivation was first required which the bulk of people simply did not have. According to the missionary argument, to a man in a state of ignorance of moral law literature was patently indifferent to virtue. Far from cultivating moral feelings, a wide reading was more likely to cause him to question moral law more closely and perhaps even encourage him to deviate from its dictates.

The case of poetry offers an interesting example of how several important strands in English culture converged to cause a profound distrust of a literary mode that was at one point unequivocally called the "art of perverting words from their primitive meaning."[2] The criticism of the corruption of language by poetry and its attendant deviation from truth when read without a context or purpose brought the Evangelicals and the Utilitarians on common ground to a point where they could reconcile their differing ideological positions. The Utilitarian hostility to poetry found its chief priest in Bentham, who categorically excluded all imaginative literature from his ideal republic because it did not serve any functional purpose and caused misrepresentations of things. To the Utilitarian denunciation of poetry as a falsification of the inherent reality of things the Evangelicals added the criticism that the ornamentation of poetry exalted sensibility over morality and self-indulgence over Christian humility. The Sunday School movement, which grew out of Evangelical involvement with the uplift of the lower classes, attempted to inspire devotional feelings in the young through tracts written in a language that emulated the simplicity and directness of the Bible. Originally written in the form of parables, these tracts (whose enormous influence established a literary reputation of sorts for Hannah More, Sarah Trimmer, and Anna Barbauld) gave a new respectability to the novelistic genre whose growth in part they stimulated.

In missionary pamphlets greater sanction was given to literature wherever it supported a pedagogical emphasis on the "moral and intellectual improvement of mankind." Literary devices such as alliteration, rhyme, and reduplication came to be seen as extremely harmful because they imposed "arbitrary fetters" on thought and resulted in an affected style. Many critics shared James Mill's Utilitarian distrust of ingenuity and argued that it diverted minds from "the correct and dignified style of prose composition in which the Greek and Latin writers (and those of all Western nations) so much excel, and which to a nation is of far greater importance than all the embellishments of poetry."[3] Furthermore, it was argued, the reader's concentration is so much on discovering the division and meanings of the syllables in the alliteration that all unity of impression is lost, for the reader is unable to take in the whole and is ill prepared to receive the impression that the story was calculated to make on him.

The emphasis on sound rather than meaning in secular pedagogical practice in British India was a frequent complaint of missionaries. Likewise, some British administrators involved with Indian education, among them A. D. Campbell, were equally vehement in deploring the current practice in the schools that converted the teaching of texts that had the potential to offer instruction in morals, even Indian texts like the *Bhagavad Gita*, into exercises in sound and memory.[4] The Evangelical antagonism to a literature that depended for its effect on sound patterns converged with Utilitarian convictions that pure sound is totally divorced from meaning and therefore emptied of all intellectual and spiritual content, without which the mind is led astray. There emerged a strong belief that texts read without any religious or cultural associations literally left readers adrift like drowning sailors in a shipwreck.

Ironically, much the same argument was made even by staunch Orientalists like Horace Wilson, who criticized prevailing pedagogical practices on the grounds that "the mere language cannot work any material change." Only when "we initiate them into our literature, particularly at an early age, and get them to adopt feelings and sentiments from our standard writers, [can] we make an impression upon them, and effect any considerable alteration in their feelings and notions."[5]

ONE OF the most relentless critics of British secular pedagogy was the Scottish missionary Alexander Duff. Along with other missionaries, Duff was greatly alarmed about the potentially lethal implications of a secular emphasis in Indian education. The climate of skepticism and intellectual defiance that had become the hallmark of Hindu College in Calcutta, where Duff also ran his own school, confirmed his worst fears. What benign officials regarded as a spirit of free intellectual inquiry fostered by English education Duff interpreted as a descent into moral anarchy. And yet, though Duff was opposed on almost every count to the official British position on Indian education (with an acrimony that ought to have alienated him permanently from administrative circles), no missionary was as successful as he in impressing upon government administrators the urgency of moral and religious instruction. Indeed, the influence he exerted on the direction of English education was staggering. Though his views are by no means a definitive assessment of British policy, his critique of secularism can be taken as fairly representative of missionary arguments for reorienting English instruction in a religious direction. This chapter will thus be devoted to an examination of his educational theory and practice.

Alexander Duff's career spanned three continents: as moderator of the General Assembly of the Church of Scotland and later professor of evangelistic theology at St. Andrew's he was keenly involved in the struggle between secular and spiritual authority that was ripping apart the Established Church at its seams. Though he eventually joined the Secession, he continued to think of his role as one of arbitration between "Unionists" and "Separatists" on the integration of the Free Church with the United Presbyterian. Though his longest years abroad were spent in India and his most enduring contributions were to Indian education, as convenor of the Foreign Missions Committee of his church he was instrumental in establishing missions in, among other places, South Africa, Egypt, Syria, Turkey, and Lebanon. News of the success of his work abroad, combined with legendary accounts of the fiery eloquence of his oratory and the fervor of his evangelical passion, reached interested Scottish Presbyterians on the other side of the Atlantic. In the winter of 1854 he was invited for an extensive lecture tour of the United States and Canada, which by all accounts left such a powerful impression that a New York reporter wrote: "Never did any man leave our shores so encircled with Christian sympathy and affection."[6]

To a greater degree than other missionaries Duff had developed a systematic and theoretical approach to the issue of secular education, which he expounded in numerous pamphlets and publications and most fully in *India and India Missions,* published in 1839. Born in Scotland in 1806, Duff was educated at St. Andrew's University, where he studied moral philosophy under Thomas Chalmers, whose influence over him was incalculable. It was Chalmers, in fact, who encouraged Duff's decision to become a missionary.[7] In 1829 Duff was invited by the Committee of the General Assembly of the Church of Scotland on Foreign Missions to become their first missionary to India. Following ordination that same year, Duff set out for Calcutta. It was not a pleasant voyage, to say the least. His apprehensions in taking up a strange new life in India were dramatically intensified when he found himself shipwrecked not once, but twice. In the first instance his ship struck a sandbank near the cape. Most of the people on board managed to scramble out of the boat and took refuge on a desolate island nearby. But Duff lost his entire library of eight hundred books, "representing every department of knowledge," which he had carefully chosen for the college he planned to set up in India. One book, however, did happen to get washed ashore; when the sailor who had spotted it went to retrieve it, it turned out (not surprisingly) to be Duff's copy of the Bible. The loss of all his books save this one had a profound effect on Duff's attitude toward the sum of human learning. Henceforth he saw the value of modern knowledge only as a means to truth and not an end in itself. "They are gone," he wrote, "and, blessed be God, I can say, gone without a murmur. So perish all earthly things: the treasure that is laid up in heaven alone is unassailable."[8]

After several weeks of being stranded in Capetown, arrangements were made for another ship to continue the journey to India. But just about a hundred miles outside Calcutta, in the confluence of the Ganga (the Ganges river) with the ocean, the ship fell victim to the fury of the monsoon rains and was hurled onto a mud bank, where it lay hopelessly crippled. Through a daring that is often born of sheer desperation, the people on board fought the swirling currents and managed to swim to a nearby island. Once on land, they took refuge in a village temple, where they remained until word of their plight reached Calcutta and rescue efforts got under way. But despite the succession of disasters on a voyage that took over eight months to complete, one blessing did emerge. According to his biographer, George Smith, the villagers who heard of the travails surmounted by Duff were so struck by awe and wonderment that many came to believe that "surely this man is a favourite of the gods who must have some notable work for him to do in India."[9]

Once settled in India, Duff quickly set his attention on the business that had brought him there in the first place. On arriving in Calcutta, he was appalled to find that the other denominations spent most of their energies teaching and preaching in the native languages to the masses, a practice that appeared to him to have minimal impact on religious and caste sentiment and seemed utterly to vitiate the efficacy of missionary labor. The practice seemed even more ludicrous in light of the fact that among the more respectable classes of the community there was a growing desire for acquiring knowledge of the English language, even if it was solely for purposes of securing government positions. Blessed with an uncanny instinct for turning opportunity to his advantage, Duff set out to reap spiritual benefits from prevailing material interests by opening a school in which nearly all studies, literary, theological, and scientific, were conducted in English. Admission to his General Assembly Institution in Calcutta was at first free. Duff reported that when the school opened on July 12, 1830, three hundred applicants turned up in three days in a hall that held only 120 people. Hordes of young Indians came begging to be taken in, crying, "Me want read your good books; oh, take me," "Me good boy," "Me poor boy," "Me know your commandments, 'Thou shalt have no other gods before me'; oh, take me," "Oh, take me, and I pray for you." These pleas were topped off by ingratiations to Duff as "the great and fathomless ocean of all imaginable excellencies." Unfortunately, as Duff himself was all too aware, it may have been the anticipation of free books rather than the attractions of Christianity that drove poor children to the school. It was not uncommon for huge numbers to flock to new schools and, once the free books were distributed, run away with them and never turn up again. And as Duff sadly remarked, book pages were often converted not into stores for the intellect but wastepaper for petty retailers in the bazaar.

Duff ran the General Assembly Institution for thirteen years, from 1830 to 1843. The enrollments swelled each passing year, making it one of the most successful institutions in the city. But in 1843 he was caught in a bitter struggle taking place in Scotland between secular and religious authority. The conflict led to the disruption of the Established Church of Scotland and the creation of the Free Church of Scotland. The matter of realigning his loyalties was a difficult one for Duff. Some of his oldest and closest ties were with the Establishment, and the most sacred associations of his life were linked with this ancient bulwark of his native land. Moreover, severing those ties meant a surrender of the results of his thirteen years of hard and patient labor in India. The fine college buildings with their complete equipment, in which he had taken such pleasure and pride, had to pass into the hands of the Established Church, which had put up the money for it, and he would be forced to begin anew and rebuild from the foundation. But Duff arrived at his decision quickly and responded to the overtures of the Free Church by joining the Secession. In time, with the help of sympathetic friends and church associates both in India and abroad, he raised enough money to establish a new institution under the patronage of the Free Church of Scotland that soon surpassed the other school in numbers of pupils and also in conversions.

Both the original General Assembly Institution and the later Free Church Institution were set up in response to what Duff considered the secular abuses of government institutions, in particular the excesses committed at Hindu College in Calcutta, later known as Presidency College, which regularly churned out what he called "gentlemen outlaws" and "privileged desperadoes." Though Duff conceded that the students at institutions like these scorned forms of Hindu worship, lived like Europeans, and conducted themselves well as public officers, he remained convinced that while their immersion in Western ideas caused them to turn their backs on their own religion, they had grown increasingly hostile to all religions, as well, including Christianity.

Duff voiced a complaint made by many missionaries in India that the most vituperative critics of Christianity they encountered in their labors were not traditional caste Hindus or Muslims as conventionally believed, but the young men who had been trained in what they termed the godless colleges of the government. The recalcitrant behavior of the students at Hindu College convinced Duff that the exposure of error did not necessarily result in the immediate embracing of truth. Ironically for British policy, the more successfully English education turned the Indians against their own religion through the exercise of right reason and judgment, the more insidiously it induced a violent rejection of the premises of all religion. Insofar as government education gave Indians receiving Western training a disposition for rational argument and scientific proofs and through it an attitude of skepticism and contempt toward their own belief systems, it could be adjudged successful. But the assertion that "as soon as [the natives] become good English scholars, they must cease to be Hindoos"[10] blandly assumed that Western knowledge had an inherently destructive effect on contrary systems, which even a staunch Anglicist like Duff realized was a gross self-deception. Critical of attempts to set intellectual liberation as the sole goal of education, he projected the policy of knowledge without religion as no less pernicious to the stability of British rule than idolatry and superstition. He attributed the Mutiny of 1857, for instance, to the secular policies of the government. In a series of letters to a friend, Dr. Tweedie, that became one of the most frequently quoted accounts of the rebellion, Duff directly linked the newfound political consciousness among Western-educated Indians to the official position of neutrality toward religion.[11] Government policy foolishly placed the Indians in a position where they were able to say, in Duff's ironic scenario of the future, that "we are very much obliged to our foreign rulers who have let us into the secret of their weakness and our own strength—the knowledge which must qualify us speedily to get quit of them, and undertake the management of our own civil and military affairs without their help."[12] Knowledge without religion produced infidels, who were the spiritual equivalent of political rebels imbued with contempt for constitutional authority. In Duff's aphoristic formula: "As Christianity has never taught rulers to oppress, so will it never teach subjects to rebel."[13]

Yet while Duff and others expressed serious reservations about the secular education given at government colleges and went ahead with plans to set up alternative Christian schools, claiming that these served the government's interests more rigorously in principle than their own schools, neither he nor other critics were prepared at the same time to dispense with literary instruction in their institutions. In both of his institutions Duff divided his classes to cover a wide range of literary instruction, beginning with the alphabet and extending to the most advanced courses of literature. Working from the simple definition of Christian education as the drawing out of all capacities that characterize the soul as spiritual being, Duff set out to identify those works that best met that definition. The works of authors such as Bacon, Locke, Reid, Dugald Stewart, and Thomas Brown were named as the most exemplary sources, but the Bible remained of course the single most important text.[14] The reading of the Bible was followed by comment, illustrative example, and amplification. The Bible was used as a classbook exclusively for religious instruction, never for parsing or syntactical and other grammatical exercises of linguistic acquisition—practices that necessarily reduced the Bible from its deserved status as "the Book of Books" to merely one among many books. More important, to avoid the error of committing what Duff contemptuously referred to as "Pharisaic idolatry," the Bible was never established as the final authority. Duff's dictum was not "Behold the Book, fall ye down before it, and worship it," but "Behold your God revealing himself through the medium of his written word; fall ye down and worship before Him."

In 1852 the curriculum at Duff's Free Church Institution prescribed the following books in its course on English literature: *Poetical Reader,* Cowper's *Poems,* Milton's *Paradise Lost,* with *Minor Poems,* Pollock's *Course of Time, Selections from Southey, Montgomery, Campbell and Wordsworth,* Macaulay's *Lays of Ancient Rome,* Akenside's *Pleasures of Imagination,* Young's *Night Thoughts,* Bacon's *Moral and Civil Essays* and *Advancement of Learning,* Whately's *Rhetoric,* Schlegel's *History of Literature,* Hallam's *Literary History of the Fifteenth, Sixteenth and Seventeenth Centuries,* Foster's *Essays, Select Essays from the North British and Other Reviews,* and various works of the London Tract and Book Society. Among texts taught in the course on natural and revealed religion were the Bible, Paley's *Natural Theology,* and Bunyan's *Pilgrim's Progress* (which was taught as a religious, not a literary text) and among those taught in philosophy John Stuart Mill's *Logic,* Reid's *Inquiry and Essays,* Thomas Brown's *Lectures,* Abercrombie's *Intellectual and Moral Powers,* Whewall's *Moral Philosophy,* Bacon's *Novum Organon,* Plato's *Dialogues,* and Butler's *Dissertation on Human Nature.*[15]

In contrast, the books prescribed in government schools reveal a different focus. There were variations from institution to institution, but the following books remained standard fare in the literature curriculum of government schools in midnineteenth century India: Richardson's *Poetical Selections* (Goldsmith, Gray, Addison, Pope, and Shakespeare), Otway's *Venice Preserved,* Shakespeare's *Hamlet, Othello,* and *Macbeth,* Pope's *Iliad by Homer,* Milton's *Paradise Lost* (the first four books), Addison's *Essays,* Johnson's *Rasselas* and *Lives of the Poets,* Paley's *Moral Philosophy,* Goldsmith's *History of England,* Bacon's *Essays, Novum Organon,* and *Advancement of Learning,* Malkins' *History of Greece,* Pinnock's *History of Greece,* Horace Wilson's *Universal History,* Adam Smith's *Moral Sentiments,* Abercrombie's *Intellectual Powers,* and Whewall's *Moral Philosophy.* In addition, specially compiled prose readers were brought out in several volumes for each class, some of which were prepared by Macaulay when he was president of the Council on Education in India.[16]

Of special interest is the preponderance of eighteenth-century neo-classical writers in the government curriculum, as opposed to the Romantic writers in the missionary curriculum. The range of texts represented in Duff's curriculum gave the lie to the missionary charge that works of the imagination were harmful to morals. Of course, poets like Pollock and Cowper are known to be favorite reading of the Evangelicals,[17] and it is not surprising that they were prescribed in the missionary curriculum. But given the claims for Christianity in Johnson, Addison, and Pope, we might well ask why Duff did not represent these writers in his course of literary studies. But this is to assume that the intention of teaching literature was to impart Christianity indirectly, when in fact we know that the Bible was openly taught as an authoritative exposition of religion in the missionary schools. Obviously, then, there was no need to get around an injunction against religious teaching as was the case in government schools, which chose the path of teaching literature to convey the message of the Bible. Literary study plainly served some other purpose in Duff's school, which must be established before the difference between the curricula in the two institutions can be explained.

The clue to the difference would appear to lie in Duff's concern that the Bible make an appropriate impact on its readers, both logically and emotionally. As various missionary publications point out endlessly, the power of the Bible lies in its imagery. If images could be regarded as arguments, reasons, and demonstrations that illustrate and reinforce the truth, the best means to conversion was, accordingly, through an appeal to the imagination. The horrors of sin and damnation were not to be understood through reasons but through images that give the reader a "shocking spectre of his own deformity and haunt him, even in his sleep."[18] The truth of Christianity was presented in vain unless it was *seen*, unless it was *felt*. To read the Bible well, to be moved by its imagery, to be instructed by its "dark and ambiguous style, figurative and hyperbolical manner," the imagination first had to be fully trained and equipped.[19] The highly imagistic poetry of Cowper, Wordsworth, Akenside, and Young clearly served this objective more immediately than did the more formal poetry of the Augustan neoclassicists.

At a glance it appears that government and missionary schools adopted two mutually exclusive curricula, one heavily classical and the other predominantly Romantic. By contrast, in English public schools of the same period the classical and the Romantic strains converged in a single curriculum bearing the impress of the nineteenth century's most famous educator, Thomas Arnold. The Arnoldian curriculum was a course of studies with a heavy stress on classical languages and literatures and classical history, and it was geared to instruct learners in the principles of law, government, and society. This content was balanced with readings in the poetry of the Romantics to teach lessons in the deeper relations between nature and the human soul. The classical-humanist and the Romantic strains in the Arnoldian curriculum together formed the Victorian ideal of what David Newsome has pithily described as "godliness and good learning."[20] The alliance between education and religion was basic to Arnold's philosophy of the curriculum, and its goal was the inculcation of a code of Christian values by which men of culture were to live.

But at the same time, this curriculum was entirely suited to the vocation of ruling. The strong emphasis on historical and philosophical texts in the literature curriculum correlated with the need for better-trained and better-informed administrators. The new demands of industrialization and an expanding empire required a specialized ruling class, "cultivated, steeped in philosophy and history, aware of its world politically and intellectually, and *interested,* in a deeper sense than either the scholar or the aristocratic amateur could claim to be."[21] The course of studies in English public schools was designed to foster those leadership qualities required of a governing elite: independent thinking, a strong sense of personal identity, and an ability to make decisions on one's own authority. Making men leaders also meant that they had to be marked off from the rest of society, and in British education this was achieved through social discrimination and a markedly stratified schooling system. As the educational historian T. W. Bamford observes, it is not generally realized how effective social or hierarchical gulfs can be in promoting leadership and the acceptance of decisions.[22]

Though the Arnoldian curriculum was meant for a ruling elite, the texts that were a part of it were also taught in India. Until the second half of the nineteenth century, Indians could not occupy government posts higher than those of clerks and lower-level subordinates, and even when they were admitted to higher positions it was obviously not to give them a role in governing, but only to carry out the work of bureaucracy. But the authors they were reading in school—Bacon, Butler, and John Stuart Mill—were not addressed to men who would be clerks and subordinates, but to those who would lead and assume responsibility for their actions. Indians receiving Western education were reading texts that taught them to be independent thinkers and leaders, but they had neither the independence nor the opportunity to lead. It would seem, then, that the political consequences of the Arnoldian curriculum in the Indian context could only be frustration and possibly rebellion, raising questions about why Indians were being given the same kind of literary education as the English elite.

In her case study of late nineteenth-century Indian education Ellen

McDonald notes the involvement in religious and social reform of many Indians educated in the Arnoldian curriculum. She cites the influence of Butlerian philosophy on well-known Bombay reformers like M. G. Ranade, a renowned lawyer, and Chandavarkar, the vice-chancellor of Bombay University, for both of whom social change was inseparable from moral reform of the individual.[23] On the basis of her finding, there is ground to believe that the Arnoldian curriculum was adapted in India in such a way that the goal of self-improvement in this context no longer meant training a ruling elite but setting educated Indians' attention on reform of their own society, a goal repeatedly articulated by Duff in his own educational writings.

The range of texts represented in Duff's curriculum belied the missionary charge that works of the imagination were harmful to morals. The more than nominal importance ascribed to literature in the education of Indian youth attending Duff's institution appears to reveal a basic contradiction in missionary practice, which becomes more apparent in light of the fact that missionary institutions were set up as alternative schools to the existing government colleges and were thus relatively free of centralized influence.

But considered in pedagogical terms, Duff's strong emphasis on a literary curriculum in his own school is less a reversal of his earlier objectives to its presence in government schools than a relocation of moral value and meaning from individual texts to the contexts in which they were taught and read. In Duff's view it was not theoretically impossible for literature to be a source of religious skepticism in one situation and a source of religious belief in another. If it were true that morality lay in texts, then selected texts could readily be singled out as more "moral" than others. Instead, Duff believed that morality lay in intention, context, purpose, and overall structure of the educational system.

Duff's determination to hold on to a literary curriculum was also shaped in large part by a perception of resistance to direct Christian instruction by Indian students who regarded the Bible as a necessary evil and barely tolerated its presence in their instruction. Though the *Calcutta Monthly Journal* castigated Duff for serving interests other than those he claimed to serve (he was accused, for instance, of being motivated by antipathy toward Roman Catholics, Episcopalians, Socinians, and other Christian sects whose religious opinions were as hateful to him as those of the Hindus), the assessment that "Dr. Duff will never be a fair reasoner until he is able in imagation [sic] to put himself in the position of the party whose wishes and interests are at stake" was not wholly true. So sensitive was Duff to native resistance that he invited parents to witness for themselves the kind of instruction their children were receiving at his school, by way of reassurance that there was no proselytizing going on there. Admittedly, many of the parents he encountered were overly consumed by suspicion of missionary intentions in forcing Bible instruction on their children. It was not uncommon for parents to withdraw their children immediately from Duff's school wherever they sensed what they saw as the "tyranny of the Bible." Some parents negotiated their needs in a more sanguine manner. Duff's biographer and former student, Lal Behari Day, records the plan his father had worked out: he would wait for the moment when his son had learned enough English to obtain a decent situation outside but was not yet intellectually advanced to understand lectures on Christianity—as soon as that moment arrived, he would instantly be withdrawn from school and placed in an office. "Let Duff Saheb do what he can," was the father's defiant challenge to the threat of proselytism.[24]

But Duff Saheb was a little more devious than even Day's father imagined. Duff had developed an elaborate system for inculcating Christian concepts through close questioning, careful relation of concepts, and association of ideas with their precise linguistic equivalent. The same associative technique was used for undermining reverence for Brahminical concepts. Day recounts his first class of instruction by Duff, in which the subject was a catechism on the cow. Duff asked his students to supply the Bengali word for cow, which is *goru*. He next asked whether they knew another Bengali word resembling it in sound, which happened, of course, to be *guru*, or Brahmin teacher. Dwelling at ample length on the patterns of similarity in form and sound between the two words, Duff quietly built up to his solemn query about what purpose was served by a *guru* and whether *goru* was not more useful than *guru*. "He then left our class," writes his student, "and went into another, leaving in our minds seeds of future thought and reflection."[25]

Duff insisted that in all the years he ran the school only three or four students ever left in protest over teaching of the Bible. A young Brahmin student who had earlier shown great hostility to Duff's comparative allusions to Christianity and Hinduism became so emotional and enraptured after reading the Lord's Prayer, the story of the Prodigal Son, and the thirteenth chapter of First Corinthians that he burst out in the middle of Duff's lecture to exclaim, "Oh sir, that is too good for us. Who can act up to that? Who can act up to that?"[26]

But Duff was never so extravagant in his claims for conversion as some of his fellow missionaries at times tended to be, drawing as they often did on the most dubious evidence bordering on the ludicrous, as with this little item from the *Missionary Register:*

> S., a little boy, came for the first time to speak concerning his soul. In our half-yearly report of the examination of the seminarists, we were obliged to characterize him as a quarrelsome little fellow. He now complained to me, that whenever others offend him in any wise, he is always inclined to BEAT THEM: such a free confession of a fault is doubtless a token for good, a proof that the Holy Spirit is active in the Soul.[27]

THE FACT that literary study won an honored place in Duff's curriculum suggests that though the secular study of literature might have been associated in his mind with moral degeneracy, this was by no means to say that he imputed to literature a natural tendency to corrupt the individual and blur his moral sense. Quite the contrary, the power of literature to inculcate virtue was less an issue than the fact that its moralities were accessible only to those who were suitably trained to read literature or had reached an advanced stage of mental development. By claiming that the force of truth rested on the moral state of the heart, Duff restricted the investigation of truth to a morally qualified inquirer whose mind had first been purged of all the prejudices, errors, and misconceptions that obstructed its advancement in true knowledge and then adequately replenished with "true" moral principles. For literature to be read as morality, a high degree of mental and moral cultivation was first required, which in Duff's view the mass of people simply did not have. For those who were ignorant of moral law there were no lessons in virtue to be gleaned from literature. Far from being a cultivator of moral feelings, a wide reading in literature was more likely to cause sharper questioning of moral law and perhaps even encourage active defiance of its commands. Duff's objections to English literary instruction at the government colleges were based on the fear that the students were inadequately equipped to read for edification. To his mind, no amount of literary study could possibly contribute toward the moral improvement of the Indians where there was no prior moral instruction. Literature could only shape and enlighten to the degree that the reader was already inherently predisposed to such enlightenment. But to expect literature to perform the work of raising the moral and intellectual level of the reader was to assume that all readers were on a comparable plane of moral development. Duff's critique raised larger theoretical questions about the nature of literary texts and their relationship to behavior and action. How useful, for instance, is literary instruction when readers have no prior sense of moral principles? Can the text succeed where nature has failed? Assuming that human nature is deficient and society fails to provide adequate models of behavior and action, can texts step into the vacuum and function as a surrogate for nature and shape moral and intellectual development? And if so, which works are the most appropriate ones for that purpose?

Duff's argument against secular uses of literature rested on a peculiarly grim Hobbesian theory of human nature as dark, proud, and selfish. If human nature were inherently good, it was perfectly reasonable to expect that the teaching of literature could proceed outside religious foundations without causing undue harm. But the predisposition of human nature for evil decisively established that nothing less than the triumph over innate depravity could legitimately be the goal of instruction. Duff's insistence on this point, drawn from a deeply felt Calvinism, highlighted by contrast the idealistic conception of human nature that informed a secular policy of education—of a concept of man as still unfallen, tainted neither by depravity nor sin, who lived in accordance to natural moral law, protecting him like a coat of armor against the actual (or potential) undermining effect of worldly knowledge. Duff's response to the secular conception was that "were human nature in a state of innocence and holiness, all true knowledge, literary or scienti... , would be not merely negatively harmless—it might be positively beneficial. But as long as human nature is guilty and depraved, such knowledge may become not merely negatively useless—it may prove positively injurious."[28] Flatly rejecting the theory that the text is independent of the moral state of the reader, autonomous in its own morality and truth, Duff sought to refocus attention on the reader as fallen, depraved, and sinful in order to reclaim his moral regeneration as an obligatory social and political goal.

The belief that virtue is an abstract quality removed from, unshaped by, and therefore anterior to worldliness led Duff to conclude that the pursuit of moral good rather than intelligence was the true object of education. He saw the struggle between good and evil, virtue and vice, order and anarchy as fraught with so much uncertainty and tension that the mere exercise of intellect was not sufficient for its resolution. From such observations he came to believe that the efforts of intelligence to create institutions like representative government could not by themselves emancipate people enslaved by religion from the tyranny of its yoke.

On the point of social utility Duff was in little disagreement with the secularists. But the issue that wrenched them apart concerned the power and authority of texts to regenerate individual souls. Morality for Duff was unquestionably a quality of the reader rather than of literature itself. But in presuming a homogeneous readership located at a comparable level of mental and moral development and moral receptivity, the secularists in Duff's view took up a position that established natural moral law as part of man's innate knowledge. The description of human nature in these terms made it more feasible for secularists to entertain a moral theory of literature—a theory of texts whose morality existed independently of the reader. The dependence of secularism on these two assumptions—that is, of a homogeneous readership and of moral law as part of man's innate knowledge—became a prime object of Duff's attack, which turned on a sharp questioning of the secularist belief in a common development of minds. Undaunted by the oversimplifications inherent in such an attack, to the extent that it meant restating in an absurdly naive way that minds developed at various paces, some more morally fortified than others, Duff plunged headlong into a line of attack that argued the inevitable emergence of a differentiated readership, so affecting interpretation of literature as to produce distortion, error, and falsehoods. The variability of the reader from individual to individual necessitated a program of instruction aimed at parity and standardization. If it was true to characterize secularism as based on the concept of an innately good human nature, then it was equally true to suggest that its ideal of perfection precluded a moral system because prescriptions are essential to ethics and superfluous when all behavior contributes to the ideal. To Duff's understanding, the conviction of innate depravity and the hope of regeneration provided the mechanism for regulation of behavior and therefore legitimized an ethical system. Such a system could not be apprehended by untutored intuition, but required the intervention of the educational process.

Duff interpreted secularism as a claim on behalf of a common development of minds that dispensed with first principles for comprehension of the world of matter. His attack fell on a derivative premise of this claim that established the formation of moral perceptions in the intellectual faculties and viewed the development of the intellect as a prelude to the cultivation of the moral sense. His own argument reversed the sequence of development in order to restore primacy to moral perceptions in intellectual formation. And though this emphasis certainly did not imply a rejection of the concept of Western literature as a product of Christian experience and history, embodying its best conscience, it did suggest that the guiding power of conscience was activated only when the reader had been shaped through prior formative influences for the reception of moral truths. In short, truth was self-evident only to those equipped both mentally and morally to receive it.

A curious contradiction characterizes this argument. However consistent, indeed predictable, belief in the priority of moral perceptions in intellectual formation might be with Evangelical convictions, that belief conflicted with the actual practice of many missionaries, including Duff himself, in the institutions they conducted. The practice rested on the premise that the force of modern knowledge (by which Duff meant both literary and scientific knowledge) was so great as to cause those exposed to it to turn away in revulsion from the errors of their own native systems. The subjects that were condemned for their secular character when taught in government institutions were included in the missionary curriculum as central subjects of study, so that while it was claimed on the one hand that truth is not self-evident, that its apprehension is possible only under certain conditions (one of which is a cultivated moral sense), it was maintained on the other that Western learning had a direct and immediate destructive effect on native superstitions, myths, and legends. Looked at objectively, there was a compelling logic to this process. If the young learner was made aware that all the facts regarding geography and history given in the Hindu scriptures were entirely fictitious, the shaking of his faith in one part of the system (the intellectual) would surely have the effect of shaking his faith in others. The destruction of that belief through instruction in scientific and literary truth was seen as the first stage in opening minds to the "purer" truths of revealed religion, and Alexander Duff, along with other missionaries, was attracted to the idea of an intellectual revolution that would lead toward a universal Christianity. The belief that Hinduism would surely fall from its foundation and the Gospel rise on its ruins—that through science and modern learning "we must all come to one religion"—was quite clearly an ideology that directed missionary labor in India.

But on two crucial points this practice was inconsistent with the avowed commitment to moral training: first, if modern knowledge had an inherent power to demolish an entrenched religious system, then it was tantamount to suggesting that its truths were self-evident; and second, if the destruction of Hinduism were able to occur so systematically and with the simplicity and elegance ascribed to it, it was difficult to avoid the conclusion that the Indians were at an acceptable level of mental and moral development to be able to participate in its demolition in the first place. Assuming the truth of both premises, the outcry over secular education appears even more perplexing and inexplicable, for if it were true that Western thought possessed the sort of self-evident, irreducible power attributed to it to cause Hinduism to come crashing down, then the educational process that Duff advocated as a form of preliminary "mind training" was simply redundant.

But this apparent inconsistency is less of a contradiction than it seems, and Duff coined a new phrase, *secular convergency,* to resolve it. The dilemma for Duff of course was to reconcile the conviction that only those who were morally prepared or trained could derive moral value from literature, with the view that Western literary knowledge had an intrinsic power to expose the falsity of existing superstitions and, by so doing, lay claims to moral authority and moral value. But he saw this dilemma as one that necessarily involved arbitrating between two basically untenable extremes. If Duff's whole argument against secularism was that it failed to replace destroyed beliefs with other, more positive values, the potential of secular learning to produce an intellectual revolution culminating in a universal Christianity then became entirely suspect.

But by a sleight of hand Duff accommodated secularism to evangelizing aims with the claim that modern studies acquired the force of religious instruction *after the fact,* that is, by virtue of its impact on destroying false religious systems. He wrote: "We must disown the bigotry of unwise pietism by patronizing the cause of sound literature and science lest by negligence we help to revive the fatal dogma of the dark ages, that what is philosophically true may yet be allowed to be theologically false."[29] When missionary institutions were first set up in India, the original plan was to introduce the higher branches of literature and science as an indispensable part of liberal education, separate from and unrelated to religious instruction, as a concession to the demand for modern studies by Indians. Duff himself raised the question whether by urging "secular convergency" he was denying the "self-evidencing power" of the Bible. But his answer was that in proportion to their demonstrated effects on eroding the grip of Hinduism, subjects that were seemingly remote from religion, like geography, general history, and natural philosophy, became divested of their secularity and stamped with the impress of sacredness. As Duff observed: "The teaching of these branches seemed no longer an indirect, secondary, ambiguous part of missionary labour,—but, in one sense, as direct, primary, and indubitable as the teaching of religion itself."[30] In short, the effect modern studies had on shaking native systems of learning contributed quite literally to the sacralization of its content. And so in achieving what religious teaching aimed at all along—the destruction of the "errors" of Hinduism—British secularism firmly and irrevocably aligned itself with Christianity. The motto outside Duff's General Assembly Institution expresses that conviction, albeit rather inelegantly: "He who enters here must moralize and religionize, as well as geometrize."[31] By redefining secularism as a handmaiden of religion in its positive aspects, Duff virtually reduced secular knowledge, as a category existing independently of religion, to the status of a non-concept. For this reason he was able to say: "Let us thus hail true literature and science as our very best auxiliaries . . . But in receiving these, as friendly allies, into our sacred territory, let us resolutely determine that they shall never, never, be allowed to usurp the throne, and wield a tyrant's sceptre over it."[32]

Duff often pointed to the example of one of his students, Guru Das Maitra, who later converted and became pastor of the Bengali Presbyterian Church of Calcutta. Guru Das was led to conversion by a curious chain of events. For two years, while studying at Duff's college, the young man had been deeply impressed by the daily readings of the Bible, and at last his disturbance of mind became apparent to his family. Alarmed by his interest in the religion they dreaded, family members attempted to divert Guru Das with the writings of Thomas Paine. But alas, the effect was quite different from what they had anticipated: the arguments of the skeptic only assured Guru Das more firmly than ever of the truth of Christianity. His decision to convert followed soon after.

POSSIBLY THE most provocative contribution of Alexander Duff is his interpretation of the East India Company's secularist policy as a conscious reaction to a cultural situation in England that worked against secularism in education. As Duff explains it, no child brought up in England could remain untouched by the all-pervasive influence of Christian culture, regardless of the attempts to subsume scriptural teaching under worldly instruction in certain institutions. The ultimate failure of secular education in England to disengage itself from religious influence demonstrated conclusively, as far as Duff could see, the powerful influence of an enveloping Christian culture in the formation of moral structures in society. It is clear that Duff virtually accepted as axiomatic a unitary theory of English civil society based on religion, influencing all forms of knowledge produced in that society.

As a rationale for evangelizing intent, Duff's argument was unambiguous and straightforward enough to warrant consideration strictly on those terms. But when a statement of intent attempts to pass itself off as cultural analysis as well, then it is obviously quite a different matter and premises that might have been accepted earlier as enabling premises for a program of action now acquired the character of a priori assumptions, whose effect was to reduce the persuasiveness or usefulness of the analysis. One such assumption was that a state of perfect symmetry existed between English civil society and Christian doctrine. To define advanced societies in terms of the closeness of fit between civil and sacred institutions on the one hand and literary and religious knowledge on the other was to render logically true and eternally valid a set of propositions whose verity was otherwise undemonstrable: first, that the concept of secular knowledge in a Christian culture is manifestly an artificial construction; and second, that in a Christian culture like the English the study and teaching of literature in purely secular terms is not merely a contradiction in terms but an unrealizable and implausible event.

The sheer governmental arrogance of insisting on literature's autonomy from the influence of religious culture led Duff to suspect that the official policy of secularism in India had been instituted in a spirit of experimentation and that India was merely being used as "a fair and open field for testing the non-religion theory of education."[33] There is no question that India had indeed become an experimental laboratory for testing educational ideas that had either been aborted in England or fallen victim to stiff opposition from entrenched traditions and orthodoxies. The official perception of the colonized culture as lacking in counteractive influences (by which was meant direct church control) caused India to be viewed as fertile ground for experimentation with untried or unfavorable ideas and for observing and recording their effects under controlled conditions.

But while Duff's criticism was at many points incisive and trenchant, the analysis remained trapped at the level of polemics. His explanation for the British experiment in secularism discounted crucial factors such as shifting class structures, the institutionalization of science, and bureaucratization of state machinery in favor of a narrowly exclusive explanation centered on the special nature of the relation between church and state in England. The characterization of Western society as a harmonious integration of civil and sacred institutions with literary and religious knowledge had profound implications for subsequent delineations of non-Western societies. If the representation of Christian society as a unitary composition were to hold true, then non-Christian society could be discussed in no other but antithetical terms, that is, as a society marked by asymmetry and dissonance and where knowledge ran counter to established institutions and structures. Cultural analysis that began with an explanation of a specific cultural situation in England thus shifted to more generalized descriptions of the nature of Indian society as somehow only arbitrarily or loosely related to prevailing forms of knowledge.

But what is particularly significant, because it reveals Duff's incessantly shifting focus and consequent equivocation, is his use of the word *knowledge*, by which he meant not knowledge indigenous to Indian society, but knowledge introduced through Western cultural expansion. Of course, from the missionary point of view cultural analysis of this sort, which ostensibly aimed at exposing government motives, had a productive value as well, in that it simultaneously made a strong case for the introduction of Christianity in India. (And much the same sort of thing characterizes Duff's reports in *The Indian Rebellion,* where the objects of attack in British secularism were then reconstructed as helpful to the missionary cause.) For if Western scientific and literary knowledge ran counter to Hinduism, which was allegedly based on superstition, ritual, and dogma, the minimum condition for an integrated Indian civil society was a religious culture that supported the new knowledge structure. Therefore, though Duff's analysis may have been outwardly critical of official representations of India as fertile soil for the engrafting of new social formations based on exclusively secular principles, the critique was expansive enough to accommodate evangelical aims as well.

Duff's exposure of the experimental motives of British secularism in India is perhaps his chief contribution to intellectual history. Not surprisingly, the kind of project he proposes is akin to what Eric Stokes, for example, has more recently attempted in *The English Utilitarians and*

India, which describes the uses to which India was put by the new middle-class mind for the translation of its political and moral ideas. Stokes offers a truly remarkable record of how many of the movements of English life tested their strength and fought their early battles on Indian soil. Only an enormous amount of cross-referencing no doubt can prove Duff's thesis, but at the same time it is useful to remember that a major pitfall might be to get drawn into the reductive form of analysis employed by colonial rulers that sought out neat correspondences between English social structure and the structure of colonial relationships, such that the multiple religious and ethnic groups of India are loosely combined to form an amorphous whole corresponding to the English working class. Part of Duff's self-appointed task was to explode some of those assumptions, but in the long run he was able to do no more than substitute his own set of equally skewed assumptions for those he felt were taking colonial India in the direction of anarchy, political discontent, and perfidy. In some respects his arguments anticipated the Anglican defense of John Henry Newman and Thomas Arnold, particularly with respect to issues concerning the accommodation of the secular to the spiritual and the intellectual to the moral, though Duff, who chose to join the splinter movement of the Established Church of Scotland on grounds of preserving freedom of the church from state intervention, would have never accepted Arnold's ecumenism or his view of church-state as an embodiment of the unity between religious morality and secular philosophy. Also, Duff's self-conscious efforts to deploy scientific and literary education for support of the truths of Christianity would have seemed unnecessary to Arnold, who rather than have his son preoccupied with science "would gladly have him think that the sun went round the earth, and that the stars were so many spangles set in the bright blue firmament."[34]

3

"One Power, One Mind"

> He that would break a fortress, first ascertains its weakest point. The nature of the poison must be well understood, before the antidote can be administered with effect.
>
> —*The Missionary's Vade Mecum*, 1847, p. 5.

IN ENGLISH social history the function of providing authority for individual action and belief and dispensing moral laws for the formation of character was traditionally carried out through the medium of church-controlled educational institutions. Until the beginning of the nineteenth century, education in England was fully integrated with the church and shared many common features—curricula, goals, practices. Even when, by midnineteenth century, the ideological supremacy of the established churches was eroded and its integration with education replaced by new institutional relationships, the churches continued to function as interest groups influencing educational development. As the British sociologists Michalina Vaughan and Margaret Archer point out in their work on social conflict and educational change in England:

The deposition of a group from a previous position of institutional domination does not spell its ultimate decline. The group will continue for as long as adherence to it offers either objective or subjective advantages to its members. As an interest group it will interact with others; while it is unlikely to dominate social institutions, it is still capable of influencing them.[1]

The aristocracy maintained a monopoly over access to church-dominated education and instituted a classical course of studies that it shared with the clergy but from which the middle and working classes were systematically excluded. The classical curriculum under church patronage became identified as a prerequisite for social leadership and, more subtly, the means by which social privilege was protected. This alliance between church and culture consecrated the concept of station in life and directly supported the existing system of social stratification; while the classical curriculum served to confirm the upper orders in their superior social status, religious instruction was given to the lower orders to fit them for the various duties of life and to secure them in their appropriate station. Thus the alliance between church and culture is equally an alliance between ideas of formative education and of social control.

Two educational movements of eighteenth-century England illustrate the powerful influence of the church in institutionalizing certain kinds of texts and excluding others. Both the Charity School movement and the Sunday School movement grew out of concern over the alarming rise of urban squalor and crime and out of a conviction that unless the poor were brought back into the Christian orbit, the relatively harmonious order that had been carefully laid would be shattered. Only instruction in sound Christian principles, it was maintained, would prevent such a catastrophe, and "such little portions of Holy Scripture as recommend industry, gratitude, submission and the like virtues" were duly prescribed. Hannah More summed up the educational philosophy of social control adopted by these institutions when she declared, "Principles, not opinions, are what I labour to give them."[2]

Apart from the Bible, required reading in these institutions consisted of religious tracts, textbooks, parables, sermons, homilies, and prayers, many of which were specially written for inclusion in the curriculum. Because of the huge demand for such works, the two movements stimulated the production of a great number of religious texts. M. G. Jones' illuminating study, *The Charity School Movement*, makes a comprehensive listing of the works produced and studied, and I mention a few titles to give an idea of their ideological bias: R. Nelson's *The Whole Duty of a Christian Designed for the Use of the Charity Schools in and about London* (1704); T. Green's *Principles of Religion for Charity Children*; Ellesby's *A Caution against Ill-company: The Dignity and Duty of a Christian and the Great Duty of Submission to the Will of God*; White Kennett's *The Christian Scholar; or, Rules and Directions for Children and Youths sent to English Schools, more especially designed for the Poor Boys Taught and Cloathed by Charity in the Parish of St. Botolph's, Aldgate* (1710); Dean Nowell's *Elements of Christian Piety, designed particularly for the Charity Children* (1715); and J. Hanway's *A Comprehensive Sentimental Book for Scholars learning in Sunday Schools, containing the Alphabet, Numbers, Spelling, Moral and Religious Letters, Stories and Prayers suited to the growing powers of Children for the advancement in Happiness of the Rising Generation* (1786).[3]

These works were part of what was labeled the "literary curriculum." The religious bias of a course of studies restricted to the Bible and catechism meant that secular writing of any kind, by which was generally meant works of the imagination, was kept out of the institutional mainstream. As late as the 1860s, the "literary curriculum" in British educational establishments remained polarized around classical studies for the upper classes and religious studies for the lower. As for what is now known as the subject of English literature, the British educational system had no firm place for it until the last quarter of the nineteenth century, when the challenge posed by the middle classes to the existing structure resulted in the creation of alternative institutions devoted to "modern studies."

It is quite conceivable that educational development in British India might have run the same course as it did in England, were it not for one crucial difference: the strict controls on Christianizing activities. Clearly the religious texts that were standard fare for the lower classes in England could not legitimately be incorporated into the Indian curriculum without inviting violent reactions from the native population, particularly the learned classes. The educational experiments in social control that had been conducted on the English poor had only limited application in India. Yet the fear lingered that without submission of the colonial subject to moral law or the authority of God, the control England was able to secure over the lower classes back home would be eluded in India.

The experience with the English working classes prompted at least one British official, the Marquess of Tweeddale, governor and commander in chief of Madras from 1842 to 1848, to seek out the same distinguishing characteristics in the Hindus and Muslims (assuming them to be a unified group): immorality, sensuality, self-indulgence, corruption, and depravity—all of which were identified as inimical to society and therefore to be combatted and controlled. Tweeddale had issued a minute in 1846 seeking introduction of the Bible as a class book. The proposal was defeated, but the fact that it was made at all suggests an ambivalence and indecision in the government's position on religion. Not only did the minute officially endorse the value of religion and a practical education, but it also insisted on its importance in making the English nation fit for the various duties of life. The substance of Tweeddale's minute included extensive comparisons between the situation at home and in India, between the "rescue" of the lower classes in England, "those living in the dark recesses of our great cities at home, from the state of degradation consequent on their vicious and depraved habits, the offspring of ignorance and sensual indulgence," and the elevation of the Hindus and Muslims, whose "ignorance and degradation" required a remedy not adequately supplied by their respective faiths.[4] In building up that foundation through Christian principles, claimed Tweeddale, the British government would not simply be teaching Christianity; it would be giving instruction "useful to the State."

The comparability of the English working classes to the Indian colonial subjects intensified the search for other social institutions to take over from religious instruction the task of communicating the laws of the social order. The uneasiness generated by a strictly secular policy in teaching English served to resurrect Charles Grant in administrative discussions. An officer of the East India Company, Grant was one of the first Englishmen to urge the promotion of both Western literature and Christianity in India. In 1792 he had written a scathing denunciation of Indian religion and society titled *Observations on the State of Society among the Asiatic Subjects of Great Britain*. The tract was as much prescriptive of British policy as descriptive of Hindu practice and custom, for Grant's proposals went far beyond the eradication of practices offensive to British sensibility to include an enunciation of strategies for ensuring British hegemony. Grant reacted contemptuously to measures or policies based on principles of mere expediency and sought to make British connections with India "permanent and . . . indissoluble."[5] Unlike many of his contemporaries, he had little faith in the power of legal and political actions to yield long-term benefits. He was convinced that if Indians were ever to find the British government better than their own, it would have to be because of "the superior personal conduct of Britons" and not the superiority of the system.[6] He fervently maintained that for England to gain a more lasting foothold in India, the situation required a demonstration of the religious and moral principles that alone validated its position. Ideally, there were two means by which this could be accomplished. The first was placing the people at close proximity to their rulers, to provide reassurance that their destinies were guided by men of principle, not rapacious vultures, for "without an uniting principle, a conjoining tie of this nature, we can suppose the country to be, in fact, retained only by mere power."[7]

But the not so exemplary conduct of Englishmen in India vitiated this objective ("by them the worst part of our manners will be exhibited"). British misconduct gave Grant the opportunity he needed to attack the deistic and rationalistic tendencies of his age:

> Discovering in their intercourse with us little of the nature of the religion we profess, [the Indians] will not of course be apt to refer the good qualities of which the English appear possessed to that source; nor will they, know that the national standard of morals formed from it has an influence even upon the conduct of those who pay no particular regard to a religious system.[8]

Grant's perception of the moral laxity of England in 1794 appeared even more horrifying in the scenario he imagined, where anarchy was pictured as wildly overrunning India, a land "so wonderfully contagious. . . . so congenial to the worst qualities of human nature." Grant's real fear was of a different order: by keeping Christian influences out of India, the East India Company left no means of explaining the superiority of England except in material terms. The dangers of material explanations lay in the possible suggestion to native minds of British susceptibility to decay, change, and contingency. The relation of British strength to its spiritual ideals was, for Grant, England's only sure guarantee of enduring hegemony, but that had no chance of being established as long as religious influence was denied. As he warned: "It is . . . in continuing as we are, that we stand most exposed to the dangers of political revolution."[9] And thus the second principle by which long-term rule in India was guaranteed: the creation of an image of the English nation as having been "formed by superior lights and juster principles and possessed of higher energies."[10]

Complementary to the restoration of Christian principles was a derogation of Hindu society and religion. Grant's critique is not remarkably original in the ground that it covers. The caste system, idol worship, polytheism, and propitiatory rites are all condemned in the most conventional terms. But in mapping out his strategy for British supremacy in India, morality, monotheism, and monorule all become linked in his thought as part of a single constellation of meaning. Grant's objections to caste, for instance, are as much the basis of an argument conjoining religion and state as a criticism of Hindu religion. Quite ignoring the symbiotic relationship of caste groups within the hierarchy, Grant held a fragmented view of caste, which formed the basis for his conclusion that the norms and rules of the particular caste group to which a Hindu belonged, rather than society as a whole, gave legitimacy to his actions, however contrary to the external interests of the body politic. He gave the example that what might be considered criminal acts in other societies are less readily defined so in a caste society where each caste group has its own system of rules and ethics. How, argued Grant, could any sense of right and wrong develop in the members of a caste society where no single moral code is upheld to enforce positive social behavior and where a universal definition of crime is virtually impossible?

Grant's intense revulsion from Hindu society was at the same time laced with a morbid paranoia. For an Evangelical writing out of Anglican England there could be no worse thought than the horrors unleashed by a disjunction between religion and state, spelling the decay of morality and law. Symptomatic of that break was the failure of religion to provide the laws by which crime is recognized as an offense against the state and against God, from which ensue corruption and depravity of character.[11] In proportion to Grant's revulsion from the polytheistic, caste society of Hinduism grew a conviction that there must be one single moral code—"one Power, one Mind"—governing society.

The idea of "one Power, one Mind" had both theological and political resonances for Grant. His objections to polytheism illustrate the fusion of these two levels, with a hidden appeal for integration of religion and state. Grant's argument is as follows: On the moral level, the existence of many gods implies choice in whom to worship, the consequence being that "he who makes a god for himself will certainly contrive to receive from him an indulgence for his corrupt propensities."[12] The multiplicity of gods in the Hindu pantheon blurred any sense of a single, universal cosmic law upon whose recognition Grant believed all social harmony rests. Instead of creating a vision of divine principles acting in uniform concert, the Hindu scheme fragmented cosmic unity and encouraged a system of multiple deities working at variance with each other. Barriers between worshipers of different deities are reinforced and a unitary code replaced by a relativistic one.

Grant continues that the unsettling fact about a polytheistic society, where kings and rulers keep company with other gods, is its resistance to a central authority:

And how are our subjects to be formed to a disposition thus favourable to us, to be changed thus in their character, but by new principles, sentiments, and tastes, leading to new views, conduct, and manners; all which would, by one and the same effect, identify their cause with ours, and proportionately separate them from opposite interests?[13]

In a society where multiple worship was complementary to multiple allegiances, Grant was not confident that brute assertion of authority was likely to overwhelm resistance to assimilation. Nor did he believe that the ameliorative project could be carried out effectively in a society that was not driven by ethical absolutes, a society where the propitiation of deities was sufficient to satisfying immediate needs and larger social objectives were consequently reduced to irrelevance. Grant considered the introduction of Western knowledge without prior changes in the structure of native religion a self-defeating enterprise. He was not optimistic that the truths of Western civilization were so self-evident as to cause an immediate transformation of archaic social structure. But at the same time he intuitively recognized that a unitary concept of God was the key to the assimilative project of British colonialism. His idea of "one Power, one Mind" encapsulated related ideas of cultural hegemony, ethical absolutism, centralized authority, and submission to an overarching law governing all individuals, without which Western knowledge was deprived of all transformative effect.

MANY YEARS after the publication of his tract, Grant's assessment of Hinduism as the linchpin of British rule rang with the force of truth to succeeding East India Company officials, for whom the realization dawned that Christian instruction, or something akin to it, could be deferred only at the peril of the English government. Sensing a weakening of the government's resistance to religious involvement, the Rev. William Keane exerted subtle pressure by pointing out, in a timely speech, that while secular European education had substantially destroyed "heathen" superstition, it had not substituted any moral principle in its place. The exclusion of the Bible had a demoralizing effect, he claimed, for it tended to produce evils in the country and to give the native mind

> unity of opinion, which before it never had . . . and political thoughts, which they get out of our European books, but which it is impossible to reconcile with our position in that country, political thoughts of liberty and power, which would be good if they were only the result of a noble ambition of the natural mind for something superior, but which, when they arise without religious principles, produce an effect which, to my mind, is one of unmixed evil.[14]

In stronger terms, he called the government's decision to exclude religion "politically mischievous," an incitement to radicals, who were bound to interpret British deference toward local feelings as a mark of political weakness. Keane's contempt for British policy was equally a contempt of emasculated authority and excessive delicacy of sentiment. Pragmatic considerations had so blurred British political sense, he charged, that only an appeal to absolute, uncontested principles could restore it. "Whatever is morally wrong can never be politically right" became a rallying cry for religious instruction. Keane's somber testimony concluded with a stirring call to duty that became the credo of the missionaries: "God is hastening us on the glorious work for which alone he sent us to India, which is to make the Gospel known to the poor heathen."[15]

The missionaries got further support from an unexpected quarter. The military officers who testified in the parliamentary sessions on Indian education joined hands with them in arguing that a secular education in English would increase the Indians' capacity for evil because it would elevate their intellects without providing the moral principles to keep them in check. Major-General Rowlandson of the British army warned, "I have seen native students who had obtained an insight into European literature and history, in whose minds there seemed to be engendered a spirit of disaffection towards the British Government."[16] While obviously the missionaries and the military had different interests at stake, with the latter perhaps not quite as interested in the souls of the "heathen" as the former, they were both clearly aiming at the same goal: the prevention of situations leading to political disunity or lawlessness. The alliance between the two undoubtedly proved fruitful insofar as it loosened the British resistance to the idea of religious instruction and made them more conscious of the need to find alternate modes of social control.

In the years following the actual introduction of English in India there was occasion to recall Grant's shrewd observation that an emphasis on the moral aspect would facilitate the introduction of Western education without throwing open the doors of English liberal thought to Indians; that moral improvement of the subjects was possible without opening up the possible danger of inculcating radical ideas that would upset the British presence in India. Moral good and happiness, Grant had argued, "views politics through the safe medium of morals, and subjects them to the laws of universal rectitude."[17] The most appealing part of his argument, from the point of view of a government now sensing the truth of the missionaries' criticism of secularism, was that historically Christianity had never been associated with bringing down governments, for its concern was with the internal rather than the external condition of man.

Complaints against the anarchical threat of English studies taught as a secular branch of knowledge were so common that a questionnaire sent out by the Baptist Missionary Society evoked little surprise when it devoted a major part of its survey to soliciting observations from various kinds of institutions on the attitudes of English-speaking Indians to matters of religion and morals. More often than not, the general response was that "the new ideas obtained by the study of English literature will undoubtedly weaken, if not destroy, superstitious prejudices; but, on the other hand, the knowledge thus attained tends to produce a supercilious pride and skepticism unless leavened with a large amount of Christian teaching, and this, in the present state of things, it is impossible to give."[18] The "present state of things" was a reference not only to the policy of religious neutrality, but also to inadequate facilities for training native preachers, insufficient funds, and native resistance to direct Christian instruction.

The controversy surrounding the instruction offered at Hindu College, Calcutta, marked increasing dissonance in the British position on education for Indians. While the cultivation of the rational faculties remained the chief aim of instruction, the climate of skepticism prevailing at Hindu College was a dismal reminder that the goal required continual modification to meet the equally important objective of nurturing socially responsible individuals. Criticism of Hinduism was matched by an equal contempt for Christianity by the college youth so that the managers of the college had to issue an order "to check as far as possible all disquisitions tending to unsettle the belief of the boys in the great principles of natural religion."[19] Some parents were sufficiently alarmed by the college's reputation for skeptical inquiry to withdraw their sons, complaining that "boys are taught to learn the higher branches of literature and science, but are not instructed in any book of morals."[20] One Hindu parent went so far as to urge that the precepts of Christ be made a class book in government and aided schools.

The principal object of the missionary attack was Utilitarianism, particularly its extreme intellectualism and scientific rationalism. For many missionaries the merging of literature and science in Utilitarian thought falsely reduced the two disciplines to comparable branches issuing from the same trunk of knowledge and engaging the same intellectual faculties. The first step toward a reconstitution of literature's role in society, therefore, was the disengagement of literature from science and a reclaiming for it of functions associated with faculties of mind other than the purely intellectual. Convinced that the secularization of literature had cut people off from the past and introduced discontinuity into their lives, many missionaries foresaw an England heading toward a crisis of mammoth proportions if the government continued to discourage influences to "replenish the soul, nurse diseased spirits to health, touch the conscience, and refine the intellect." The disastrous effect that the blurring of literary and scientific knowledge had produced on the morals of Indian youth, with its attendant substitution of reason for divine will, pointed to a causal relation between secular study of literature on one hand and moral decay and subversion of moral law on the other.

The long-term effect of the missionary clamor was a redefinition of reason in alignment with notions of duty and social obligation. Missionaries hostile to the basic premises of secular education unleashed every available weapon in their arsenal to prove that the equation of reason with individually realized truths unwittingly fortified the position of Hinduism. Through extensive references to Hindu scriptures, Alexander Duff set out to demonstrate that the central value of self-reliance affirmed by Hinduism placed the worshiper in a false relationship of oneness with the Absolute, transforming God from a being external to man, demanding submission to his righteousness, to a being internal to man. By the terms of this analysis, the Hindu form of worship was no more than intellectual self-adoration, producing not morality—the complete submission of man to the righteousness of God—but the illusion of self-sufficiency.

Duff's reading ironically challenged the conventional British derogation of Hinduism as a religion that subordinated self to caste and community. While denouncing Hinduism as a religion that promoted intellectual rather than moral worship, Duff negotiated the conflict between individual conscience and submission to God to accommodate Utilitarian ideas of social cohesion and obligation. The Hindu concept of God struck at the root of all morality through a peculiar syllogism that Duff saw as characteristic of Eastern religions: Whatever man does, God does; every man is God, but God is not responsible to any. Therefore, man, who is God in the Hindu scheme of things, cannot be responsible to any. In short, because there is only one being—Man/God —who is absolved of all responsibility, there is neither right nor wrong in human actions.[21]

Though a body of opinion in England still advocated minimum interference in Indian religious faiths, in the hope that education and knowledge would ultimately guide the Indians to Christianity, the group of missionaries who had argued for more unambiguous, direct means began to make a dent on the government's thinking. The British government officially remained committed to a policy of religious neutrality, but indirectly gave tacit encouragement to the missionaries through their own example. For instance, government schools prescribed spelling-books for teaching English, but often, such as in the school at Banares, these books contained passages at variance with polytheism. In the name of teaching the mechanics of the English language, the British government saw no violation of. its own injunction against religious interference by providing religious instruction indirectly.[22] The paranoia that normally dictated colonial policy alternated with a familiar smugness about the Indian character, for "upon that principle of acquiescence in whatever the State does, which seems to regulate the minds of the natives, there would have been very little opposition raised to it."[23] Indeed, as long as Indians remained unaware of the connection between the diffusion of knowledge and instruction in Christian principles, the government was content to turn a blind eye to religious instruction. But if they were ever to become suspicious, as one cautious observer remarked, "all efforts on their ignorance would be as vigorously resisted as if they were on their own religion. The only effect of introducing

Christianity into the schools would be to sound the alarm and to warn the Brahmins of the approaching danger."[24] The safest solution was to keep Indians at the level of children, innocent and unsuspecting of the meaning of their instruction, for once enlightened, there was no predicting how hostile they would turn toward those who were educating them.

Maintaining a delicate balance between "pagan" ignorance and subversive enlightenment put enormous pressure on the British, often leading to disastrous results. In 1818 British troops moved into Rajputana (now called Rajasthan), a province in the western part of India. Confident that the presence of new schools would wean Indian youth away from the ill habits of their parents, the Marquess of Hastings sent the formidable Serampore missionary William Carey to Ajmere for this purpose. But there Carey made the mistake of introducing the Bible as a schoolbook. Instantly the parents were up in arms and refused to send their children to school until it was withdrawn. But generally the experience of the missionary societies was somewhat different, as in the case of the Calcutta Diocesan Committee of the Society for Propagating Christian Knowledge. When it introduced some of the less "controversial" Scriptures as lessons, it initially encountered considerable distrust from the parents, but suspicion gradually faded into acceptance when the parents perceived that the choice was a grim one: either this education for their children or none at all. From such experiences, not a few missionaries delighted in painting a picture of the Indians as a people who were quite ready to sacrifice their prejudices and offer themselves to the worship of Christ if it meant they could get a school for their children in the bargain.[25]

The gingerliness with which colonial administrators approached the issue of instruction in the Bible led to what some missionaries felt were practices of only secondary and perhaps even unsound value, such as treating the life of Christ as biography or teaching the Scriptures in colleges for purely secular reasons like preparing students for the law.[26] The government schools would not even risk teaching the Bible as a historical work. The proscription of the Bible in schools and colleges was a sensitive issue, but much more for the British, apparently, than the Indians. As was often remarked, fear of the Bible was really an English, not a Hindu, one and had its origins in the objections of Roman Catholics. If Indians had any fear of the Bible at all, it was primarily in its political rather than its theological character. The Rev.

Keane tried to reassure Parliament, to no avail, that "the Hindus despise our Bible; they do not believe it is the power of God to upset their whole system; when they do, then I believe they will try to keep it out of the schools if they can."[27] The Hindu indifference to the Bible was in fact urged as an excuse to include it in government-aided schools, for "they . . . cared as little for the Bible in its religious character as we do for Homer" or "as we in our school-boy days cared for the mythology of Ancient Greece and Rome."[28]

STRUCTURAL CONGRUENCES established between Christianity and English literature fortified a sense of shared history and tradition. Missionaries ably cleared the way for the realization that as "the grand repository of the book of God" England had produced a literature that was immediately marked off from all non-European literatures, being "animated, vivified, hallowed, and baptized" by a religion to which Western man owed his material and moral progress. The difference was rendered as a contrast between "the literature of a world embalmed with the Spirit of Him who died to redeem it, and that which is the growth of ages that have gloomily rolled on in the rejection of that Spirit, as between the sweet bloom of creation in the open light of heaven, and the rough, dark recesses of submarine forests of sponges."[29] This other literature was likened to Plato's cave, whose darkened inhabitants are "chained men . . . counting the shadows of subterranean fires."

If not in quite the same colorful terms, other missionaries pointed out that though the government claimed it taught no Christianity, a great deal was actually taught, for English education was so replete with Christian references that much more of scriptural teaching was imparted than generally admitted. The Rev. William Keane attempted to persuade officials that

> Shakespeare, though by no means a good standard, is full of religion; it is full of the common sense principles which none but Christian men can recognize. Sound Protestant Bible principles, though not actually told in words, are there set out to advantage, and the opposite often condemned. So with Goldsmith, Abercrombie on the Mental Powers, and many other books which are taught in the schools; though the natives hear they are not to be proselytized, yet such books have undoubtedly sometimes a favourable effect in actually bringing them to us missionaries.[30]

Pretending that a policy of religious neutrality was in force was sheer self-deception, noted the Rev. J. Kennedy, proclaiming somewhat magisterially, "Let the books imparting useful knowledge, or giving the highest products of the European mind, be pruned as they may of Christian references, the Christian element will remain in some degree to tinge the instruction imparted, and give it a Christian tendency."[31] And as a writer for the *Calcutta Review* remarked, even though the Bible was proscribed and religious chapters on passages from English books expunged, "who will succeed in robbing Shakespeare of his Protestant common sense, Bacon and Locke of their scriptural morality, or Abercrombie of his devout sentiment?"[32]

The literary enterprise of familiarizing the Bible amongst "benighted" peoples was at various points framed in the imagery of empire building. The *Madras Christian Instructor and Missionary Record* asserted that

> the genius of literature . . . clearly sees that in the missionary brotherhood she has found the men who are to extend her empire to the ends of the earth, and give her throne a stability that will be lasting as the sun. She beholds them subduing language after language, reducing them to the laws of grammar, and fixing them in the columns of the lexicon. She sees, with grateful wonder, the schoolhouse rising in the desert, and hears in the depths of its solitude, the creative crash of the printing-press, as it pours forth its intellectual bounties.[33]

Yet while appearing to represent the end-point of comparative analysis it is worth noting that the structural correspondence between English literature and Christianity did not immediately develop from a sense of shared history between religion and literature or from a belief in a common culture of values, attitudes, and norms. To recall, the relationship between literature and religion was often perceived in antithetical terms by both Company officials and missionaries in the initial period of England's commitment to Indian education. The meager faith missionaries vested in literary texts to enhance the moral tone of society sprang in part from the conviction that an unusually high level of mental and moral excellence was first required before English works could truly be enjoined to the moral enterprise. Given the fact that the majority of people were believed to fall below that level, literary instruction did not present itself as an effective instrument for inculcating morality. On the contrary, for readers ignorant of moral law literature seemed to provide no direction toward understanding or obeying its dictates. Many missionaries feared that far from cultivating moral feelings, untutored and unregulated reading would conceivably cause a closer questioning of moral law, stimulating readers to act against accepted norms.

The hostility to certain literary forms, particularly poetry, accentuated the lines of opposition between literature and religion. The essence of poetry is deception, insisted one writer for the *Asiatic Journal*, adding that the cultivation of an art form that is so contrary to truth could only create a nation of deceptive people. He based his claim on the observation that what would be considered lies in plain prose are acceptable in poetry, because such lies go under the guise of poetic conventions like hyperbole and conceit: "To assert one thing and mean another is not termed deceit, but 'hypostasis': where a person really does what he declares he will not do, it is only an 'aposiopesis' in a poet, but is considered a most dishonourable act in any other person."[34]

But this is not to say that all poetry was unconditionally dismissed as deceptive, and the critic for the *Asiatic Journal* cited above was quick to draw attention to the example of the Bible, where the directness of the language and the close correspondence between word and concept eliminated all possibilities of equivocation and ambiguity. If a given term is understood to denote one object before it is used figuratively to signify another, its proneness to deception is correspondingly reduced.[35] As a higher-level activity, figuration was deemed acceptable when preceded by the stage of exact signification. The figuration in Oriental literature, bypassing an earlier stage of precise signification and thwarting and even reversing the normal development of a culture, was held responsible for the flawed moral growth of Indians. The emergence of poetry at a later stage in both the individual's and the culture's growth ideally provided the conditions for a truly significant moral impact, at a point when morality and imagination were so finely attuned that they constituted a perfect equilibrium.[36]

Nonetheless, even when literature had gained considerable importance and was enlisted as an auxiliary to religious instruction, as was true in Duff's General Assembly Institution and later Free Church Institution, literary understanding was still held secondary to the goal of conversion by many missionary societies, which would not accept literary education as a complete substitute for religious instruction. Though grand, extravagant claims may have been made in missionary publications about Christian influence in English literature (primarily to influence government policy on neutrality), the inclusion of literature in the missionary curriculum was made in many instances for pragmatic rather than philosophical reasons. Limitations in resources to disseminate Christianity required missionaries to fall back on alternative methods. The training of native preachers to carry the Christian message to the native population was an enormously difficult task, and adequate facilities simply did not exist for a huge undertaking of that kind. The preachers who were trained under the existing conditions were frequently criticized for being intellectually weak. Native deficiences were explained in terms of an insufficiently developed indigenous literature capable of providing support for elucidating moral concepts.[37] In its absence, Indians depended on oral instruction given by missionaries, who in turn lacked enough knowledge of native languages and of native modes of thought to convey the exact theological nuances. English literary study acquired the status of an institution in place of the one that the missionaries would have preferred to have available, but failed to secure because of insufficient funds and manpower, for training Indian preachers. To offset the financial constraints, one report recommended that native preachers be educated in English first so that "by this means they would have access to a wholesome literature, and independently of the aid of a missionary, might continue to improve their morals."[38]

At the same time, however, though prospective Indian preachers were educated in English literature to prepare them for participation in missionary activity, they were not considered choice candidates as future teachers of English.

> Those schoolmasters feel an utter abhorrence to all liberal notions of science and religion; and although their employers may insist on the introduction of books having a moralizing tendency and leading to correct notions of God and his works, yet when their conduct is not *narrowly watched,* they avail themselves of every opportunity (and a schoolmaster has many) to throw ridicule upon the new instruction [emphasis in the original].[39]

And so even though English literature may have been employed to teach the natives elements of religion, it was not successful in turning them to a full embrace of its principles.

But perhaps the argument most persuasive for missionaries for the provision of literary training in their schools was the one that demonstrated that Christian instruction tinged with a literary emphasis invariably produced favorable effects. A report commissioned by the Baptist Missionary Society observed that "[the Indians] are more susceptible to religious impressions, through a skilful use of the frequent allusions to Christian truth found in the prescribed course, and an indirect reference to the Scriptures, than in the time specially devoted to Christian teaching."[40] The stereotypical representation of Indians as children is implicit in this characterization, which attributes missionary success in arousing Indian curiosity in Christianity to the literary mode of parables and storytelling in the Bible. Narrative, plot, event, and character were pinpointed as literary techniques that immediately arrested the students' attention, conveying theological messages more effectively than a strictly doctrinal approach. The style of preaching also tended to follow a literary structure and took on literary characteristics both of the Western tradition (with "lightning flash of metaphor," "convictive parallelism of analogy," and "instructive imagery of parabolic illustration"[41]) and the native modes of storytelling, recitation, and singing. Furthermore, the successful adaptation of preaching style to literary modes encouraged similar explorations in a "lighter and freer style of tract literature."[42]

In the final analysis, however, the missionary interest in literary in- struction eludes explanation in terms of strategy alone. Indeed, the missionary use of literature is equally a measure of the defeatism that increasingly characterized the evangelizing enterprise. Large-scale con- version of Indians had been reduced to a myth and an illusion, acquiring the force of a painful reality to devoted missionaries who had conse- crated their entire lives to mission work in India. Many were dis- heartened by the disparity between the culture of the school and that of the home, where "Moses and Matthew have to give way to Krishna and Doorga [Hindu deities], and the prayer to the Pooja." "What do you do," wrote a writer for the *Oriental Herald*, "when the tender plant, after suffering during the day the Christian manipulation of the Mission- ary, goes home at night to be twisted in another direction by the prejudices of a Hindoo family?"[43] Severed from fait! in their truth, the facts of Christianity were stripped of all sacred instruction, and it was no wonder that "such instruction did no more to convert Hindu children to Christianity than the study of Greek and Roman classics at English schools and universities to convert British youth into pagans."[44] Chris- tianity to the Hindu remained merely an assemblage of facts to be learned and memorized, not to be experienced or made his own.

The number of those actually converting (that is, adopting the Chris- tian faith through baptism) was woefully disproportionate to the efforts expended. And though some, like the bishop of Calcutta, did insist that conversion was still a viable goal and that "giving [the Indians] access to our literature and habits of thinking and the familiar use of it would tend very much to dissipate the prejudices and the indifference which now stand in the way of conversion,"[45] more realistic missionaries recognized the futility of setting conversion as the goal of literary instruction. Rather, they urged that the goal be remodified to aim for the adoption of Christian *sentiment* if not of Christian doctrine.[46] The result of such compromise was the increased importance of the educational function of English literature, which, once freed of the obligation to convey doctrinal truths, took on more moralistic, humanistic functions. English literature may have acquired the status of an independent institution serving the functions of religious instruction, but it never quite replaced it altogether. The end point of constant negotiation and accommodation, the interlocking of secular and religious knowledge signaled an acceptance of intellectual Anglicization as a legitimate goal of conversionary attempts.

PROVOKED BY outspoken missionaries like Alexander Duff, William Keane, and William Carey on the one hand and fears of native insubordination on the other, increasing numbers of British administrators, including Charles Trevelyan, Holt Mackenzie, and William McNaughten, discovered a wholly unexpected ally in English literature to maintain control of their subjects under the guise of a liberal education. The discovery came about almost fortuitously. Though literature continued to be taught "classically," with the emphasis on the history and structure of the language, its potential usefulness in leading Indian youth to a knowledge and acceptance of Christianity quickly became apparent. For example, without once referring to the Bible, government institutions officially committed to secularism realized they were in effect teaching Christianity through Milton, a "standard" in the literary curriculum whose scriptural allusions regularly sent students scurrying to the Bible for their elucidation. (The Bible was in every library and was easily accessible to any student who cared to read it.) Bacon, Addison, and Johnson, also full of scriptural illustrations, had the same effect.

Several steps were initiated to incorporate selected English literary texts into the Indian curriculum, on the claim that these works were supported in their morality by a body of evidence that also upheld the Christian faith. In their official capacity as members of the Council on Education, Macaulay and his brother-in-law, Charles Trevelyan, were among those engaged in a minute analysis of English texts to prove what they called the "diffusive benevolence of Christianity" in them. The process of curricular selection was marked by weighty pronouncements on the "sound Protestant Bible principles" in Shakespeare, the "strain of serious piety" in Addison's *Spectator* papers, the "scriptural morality" of Bacon and Locke, the "devout sentiment" of Abercrombie, and the "noble Christian sentiments" in Adam Smith's *Moral Sentiments* (which was hailed as "the best authority for the true science of morals which English literature could supply"). The cataloging of shared features had the effect of convincing detractors that the government could effectively cause voluntary reading of the Bible and at the same time disclaim any intentions of proselytizing.

A self-appointed committee comprising Alexander Duff, Charles Trevelyan, and W. H. Pearce (who was then superintendent of the Baptist Mission Press) proposed to publish on the first of every month a select list of books recommended for general introduction into schools and libraries. In making the selection the committee was supposedly guided by the principle of practical utility, considering the works in every field of knowledge, including the religious, the literary, and the scientific. Nothing was to be rejected unless it had a corrupting influence on morals.[47] As can be imagined, the Calcutta educated public reacted with indignation to the arrogance of this self-installed group (which was contemptuously labeled the "triumverate of the spelling-book") in presuming to direct public taste and regulate public morals, to stamp one work with the mark of error and another with the brand of immorality according to the measure of its own infallible judgement, and to reestablish, upon its own private authority, the antiquated office of licenser.

Implicitly, the Duff-Trevelyan-Pearce team set out to counteract what it perceived as the lethargy of the Calcutta School Book Society in publishing a sufficient number of English books. The School Book Society, on the other hand, confessed helplessness in selecting English books according to stipulated regulations set by the governor-general-in-council—that selected books should contain no religious references —for "much the largest proportion of our English literature, from the speller to the most abstruse works on moral and political philosophy, contains repeated admission of divine authority of Christian faith."[48]

This fortuitous insight into the infusion of English literary texts with Christian references, literally stumbled upon by unsuspecting British officials, provided the solution to the dilemma first raised by Charles Grant. Charles Trevelyan revived that theme to argue that literature was supported in its morality by a body of evidence that also upheld the

Christian faith.[49] With both secularism and religion appearing as political liabilities, English literature appeared to him to represent a perfect synthesis of these two opposing positions, inclining the reader's thoughts toward religion while maintaining its secular character. The Duff-Trevelyan-Pearce committee magisterially interlocked the strength of English literature with the superiority of Christianity. The insistence of these shared features with the elevating religion of Western man had the effect of winning for English literature a higher cultural status and indeed even a greater pragmatic value.

Given the conviction that it was of comparatively little use to teach the people reading if their studies were confined to the legends of Hindu gods, the British task was to supersede these tales with the moral texts of Christian England, "a literature so full of all qualities of loveliness and purity, such new regions of high thought and feeling . . . that to the dwellers in past days it should have seemed rather the production of angels than men."[50] That Indian defects of character could be traced to ancient Indian literature was the thrust of the British assessment of Indian literature, which taught that "revenge is to be cherished, and truth is not to be rewarded as a virtue, or falsehood as a crime."[51] In fact, it was claimed that the chief reason for the Indians' opposition to the education of females before the nineteenth century was that Hindu literature was basically immoral and sensuous and that no Hindu woman who acquired learning could later make claims to respectability. In South India for example, the only girls who were literate were the nautch, or dancing girls. It was also widely reported that Hindu society prevented its women from reading by convincing them that they would become widows if they did so.[52] Charles Trevelyan argued eloquently for bringing women into the fold of education by providing them with literature of a less corrupt and immoral nature; hence, if only for the socially worthwhile cause of female education, the supplanting of Oriental literature by the purer, cleaner literature of England was all the more imperative.

But if reform of character was the larger objective, neither the missionaries nor the officers of government committed to secular education could reach an agreement about which texts in English literature supplied the best values. The government may have enthusiastically supported the teaching of English literature for the purpose of Christian enlightenment, but the practice in missionary schools did not give the impression that there was undiscriminating acceptance of this view.

There was, for instance, some objection to the teaching of Shakespeare and other dramatists in missionary schools, and it came from a view that Shakespeare's language (which contains words like *fortune, fate, muse,* and *nature*) reflected a pagan rather than a Protestant morality and would therefore exert an unhealthy influence on the natives.[53]

To be sure, the missionary description of Christianity's affiliation with literature was appropriated in its entirety by government officers. But while the missionaries made such claims in order to force the government to sponsor teaching of the Bible, the administrators used the same argument to prove that English literature made such direct instruction redundant. The successful communication of Christian truths through English literature was affirmed by the observations of clergymen and missionary visitors to the government schools, who frequently were heard to express astonishment at the accuracy and extent of a literature student's knowledge of Christianity. Judging by the enthusiastic accounts of those appearing before Parliament's Select Committee on Indian education, there was little exaggeration in the statement that "there is more knowledge of the Bible in the Hindoo College of Calcutta than there is in any public school in England."[54] Charles Trevelyan went so far as to claim that there were as many converts from the Hindu College as from missionary schools; in addition, he insisted, they remained more lasting believers of Christianity precisely because their literary education had served to develop their critical understanding more sharply than a purely religious education would have done.

DESPITE THEIR success in forcing government to recognize the need for a religious emphasis in education, many missionaries had reservations about the analytical, intellectual approach to Christian themes adopted in government institutions, sensing that conviction was not equivalent to conversion. Not a few responded with skepticism to the government claim that their subjects displayed new interest in the Bible and other Christian literature, cynically interpreting such gestures by Indians not as a show of reverence for the sacredness of the Scriptures but respect for their rulers.[55]

But unlike the Evangelicals, government administrators were less interested in the conversion of their subjects or the reform of Hindu society than in the possibilities offered by Christian instruction for strengthening commercial pursuits, increasing productivity, and streamlining the administration of government. Francis Warden, succinctly expressing the administration's willingness to renegotiate the absolutist objective of conversion to Christianity set by missionaries, settled for the more pragmatic objective of producing reliable, industrious servants of empire: "If education should not produce a rapid change in their opinions on the fallacy of their own religion, it will at least render them more honest and industrious subjects."[56] If the moral and religious content of literary instruction happened to support the needs of bureaucracy and increase industrial productivity, there was nothing to prevent its appropriation by secular administrators, despite the avowedly strict adherence to religious neutrality. The recruitment of a morally upright, honest, and trustworthy native population was increasingly recognized for its usefulness in lowering the expenses of administration, then largely run by officers specially recruited from England, who often required intensive training for the Indian situation.

In 1844 Lord Hardinge, governor-general from 1844 to 1848, passed a resolution assuring preference in the selection for public office to Indians who had distinguished themselves in European literature.[57] With this act he gave literary study a material and worldly motive that set the general aim of the "intellectual and moral improvement" of the subject population in a wholly new perspective. Not only did he draw upon a common body of assumptions about literature as a repository of certain moral and religious values to argue that they provided the most suitable basis of a public servant's education; he also made explicit the hitherto tacit belief that literary study regulates public behavior and provides social control.

In teaching natives to place social duty above self-interest, religious and moral values were established as prerequisites for admitting Indians to public office. "Can he be trusted with money?" was inevitably the first question asked before appointing a native Indian to a responsible office, and countless examples were drawn from Indian literature to show that the native culture was deficient in fostering the qualities necessary for public service.[58]

Two complementary arguments directly linked public employment with moral and religious education. On the one hand, if Indians of integrity and honesty were to occupy public office, the moral base of Indian education first had to be suitably developed to provide the appropriate training. But at the same time, the only real way of improving the colonial subjects was not simply by providing education, but by employ-

ing them in duties of trust and responsibility. In short, public employment offered reinforcement of the theoretical instruction in morality given in school. If a theory of education was to be a theory of government in the making, the application of abstract principles acquired in schooling was indispensable in order that they not merely
remained a "mixed mass of ideas" floating in the mind, but were selectively acted upon by the learner in his response to the demands of
state.[59]

James Mill made one of the first systematic arguments linking the
employment of Indians with prior instruction in English literature, even
if through translations. Seeking to reorganize the legislative functioning
of the presidencies, he established two criteria for recruitment into the
legislature: first, that the recruits have the "requisite knowledge" to do
their job well, and second, that they have "adequate motives for fidelity,"
by which he meant not only honesty but also diligence in the execution
of any task requiring trust. While conceding that it was impossible to
secure in one man all the different kinds of knowledge needed for
legislating in India, he suggested that the legislative organ should consist
of as small a number of persons as possible possessing the requisite
capacities and skills among them. For this purpose he believed that one
of them should be a person well acquainted with the laws of England. A
professional person from England was the most suitable for that purpose. Along with this official he proposed that there should be another
official, the most experienced of the Company's servants, who would
not only be conversant with the details and business of the government
but also have a thorough knowledge of the native character and the local
situation.

Finally, to maintain close contact with the colonial population Mill
urged (over and above the objections of the chief justice in Bengal) that
a native "of the highest character and qualifications" be drafted into the
legislative work of the government.[60] By selectively giving Indians a
position in the legislative council, Mill wished to enjoin their accountability to public opinion, which he believed to be a more useful method
of teaching "responsibility of character" than conventional forms of
punishment and, therefore, a more powerful instrument of social control.

But on the question of English for public employment Mill was
ambivalent. When asked whether he thought that the dissemination of
the English language would promote the induction of Indians into

public service, he answered, "I am not sure that natives would become one whit better adapted for the greater part of the employments in which we should place them, by having the English language, excepting in this, *that by becoming acquainted with English literature, they would have a chance of having their understandings better enlightened"* (emphasis mine).[61] But even that advantage was better served by the translation of European books into Indian languages:

> I do not see for example how, for the administration of justice to his countrymen as a moonsiff, a native would be better qualified, caeteris paribus, by knowing the English language. The other great branch of the local administration is collecting the revenue; acting under the English collector in dealing with the natives; fixing their assessments and realising the demand. In this, also, it does not appear to me that there would be any peculiar advantage to the native in his knowing the English language, provided only the Englishman knows the language of the native.[62]

Mill's emphasis on the literature rather than the language of England is consistent with his conviction that the chief priority of British rule was not assimilation of the natives, as many of his colleagues argued, but control. An Indian who thought and behaved like a European instead of merely speaking like one was deemed better suited to fulfill public duties, for "without his being found troublesome by pertinacity in his own opinions, compliance, I think, would be more likely to be the general habit of any native so chosen."[63]

While Mill believed that giving Indians positions of responsibility had a reinforcing effect on their sense of duty to society, Charles Trevelyan maintained that the same objective could be achieved by a professional training in law.[64] After a course of study in English literature, the study of law would allow Indians to see that the abstract moral ideas they had acquired could be put to practical use. Trevelyan, who had on various occasions expressed great concern about the intellectual decline of educated Indians after leaving school, noted that "the main thing is to open to them a proper field of mental and moral activity in after-life." In professional training in law after a school education he saw the best means of achieving this objective, which in turn would make them "good servants of the State and useful members of society."

In 1826 a committee on examinations met to give a proposal to the government that literary attainments should be made "conditions of appointment to the law stations in the courts and of permission to practice as law officers in those courts."[65] Though at this point there was no official recognition of English as a qualification for service, the priority given to "literary attainments" (by which even Sanskrit and Arabic could qualify) reinforced James Mill's argument about the importance of English literature (even in translation) over the English language. The connection between literature and the profession of law is an old and powerful one in Indian education. The Hunter Commission of 1882 noted that law was in many ways eminently suited to the bent of the Indian mind and that the first marks of progress along European lines were made by Indians who occupied judicial roles. Apart from the obvious contribution of literature in providing the required training in eloquence and the power of debate, it imparted a sense of "moral rectitude" and "earnestness of purpose."[66]

Law was frequently referred to as the most important subject in the Indian curriculum, the preparation for which required familiarity with the works of European authors and "with the results of thought and labour of Europeans on the subjects of every description upon which knowledge is to be imparted to them."[67] The alliance between literature and law brought in a greater number of native judges into the civil courts who commanded the respect of Europeans and Indians alike. Praise from Europeans was mixed with some amount of self-congratulation, for native successes were attributed to the progress of education and to "their adoption along with it of that high moral tone which pervades the general literature of Europe."[68] Ironically, the first concessions of India's creative development were made not in reference to its poets or artists, but to its English-educated lawyers and judges: "Modern India has proved by examples that are known to and honoured by all, in this assembly, that her sons can qualify themselves to hold their own with the best of European talent in the Council Chamber, on the Bench, at the Bar, and in the mart. The time cannot be far distant when she will produce her philosopher, her moralist, her reformer."[69]

Even more important than the European approbation of the judges' mettle was the high esteem in which native judges were held by their own people. The British had long insisted that Indians suffered from self-distrust, preventing them from behaving in truly moral ways. But to see native judges reach advanced positions in government offered possibilities of raising the national character in the estimation of the people themselves. The "healthy influence," for example, that pleaders of unimpeachable character exerted on many a district court, where chicanery and many questionable devices had earlier prevailed, reinforced the fondest

British belief that "all classes, though they may not practice, yet know how to admire real honesty, and integrity of purpose."

Not only then did British educational ideology set maximum advantages from the employment of morally trained men for those who ran the country, but such employment was impressed upon the general public as beneficial to its own moral character. The importance of English literature for this process could not be exaggerated; as the source of moral values for correct behavior and action, it represented a convenient replacement for the direct religious instruction that was forbidden by law. Inasmuch as the missionaries were gratified by the government's recognition of the need for moral instruction, they must surely have been dismayed to see that the government interest lay less in Christianizing the "natives" than in preparing them for participation in the work of empire. After all, the missionaries' chief motive in pointing to the shared features of Christianity and English literature was to draw attention to the fact that a subject already included in the Indian curriculum was a vast repository of Christian values, so where was the harm in teaching the Bible as well? The government listened keenly to the first half of the argument and promptly ignored the second. A discipline that was originally introduced in India primarily to convey the mechanics of language was thus transformed into an instrument for ensuring industriousness, efficiency, trustworthiness, and compliance in native subjects.

4
Rewriting English

> [The Indians] daily converse with the best and wisest Englishmen through the
> medium of their works, and form ideas, perhaps higher ideas of our nation than if
> their intercourse with it were of a more personal kind.
> —C. E. Trevelyan, *On the Education of the People of India* (1838), p. 152.

WHILE IDENTIFICATIONS between English literature and Christianity were occurring at one level, at another level the asserted unity of religion and literature was simultaneously disavowed, as evidenced in a series of contradictory statements. The most directly conflicting of these maintained, on the one hand, that English literature is "imbued with the spirit of Christianity" and "interwoven with the words of the Bible to a great degree" so that "without ever looking into the Bible one of those Natives must come to a considerable knowledge of it merely from reading English literature."[1] But in the same breath a counterclaim was made that English literature "is not interwoven to the same extent with the Christian religion as the Hindoo religion is with the Sanskrit language and literature."[2] Charles Cameron, who succeeded Macaulay as president of the Council on Education, provided an illustration for the latter position by arguing that though Milton assumes the truth of Christianity, his works do not bear the same relation to the doctrines of Christianity as does Oriental literature to the tenets of the native religious systems. But when pressed by his examiners to explain the point further, Cameron refused to elaborate, admitting only "a difference in degree."[3]

Although it is possible to read the dissociation of English literature from religion as the reactionary response of a cautious British administration, intent on avoiding all imputations of interference in native religions, the explanation does not quite capture the internal maneuverings and realignments that were occurring parallel to the enlistment of literary education in religious instruction. Nor does it adequately acknowledge continuities in the British ideology. For the same reason, to attribute the shift solely to differences between the Evangelicals and the Utilitarians and to increasing Utilitarian influence in educational policy is to assume that there was no coherent or organic relationship between the religious and the secular motives. Rather, the return to secularism is less a rejection of an earlier pedagogical approach stressing the identification of literature with religious value than a secular reinscription of ideas of truth, knowledge, and law derived from the sacred plane. The effect is the gradual removal of religion and traditional religious explanations from one sphere of knowledge after another; the setting up, within each of these spheres, of a secular orientation and autonomous explanatory laws; and ultimately the confinement of religion to matters of religious faith alone, excluding even morals.

With the disavowal of Christianity occurs a subtle but palpable shift in emphasis from the centrality of universal Christian truths to the legitimacy and value of British institutions, laws, and government. It is pertinent to question why affirmation of British institutions required denial of Christian influences in literature, particularly when movement between the theological and the political levels was possible without such repudiation as demonstrated by Charles Grant in his argument for the introduction of Western literature and Christianity into India. Grant's formulaic "one Power, one Mind" appealed to two interchangeable levels of meaning, the case for monotheism applying equally to that of centralized rule. Offensive to British religious sensibility on one level, Hindu polytheism threatened British political interests on another in its dispersal of authority in multiple figures and in its opposition to centralization in any form. Grant's plea for instruction in Christian doctrine to render subjects better disposed to British political authority indicates how subversive of that authority a polytheistic society appeared to him.

But given the claims of Christianity, no real purpose seems to be served by Charles Cameron's denial of the relation between English literature and religion at the very moment of his affirming it. In the absence of further explanation by Cameron himself, what is one to make of the alleged "difference in degree" between that relation and the one obtaining between Indian literature and Indian religion? What possible connection exists between disavowal of Christian influence and affirmation of British institutions, values, and laws?

The answer to these questions is partly the subject of Homi Bhabha's "Signs Taken for Wonders," which addresses the problematics of colonial representations of authority. Bhabha provides a compelling philosophical framework for analyzing native interrogation of British authority in relation to the *hybridization* of power and discourse, the term Bhabha uses to describe the effects of the relative transparency of colonial presence on the acknowledgment of its authority. A double vision inheres in a text recognized for its status in culture (which Bhabha would call a "transparent" text). For every truth expressed in that text there is a falsehood displaced and regulated. Metaphors drawn from photography best illustrate the gradual emergence of the image through a process of reversal, enlargement, and projection. If the acknowledgment of authority depends exclusively on the "immediate, unmediated" visibility of the rules of recognition, then the Christian text unequivocally and tautologically conveys the presence of authority through being a *Christian* text, displacing all non-Christian texts as a source of value. In other words, Christianity provides at once the frame of reference and the rules of recognition for the acceptance of its own authority.

But paradoxically, the more strongly felt the presence—the more transparent the authority—the more resistance is engendered. Bhabha illuminatingly points out that resistance to authority is

> not necessarily an oppositional act of political intention, nor is it the simple negation or exclusion of the "content" of another culture. . . . It is the effect of an ambivalence produced within the rules of recognition of dominating discourses as they articulate the signs of cultural difference and reimplicate them within the deferential relations of colonial power— hierarchy, normalization, marginalization, and so forth. *For domination is achieved through a process of disavowal that denies the* différance *of colonialist power*—the chaos of its intervention as *Entstellung,* its dislocatory presence

—in order to preserve the authority of its identity in the universalist
narrative of nineteenth-century historical and political evolutionism [em-
phasis mine].[4]

The culturally unambiguous text, the transparent text that draws
attention to itself as the voice of authority, expresses its truths by displacing others, which are then designated as falsehoods. The culturally
ambiguous or *unassertive* text, on the other hand, makes no claims for
authority or truth. Its contents are not presented as assertions of truth
but as ideas developed in the crucible of history. The validity of one idea
over another is not established by arbitrary truth claims but by the
progress of history, which alone has the power to test the relative
applicability of ideas to contexts other than those from which they
derived. Christianity and Hinduism are opposed religions only in an
ahistorical perspective. Historically considered, they are part of a single
continuum of development, their apparent differences the effect of historical change and movement. Concepts like absolute truth have no
place in the relativized domain of history, where there is only formation,
process, and flux.

But the moment texts express "truth," they cease to be part of history.
At that moment they become transparent. Ambivalence characterizes
the text caught in the nexus between process and state, observation and
assertion, identity and difference. Paradoxically, it is the text's instability
on the issue of its identity—is it historical process or cultural artifact?—
that generates resistance to itself. The effect of uncertainty estranges the
symbols of a Christian nation enshrined in its literature, and the possibility of routinized responses to them is consequently problematized.

Disavowal is at once an effort at resolution between these two contrary states and a justification of two mutually exclusive effects, one
seeking identity within history and the other seeking differentiations
outside it, transcending history. With disavowal, the conditions for
recognition of authority in the text are changed, even though the text
still remains the same. The equation between the English nation and the
Christian God is rewritten as (but emphatically not supplanted by) an
equation between the English nation and *new forms of knowledge* produced by historical development and material progress.

The religious imperative inexorably commanded Indian education
toward a situation where, unless another frame of reference for recognition of the authoritative structure of instruction was established, the
transparency of motive and intention treacherously threatened to

destroy the whole edifice of British political control from within. The conflict of truth claims visibly marked the intention of conversion, over-lying the content of instruction to render its truth value immaterial. The Serampore missionary William Carey often exasperatingly exclaimed that Christianity in India had of necessity to build into itself the activity of ratiocination, as those who were the object of conversion refused to accept Christian doctrines without rigorous proof. Christian instruction in India, he pointed out, required a different strategy than would nor-mally have been followed in England, resorting more regularly to vali-dations and proofs to overwhelm native resistance to Christianity.[5]

Disavowal, validating belief by the techniques of modern knowledge, deflects from the Christian text's self-referential, self-confirming aspects. The strategic value of disavowal confers upon modern knowledge, as a product of historical development and increased human capacities for reason, the status of independence from systems of belief based on pure faith. Proving what faith only proposes confirms far more than the mere truthfulness of religious belief. More important, the progress of knowl-edge provides the groundwork for demonstrating the increased capacity of the human mind to penetrate mysteries understood only otherwise as hieratic phenomena.

The dissociation performed by Charles Cameron is therefore less a denial of Christian influence in European literature than a rewriting of Christianity as empirical knowledge. This is quite different from the enlistment of Christianity in an intellectual revolution in the expectation that the act of thinking and reasoning from the force of evidence would culminate in a universalism of belief ("we must all come to one religion," wrote Charles Grant) destroying the gigantic edifice of Hinduism. How-ever strongly Charles Grant and other Evangelicals may have invoked reason as a means of attenuating the hold of Hinduism, their Christian-ity was firmly rooted in the tenets of revealed religion. While embracing the rigor, discipline, and precision of empiricism's most exemplary dis-ciplines, science and history, Evangelicalism vigorously resisted their explanatory frameworks. Thus, even though it was said that liberal education could not be imparted without unshackling Hinduism, this was not to confer an autonomous status on modern knowledge, to which Christianity was merely a support. On the contrary, in the eyes of missionaries Western empiricism was invested with extraordinary reli-gious power as an effect of its defying "any man to state a single proposition relating to math, physics, metaphysics, or morals that does not infringe upon Hinduism" and as an effect of its affirming that "there is no truth or reality in the universe of which Hinduism is not a direct contradiction," making it "impossible to enunciate a single truth without contradicting and controverting Hinduism."[6]

The dual tension in the content of Christian instruction did not go unnoticed by colonial subjects. Though educated young Indians had few objections to studying the life of Christ, they were violently hostile to particular doctrines of Christianity, especially revelation and grace. On the evidence of college debates, essays, and literary contests at Hindu College, for instance, it is apparent that students were quite adept in querying the conflicting purposes of the instruction given them. If Christianity were truly a religion based on reason, evidence and history as projected, many asked, why did confirmation in that religion depend entirely on accepting two central doctrines that demanded faith rather than the exercise of reason? Many of the debates held at Hindu College revolved around the paradox of Christianity being structured on the twin principles of revelation and reason, setting it off markedly from other religions that were informed by either one or the other principle.

The forced distinctions between religions that doctrine imposed impelled questioning students toward postures of ecumenism. The growing fascination of English-educated Bengalis, such as Rammohun Roy, with Unitarianism, for instance, is a measure of their intense dissatisfaction with the doctrinal aspects of Christianity and their ambition to intellectualize it in much the same way that they sought to refine Hinduism.[7] The manifesto of the Calcutta Unitarian Committee, formed in September 1821, included the following response by Rammohun to the question asked of all who joined: "Why do you frequent a Unitarian Place of Worship, instead of numerously attended established Churches?" Answered Rammohun: "Because Unitarians believe, profess, and inculcate the doctrine of the divine unity—a doctrine which I find firmly maintained both by the Christian Scriptures and by most of our ancient writings commonly called the Vedas."[8]

The British disavowal of doctrinal influence reflects a perception of the relation of Christianity to the empirical branches of science and history as having to exist in more than neutral or passive ways. The representation of Christianity as inherently predisposing individuals to rational scrutiny ascribes an ambiguous, even fortuitous relation between belief and evidence. More important, such representation inevitably reestablishes that same frame of self-reference to account for the truthfulness of its belief system. Secularization, of which disavowal is its expressive vehicle, confers a new value and importance on literary study as the medium through which religious truth is reinscribed as a form of intellectual production: the Christian text is desacralized in proportion to the presentation of its "truths," not as immanent or constitutive of an immutable system of objective reality, but as produced by mind, itself a product of the evolution of history, society, and culture. The history of human intelligence being inseparable from human history, the shift from the text to the mind producing it necessarily establishes texts in relation to other human institutions. The determination of truth cannot now be confined to the text but requires an expansion of its boundaries to include a larger, more relativized view of history—of the text evolving with other institutions, language, norms, and laws.

So even as the religious motive introduced a new tone and direction to Indian education, there occurred a subtle shift in purpose from an assertion of Christian truths to an endorsement of British laws, institutions, and government. Religious influences are carefully screened out in the process, culminating in a revivified, albeit homogenized conception of literature as entirely constituted by language to which new cultural values are then attached.

The secularization of Christian truths in the literary education of Indians moves through three distinct but overlapping stages: its direction is set by the relativization of cultural absolutes, producing a heightened emphasis on the intellectual motive in literary instruction, as well as an alignment of the functions of literature with those of history. The argument that Allan Bloom has recently advanced in *The Closing of the American Mind*, that cultural relativism anesthetizes critical judgment in the act of equalizing all value, resists considering that, historically, cultural relativism has had more than the meaning he ascribes to it. In any event, the view that discrimination is possible only when absolute standards are available assumes an individual mind emptied of all personal identity, culture, and history, a mind reduced to passivity and acquiescence. British colonial administrators were more astute in recognizing the absurdity of such assumptions, at least for the purposes of achieving success in their educational goals of political control and assimilation. The British perception of the relativization of moral value as a powerful means of ensuring intellectual control over the native population is the subject of this chapter. The next chapter will deal with the British pedagogical use of historical analysis as a method of teaching colonial subjects to identify error in their own systems of thought and, simultaneously, confirm Western principles of law, order, justice, and truth.

IN UNEXPECTED ways, affirmation of British secular institutions and laws gained fresh momentum as a result of the Anglicist-Orientalist controversy immediately preceding Macaulay's minute of 1835. Among the Orientalists, those who were most directly drawn into the debate were James Harington, J. P. Larkins, W. W. Martin, John C. Sutherland, Henry Shakespear, Holt Mackenzie, Horace Wilson, Andrew Stirling, William B. Bayley, Henry Prinsep, Nathaniel Halhed, and John Tytler. What united these men, disparate in temperaments and interests, was their intense involvement with Indian political and cultural life, all at about roughly the same time, from 1805 to 1820. Wilson was undoubtedly the most renowned of the group. Originally attached to the medical service of the East India Company, he arrived in Calcutta in 1808. His translations of Kalidas and the *Rig-Vedas* and his editions of Sanskrit grammar and the Hindu law earned him a wide reputation, whereupon he became secretary to the Asiatic Society of Bengal (1811–1833). From his position as secretary to the Committee of Public Instruction he advocated numerous reforms of the Indian curriculum, including the introduction of European science and English literature alongside the teaching of Oriental languages. Henry Prinsep and Nathaniel Halhed were second only to Wilson in dedication to public service combined with scholarship in Sanskrit grammar.[9]

An indirect and somewhat ironic outcome of the debate between Orientalists and Anglicists, among whom the most prominent were Macaulay, Charles Trevelyan, and Alexander Duff, was a reformulation of the objectives of educational policy. The Anglicist-Orientalist controversy grew out of a proposal, mooted by the General Council of Public Instruction in Calcutta, to withdraw funds from the support of Oriental learning in favor of the promotion of the English language and literature. The conflict was not simply over language or literature, but the status of knowledge itself. The debate was conducted in terms that transformed the choice between languages into a choice between the promotion of truth and the propagation of error. The Orientalists continued to insist that European learning should make its own way instead of being forced on the people through the single channel of English instruction. The relative success of missionaries in providing modern instruction through the vernaculars encouraged Orientalists to believe that the truths of European or English literature and science would be better received "by the effect of conviction alone" than by withdrawing all support to the Oriental systems of learning in order to make way for the European.

But the Orientalists had to contend with the Christian framework within which their opponents' argument resolutely operated, regardless of whether the Anglicists themselves were by inclination secularists or not. The Anglicists identified their position so completely with the Christian and drew upon Christian principles to sanction their arguments so consistently that supporting Oriental literatures without invoking the Christian framework was tantamount to endorsing the non-Christian view of life they conveyed. Thus in supporting the Indian languages the Orientalists were placed in the unenviable position of appearing not only to wish to promote error but to reject Christianity itself. It was an argument the Anglicists had little hesitation in using at the slightest opportunity to discredit their opponents.

William Wilberforce, shrewdly discerning the Achilles' heel of the Orientalists, translated their ambivalence toward Christianity into a benevolent view of Hinduism, which he then traced to a (at least for many of his fellow Englishmen) wholly contemptible origin—French Enlightenment skeptics like Voltaire, who deliberately cultivated the myth that "the principles of the Hindoos are so good, their morals are so pure, better than our own," in order to discredit Christianity.[10] An appeal to the horrors unleashed by political anarchy in France was sufficient to alert the English Parliament to an Orientalist project of subverting Christianity. Unless the Orientalists were prepared to admit that they were indeed denying Christianity, they found themselves in a situation where they had no other choice but to appropriate the techniques and strategies of the Anglicists to promote their case.

Caught in a hopelessly untenable position, the Orientalists were pressured into the realization that the only justifiable grounds for the teaching of Oriental literature were the political. Sensing the possibilities of maneuvering around their opponents by appealing to their strategic interests, a group of Orientalists responding to James Mill's 1824 dispatch[11] refocused the issue by questioning the political wisdom of an educational policy that directed the learner to truth by blocking out error. Anglicism was especially vulnerable to the charge of depriving Indians of familiarity with their own system of learning. Not a few Anglicists were acutely aware of the liability of a policy that lulled colonial subjects into passive acceptance of their rulers' culture without adequately fortifying them against the "errors" in their own tradition. The Anglicists might have found themselves on sturdier ground had the indigenous tradition already been reduced to irrelevance in Indian cultural life. But as long as the traditional learning continued to flourish in other types of institutions and was indelibly woven into the fabric of Indian society, barring Indians from knowledge of it merely encouraged two independent, parallel systems. As a result, the Anglicists had enormous difficulty contesting the Orientalists' main criticism that without significant interaction between the two systems, the impact of Anglicism on the indigenous tradition was virtually negligible.

The failings of Anglicism to produce effective change constituted the basic thrust of the 1824 letter. Persistently it remonstrated against the omission of Oriental learning as jeopardizing British rule because, in the absence of a native population trained to be critically aware of its own traditions, the authority of the priestly classes was left virtually intact. By this logic, removing Indians from familiarity with the tenets of that system was analogous to removing physicians from a knowledge of the very disease they were expected to cure. In conclusion, the letter advised that if a class of enlightened teachers and translators was indeed the object of British policy, it was imperative "to qualify the same individuals highly in their own system as well as ours, in order that they may be as competent to refute errors as to impart truth, if we would wish them to exercise any influence upon the minds of their countrymen." [12]

In sum, the Orientalist defense rested on the argument that if the educated Indian was to be enlisted in the cause of overwhelming priestly authority, the official educational policy had to reflect this political goal more clearly than was then the case. The exclusiveness of a policy that favored English and eliminated the native languages deprived it of any real political force, for by locating truth in a single cultural tradition to be apprehended solely through direct instruction in it, the Anglicist doctrine effectively suspended all confrontation with error, disabling serious, critical questioning of the native tradition. The reversal of this situation entailed a conception of truth not as *a priori* but as a process involving active dialectical effort. Such a conception necessarily demanded a broadening of the content of education and the inclusion of error as an object of instruction.

Indeed, as the Orientalist John Tytler wrote to Macaulay in response to his Anglicist doctrine, the disinterested love of knowledge demanded that the study of indigenous language, history, and culture be promoted in tandem with European learning:

> If we destroy it [Oriental studies] we shall degrade both ourselves and the people we undertake to improve. A history of the successive systems of Science and philosophy though it may not teach the true nature of things will yet afford much valuable information of another kind. It will teach what mankind have thought and how they have reasoned about these things and the successive steps by which they have arrived at Truth: It is in short the history of human opinions and this is at least as important as that of human actions.[13]

Dismissing the Anglicist view that Western systems of learning inherently possessed a self-evident power to demolish Hindu error, Tytler redirected attention to the analysis of the properties of truth as a prerequisite to the task of distinguishing error. His project of cultural decontextualization contested the imperative of presenting truths in absolute form in order to persuade disbelievers of their validity. Though Tytler scrupulously avoided going so far as to suggest that Oriental learning had claims to "state of the art" knowledge, he conceded a vital place to it as a stage in the development of human knowledge or the "history of opinions." The historical sense crucially redefined truth in more relativistic terms as knowledge that developed not independently of man's intellectual development and history, but rather as a product of human development. From this standpoint Oriental studies acquired legitimacy as a necessary stage in the growth of knowledge. At the same time, of course, accommodation of two radically different versions of reality did not necessarily endorse Eastern learning in any way or render it comparable to Western thought. Nor did it imply approval of the patently false premises upon which Oriental studies were supposed to rest.

To be sure, missionaries, particularly those working out of Serampore, had long made an argument for error as the basis of instruction in Christian truth and thus unwittingly participated in a shift encouraged by the Orientalists in the direction of a relativistic secularism. The missionary practice, of which Alexander Duff's catechetical instruction is a good example, suggested a conception of truth understood not as predetermined goal to which the learner moved in an undeviating, unerring path, but as dynamic activity forcing the learner to sift out error from all that he encountered. Far from being an annoying nuisance, the native languages were regarded by missionaries as absolutely crucial to the determination of truth. As Kenneth Ingham's study clearly shows, missionaries played a vital role in setting up printing presses, undertaking the publication of schoolbooks, translating the Bible into the various Indian languages, standardizing the indigenous languages, and encoding the literatures in script form.[14] The Serampore missionaries had not for a moment believed that the mere substitution of the Indian languages and literature by English would automatically lead to the sharpening of the Indians' intellectual faculties. Rather, they felt an intermediate step was required before the Indians whom they wished to see trained would be in a position to perceive the truths embedded in English literature. That step was defined as submitting the Indians to a rigorous examination of their own literature. To criticisms that this manner of instruction would only encourage them to continue in their own beliefs the arch response was that "truth need fear nothing from inquiry—ignorance alone perpetuates error."[15]

The "difference in degree" between Western and Eastern literatures, which Charles Cameron hesitated to specify when interrogated in the parliamentary sessions on education, had long been intuited and, in fact, had already been named by missionaries. Western literature is often described in missionary publications as a form of intellectual production, in contrast to Oriental literature, which allegedly set itself up as a source of divine authority. The Serampore Baptist missionary William Carey best expressed the missionary viewpoint when he lamented, in comparing the Hindu epic the *Mahabharata* to Homer, that "[were] it, like his *Iliad*, only considered as a great effort of human genius, I should think it is one of the first productions in the world, but alas! it is the ground of Faith to Millions of men; and as such must be held in the utmost abhorrence."[16]

Carey's distinction emphasized an arbitrariness in Oriental conceptions of truth, whose claims were supposed to derive from the power of the explicator (the class learned in Arabic and Sanskrit) to mediate between the popular mind and sacred knowledge. But though Carey made a sincere effort to understand the power of the sacred in Indian society, by and large he shared the failings of many of his fellow missionaries in their blindness toward the immense cultural position of the learned classes, particularly the Muslim learned men *(maulvis)*. The failures were often related to problems of interpretation, of gross misunderstanding of the cultural functions of the *maulvis* as interpreters and not simply teachers of the sacred texts. In a scathing critique of missionary ignorance of the symbols of native cultural power and the great harm caused thereby to British rule in India, a writer for the *Asiatic Journal* cautioned his readers that knowledge of Oriental literature involved far more than mere reading and translating of the texts.

> Being ill-acquainted with the language of the people, and unable to read the Alcoran in the original, [the missionaries] often attack imaginary doctrines and creeds which the Mahommedans do not profess. The Alcoran, it is admitted, includes absurd, puerile and immoral dogmas, but the teachers of Islamism, in their glosses and commentaries, contrive to palliate these ridiculous passages and render them plausible by some explanation. These explications the missionaries ought carefully to study, that he may direct his refutation to them. This requires a profound acquaintance with the Arabic tongue, which the majority of these travellers despise.[17]

The writer of this article was shrewd enough to see that significant shifts in cultural power would come about only through a confrontation with the interpretations and not simply the texts alone and that to challenge the explications was to challenge the explicator and loosen his power over the people. Harold Bloom's reminder in *A Map of Misreading* that "all interpretation depends upon the antithetical relationship between meanings, and not on the supposed relation between a text and its meaning" (p. 76) has as much relevance in this context as in any other. The Protestant orientation to texts as the sole source of authority frequently blinded missionaries to the basic fact that the sacred texts of the East are not finite but cumulative, consisting of interpretations layered one on top of the other through successive readings. In failing to see, for example, that the Koran is more than a single text, that it is in fact a complex unit that includes the text *and* its interpretations or explications, their efforts at conversion through an appeal to reason completely missed the mark.

Carey's distinction, linking the authority wielded by the native learned classes to the literature they superintended, contained the outlines of a strategy for undermining their role as sole explicators of texts construed as divine knowledge. If by blurring the lines between literature and religion the Indian learned classes had arrogated all power to decipher texts, an erosion of that power base—a relocation of authority away from the explicator—had undoubtedly to come from the action of texts, understood as independently verifiable by human reason.

That process is brilliantly summarized as willed strategy in a report filed by the president of the Board of Education at Bombay in April 1853:

> For my own part, I believe that Providence dictated this policy [of religious neutrality] as the means of riveting the power of England over this country; but it is clear that we cannot expect a blessing to rest upon a violation of the public faith, solemnly pledged by conquerors to those submitting to their authority.
>
> And what, I would ask, is the course to be followed by a great and generous country under such circumstances? Its faith is pledged, and the opinion of its scrupulous good faith is the keystone of the arch which supports its mighty power over these lands. Surely, surely there is but one course open.
>
> We have the subtle Brahmin, the ardent Mahomedan, the meek, though zealous, Christian missionary, each and all relying on this promise of non-interference, and pressing the evidence of his respective faith on the attention of the people of India; and when this people look up to the Government and say, "You tolerate all religions; all cannot be true; show us what is truth," the government can only answer, "Our own belief is known to you; we are ready to give a reason for the faith that is in us; and we will place you in a situation by which you may judge whether those reasons are convincing or not. We will teach you History by the light of its two eyes, Chronology and Geography; you will therein discover the history and system of every religion. We will expand your intellectual powers to distinguish truth from falsehood by the aid of Logic and Mathematics; and we will, in the sciences of Astronomy, Geology, Chemistry and Botany, lay open to you all we know of the firmament above, of the nature of the earth on which we live, and the organization of the flowers which enamel its surface; and with your perceptions of the power and wisdom of your God and ours, thus cleared and enlarged, we may safely leave you to distinguish truth for yourselves . . . Each member of the Board of Education, be he Christian, Mahomedan, Hindoo or Parsee, is engaged in one common object; viz., the advancement of truth. We differ only as to that which is truth, and, like other discreet men, we never talk on that respecting which we are sure to differ.[18]

Though a policy of non-interference may have been originally adopted for reasons of expediency, in this report it is rapidly transformed into a medium of self-presentation. As a symbol of free intellectual inquiry, religious non-interference generated an image of the Englishman as benign, disinterested, detached, impartial, and judicious. Indeed, British authority depended vitally on the stability of the image and on the consistency with which it was preserved and relayed to the native mind. From this standpoint, violations of the policy of religious neutrality were of more than military consequence: in more far-reaching ways, by breaching the "good faith" through which the British exercised their authority over the natives, they threatened to unmask the illusions that British rule in India required for its legitimation—illusions of trust, honor, and obligation.

Yet in a land where, as the missionary Joshua Marshman said, both Hindus and Muslims were known to attach high religious feeling even to secular education, it was political folly to leave British noninterference to be interpreted by the Indians in their own way, such that it might be construed "not as liberty of conscience but as carelessness about any religion."[19] Interpreted so, religious toleration had the potential of earning for the British not the image of benevolence and noncoerciveness but its very converse—an image of irresponsibility, indifference, and disdain of duty. If the rulers' faith was perceived to be shallow, much the same could be expected of their oaths.[20] British pledges of respect for the beliefs of others had no content, no value, if the inference to be drawn from neutrality was that no discernible belief system lay behind them.

The only escape from this predicament, albeit one fraught with risks, was to convince the Indians, as the report advised, "that the government cultivate their own religion."[21] Doing this without seeming to coerce it on their subjects took England back to the position outlined by Charles Grant. As with Grant, here too beyond the crossroads of the dilemma stood English literature, offering itself as both subject of study and method of analysis—the means through which the claims of Western belief were at once asserted and the grounds of its truthfulness vindicated. What made this twofold activity possible, as the president's report implied, is English literature's double stance toward reason and faith, utility and tradition, and empiricism and revelation—a stance obscuring its affiliations with institutional religion (and the entire system of social and political formation of which it was a part) through its appeal to an objective, empirical reality apprehended solely by mind.

Charles Cameron's reticence before his examiners takes on more meaning in this context, for his reluctance to affirm unambiguously literature's relation to Christianity undoubtedly stemmed from an awareness of the operational value of English literature's double stance in reinforcing the validity of the knowledge to be imparted and, by extension, of the authority of those imparting it. Further, literature's doubleness enabled the validation of Christian belief by the disciplinary techniques of European learning while at the same time deflecting attention from its self-referential, self-confirming aspects. Its power rested on the idea that European disciplines, being products of human reason, were independent of systems of belief based on pure faith. Therefore, by proving what faith merely proposed, they confirmed far more than the mere truthfulness of Christian belief; more important, they demonstrated the power and authority of the Western mind to penetrate the mysteries of the natural and phenomenal world.

The Protestant Reformation provided a historical model for the relocation of authority in the body of knowledge represented by English literary texts. The characterization of English literature as intellectual production implicated a different process of reading, requiring the exercise of reason rather than unquestioning faith. On the point of literary truth there is no fiercer testimony than Alexander Duff's rebuttals to early Orientalist claims that Indian literature was no different than English literature in its predilection for the absurd and the incredible. (One Orientalist, for example, cited Milton's description of Satan in Hell as "too gross and ludicrous . . . a conceit truly diabolical.")[22] Duff categorically dismissed any comparison of the study of Indian literature with the study of Western literature on the grounds that classical literature was read in Europe as literary production and not as divine authority, as it was in India. Duff persistently discriminated between mental capabilities as proof that the Western orientation to literary study permitted myth to be read as fable without any practical influence, whereas in India the principles and facts of myth were taught and believed in as truth. While conceding that English literature had its "foul spots," works that defied the norms of propriety and decorum, Duff maintained that it was preposterous to compare the literature of England, which he characterized as a "complete course of sound knowledge free of error in every branch of inquiry, literary, scientific, and theological," with the literature of India, which could not produce "a single volume on any one subject that is not studded with error, far less a series of volumes that would furnish anything bearing the most distant resemblance to a complete range of information in any conceivable department of useful knowledge."[23]

But Duff's moral emphasis gave way to other concerns that were more pragmatic and empirical in nature, and these can be seen in the British critiques of the Indian propensity to confer upon myth the status of a historical genre. The British objection to the Hindu epics the

Ramayana and the *Mahabharata* rested on the claim that they pretended to do the work of history, whereas Western literature had no such pretension and made a clear distinction between works of the imagination and records of history. The supposed blurring of historical and mythical consciousness in Indian literature, contributing to its falsehoods and inaccuracies, was the chief point of attack by two of the most celebrated critics of Oriental art, James Mill and Hegel. Mill refused to accept the *Ramayana* and the *Mahabharata* as history as some Orientalist scholars did; he refused even to accept them as allegory and argued that efforts to do so were only ways of softening their deformities.[24] Both Mill and Hegel equated historical composition with intellectual maturity and pointed to the absence of historical records in certain societies as proof of their low position in the scale of civilization.[25] Mill maintained that societies reach stability, coherence, and identity when they are able to make use of "permanent signs" and to preserve their understanding of events through historical records. In his view the use of arts and letters to record events coincided with the advance of culture, which he defined as the ability to observe with accuracy. On the basis of this definition, he argued that epic poetry forestalled such advance by replacing precision of observation with a sense of mythic wonder and by celebrating events solely for the pleasure of the emotions, thus encouraging exaggeration above accuracy.

Mill's disdain for poets who assume the role of historians was not idiosyncratic. Leading nineteenth-century periodicals such as the *Quarterly Review*, the *Edinburgh Review*, the *Asiatic Journal*, the *Oriental Herald*, and the *Calcutta Review* regularly published articles and reviews condemning the historical inaccuracies of Indian literature. In a review of Tod's famous historical work on the antiquities of Rajasthan, for instance, the *Quarterly Review* lamented that the annals of earlier cultures were lost in the mists of a mythic or fabulous period peopled by dimly humanized forms of gods or men magnified to superhuman stature. The same critic claimed that genuine historical records (defined as being "less imaginative") were to be found only among the heterodox systems of Buddhism or Jainism. Distinctly echoing Mill, who held that the inflated, metaphorical style of describing events failed to convey any real sense of what actually occurred, the reviewer condemned the poetic imagination for throwing a veil over events and characters: "Until history has condescended to the sober march of prose, it does not restrain itself from the license of fiction, or assume the authority of truth."[26] The alignment of poetry with falsehood and prose with truth and accuracy successfully dismissed Oriental epic narratives as nothing more than illusion and error. Furthermore, the Utilitarian premises upon which this judgment rested—that what is good is "useful" and what is bad is imaginative—provided literary criticism not only with a principle for setting one genre above another but for also totally excluding certain genres from consideration as serious art.

The imprecision of Indian literature was not only represented as aesthetically repugnant to human sensibility, but also deemed to be politically treacherous. A history of perfidy and calumny was painted as the legacy of Oriental historical accounts and their exaggerations seen as a devious strategy of early writers to falsify, obscure, and mystify events in order to conceal their own violence, injustice, and usurpation of power.[27] Indian historical literature was depicted as entirely constituted by narratives of royal personages and royal pastimes that deliberately avoided showing the operations of power or the bearing of political and other events on the condition of the people.[28] Elliott and Dowson's *History of India as Told by Its Own Historians* (1867) employed a unique method to expose Indian "pretensions" to literary or historical truth. As the title suggests, the authors deliberately present historical narratives written by Indians in order to show that in Indian histories "there is little enabling us to observe the practical operation of a despotic government and rigorous and sanguinary laws, and the effect upon the great body of the nation of these injurious influences and agencies."[29] The act of reading and writing true history and true literature was, in effect, identified with an act of demystification to dislodge those who, under the cover of misty romances and allegories, had installed and perpetuated their rule over the people.

The Elliot and Dowson rewriting of the "despotic Orient" typically provided ballast for the view that a literature claiming to provide divine revelation diluted the capacity of the individual mind to resist the manipulations of a priestly caste. By the terms of this argument, not only did Oriental literature lull the individual into passive acceptance of the most fabulous incidents as actual occurrences; more alarmingly, the acceptance of mythological events as factual description stymied the mind's capacity to extrapolate a range of meanings for analysis and verification in the real world.

Reason is thus made synonymous with the moral imagination and the moral imagination, in turn, with the ability to make discriminations and choose judiciously from a wide spectrum of possible meanings. The association of reason with an approach to literary texts as types of human activity reinforces the logic of Protestantism: the products of human consciousness are required to submit to interpretation because their creating subject is man, not God, man in all his imperfection and fallibility. Because interpretation by definition entails a plurality of response, the receiving mind is pressured all the more to weigh the truth value of each possibility, thereby activating rational processes of discrimination and judgment—intellectual skills held by the British to be utterly alien to a literature conceived as divine agency.

Furthermore, once established as an example of human invention drawing its material from a rationally perceived world, English literature lent itself more readily to representations of intellectual rigor and of disciplined reasoning from the force of evidence. The elevation of individual and closely observed experience over received tradition provided an empirical basis objectifying the knowledge contained in its body of texts. The Cartesian influence is especially strong in the argument that the element of doubt attending upon the senses sets the mind in a state of intellectual ferment, forcing it to do battle with error until a full knowledge of the truth is reached. An individually realized truth, being neither *a priori* nor predetermined, defies the arbitrary definitions laid down by class or caste. Since it would have proceeded through the stages of rational investigation—of detached observation, analysis, verification, and application—its claims to universal, objective knowledge are presumably greater than the claims to truth of received tradition.

NOT ALL Orientalists assented to the project of destabilization of the learned classes. Though supportive of the plan to include both Western and Oriental systems of learning, Horace Wilson was skeptical about the wisdom of undermining the position of the *maulvis* and *pundits,* an action that he felt adversely affected the traditional respect for learning in India and in turn prevented young Indians from deriving tangible benefits from Western education. The dangers of creating a separate class of English scholars and excluding the learned men from the political system of India were for him too real to be minimized. An arch foe of Macaulay, Horace Wilson continued to insist that the learned classes' hostility had been aroused less by the introduction of English than by the termination of funds supporting Arabic and Sanskrit. His reluctance to antagonize the learned classes took the form of a vigorous defense of the cultural value and importance of the Indian classical languages, the "congenial imagery and sentiments" from which the Indians would never be weaned away, no matter how strongly the claims of the superiority of Western culture were advanced.[30]

Wilson proposed a compromise, advising that the *maulvis* and *pundits* be employed as teachers and translators of Western texts. Agreeing in the main with Mill's letter of 1824 that the most effective agents for change are those educated in the very errors that are to be reformed, Wilson refined the "Trojan horse" strategy of destruction from within, to urge that the traditional men of learning of India also be co-opted as "additional instruments in our power."[31]

Up to a point Wilson's argument was acceptable to the General Council of Public Instruction. But he drew much sharper reactions when he advised that England interest itself in the intellectual and literary efforts that were traditionally venerated by India's learned men and, through them, lead the Indians to "chaster models of taste." The vehemence with which Wilson was denounced by even his fellow Orientalists, leave alone the Anglicists, exposes the fundamental ambiguity underlying the support of Oriental learning. Oriental studies were allowed a place in the curriculum on the understanding that language pursued as a means to an end (for instance, conducting legal business) was less likely to exert a disruptive influence than when pursued as an end in itself. The encouragement of Oriental learning was tolerated only to the extent that it remained a field of legal research, Arabic and Sanskrit being closely tied to Muslim and Hindu law respectively. And when the laws were made intelligible to the people, there was every likelihood that even these languages would cease to be cultivated except for philological or antiquarian purposes. But under no circumstances was the Bentinck administration or any other administration following his willing to support Oriental learning if it meant the perpetuation of Oriental languages and literature as the *source* of intellectual values, morals, and religion.

The same thinking underscored the argument made in the proposal for the establishment of the universities of Madras, Bombay, and Calcutta in 1857 along the pattern of London University. Charles Cameron, who succeeded Macaulay as president of the Council on Education and campaigned vigorously for a centralized university system, went so far as to call for the total exclusion of the classical languages of India— Sanskrit, Arabic, and Persian—on the grounds that they were inextricably bound with systems of "pagan theology."[32] Any course of study in these languages, he insisted, would only perpetuate the errors that were the cause of the intellectual degradation of the Indian people. Instead, he proposed that students be examined in the vernacular languages, which did not yet have a literary tradition comparable to that of the classical languages and through which Western knowledge could be more directly disseminated without having to pass through what he considered the filters of prejudice, ignorance, and error. Such a scheme, which is nothing short of an attempt to separate language from literature, was advanced as the primary means of developing a new national literature from which the disruptive elements of religion are screened out.[33]

The distinctions drawn between English and Indian literature in their relation to religion culminate in a purified, even sterilized conception of literature as constituted entirely by language. Disavowal of religious influence on literature acquires its most severe form in a plan that virtually endorses a classical approach to literary studies, establishing language rather than belief and tradition as a source of value and culture. By 1855 statements such as the following, analyzing the spread of English education to other provinces of British India, were increasingly common:

> If [Indian students] are to be imbued with the spirit of English Literature, which all in government colleges seem to have in view, they should learn something of that source from which it draws so much of its glorious inspiration. It is in this respect that all English studies have been imperfectly carried on in India, the native students being utterly ignorant of the spirit of antiquity and all classical references, and what is worse, knowing nothing of those elements which enter so largely into the structure and history of the language.[34]

The drift toward a classical emphasis in English studies in India is especially remarkable considering that the classical curriculum that still held full sway in England as late as the 1860s remained the center of a raging controversy on whether "training of the mind" was compatible with "useful knowledge."[35] At a time when utility was a rallying cry for reform of Oriental learning, English studies took a surprising direction in India, veering toward the same practices that were under fire in the homeland. Wherever new schools were established and a course in Oriental literature set up alongside a course in English literature, a classical approach invariably marked the teaching of English.[36]

THE REVIVAL of a classical pedagogy of English literary instruction in India coincided with the declining status of polite language and literature in England.[37] The growth of a mass British reading public had created what many alarmed critics saw as a distaste for fine reading and, more seriously, threatened the survival of all intellectual greatness and refinement. In proportion to the decline of "refined" reading there occurred an increase in works of amusement; the revolution in literary production, both in the number and nature of its publications, was brought about by the increased wealth of the higher classes and the increased literacy of the lower classes. Half a century earlier, only well-educated people constituted a significant reading population; by the 1820s the rate of literacy ensured a wider reading public. The changing constitution of the English readership, influencing the type of literature that was being consumed, produced, and taught, augmented the fear of the established classes that other nations, particularly France and Germany, were advancing on England with more "useful" and "ennobling" productions. Amusement had become almost the exclusive business of life in England, threatening the extinction of all intellectual greatness and refinement. In an age of mass readership, literature seemed to have become a mere reflection of current sentiments and to have abandoned almost entirely its mission as an "enlightener" and "improver" of men.

The lack of literary culture in the middle-class environment from which a typical secondary school boy came was replicated in the schools.[38] Contemporary periodicals deplored the neglect of English classics in the schools and demanded reform in the pattern of English studies if English youth were not to be lost forever to declining tastes.[39] Partly to offset the antiintellectualism of the English public schools, book societies were established in the hope that the taste for works of a "more instructive and scientific nature" would be inculcated again, "for the diffusion of knowledge and science invariably creates a numerous class of intelligent readers, whose minds can be gratified only with the works of a superior order."[40] The Cheap Book Society in Ireland provided an encouraging example of the success that book societies were able to achieve in combatting lowbrow vulgarity and enhancing taste.

A grafting of English literary achievements onto the cultural system of the colonies further assured the survival of British culture, leaving a "monument more imperishable than the pyramids of Egypt."[41] The grafting had already begun to bear the fruits of success in the linguistic habits of Indians. Charles Trevelyan, brother-in-law of Macaulay and one-time president of the General Council of Public Instruction, proudly exclaimed that the educated Indians "speak purer English than we speak ourselves, for they take it from the purest models, they speak the language of the *Spectator,* such English as is never spoken in England."[42] If Calcutta citizens spoke the language of the *Spectator,* it was by no means accidental, for editors of Calcutta journals and newspapers deliberately wrote in an Addisonian style under names like "Candidus," "Verax," "Oneiropolos," and "Flaccus" and on subjects not having the remotest bearing on Indian life, such as the fashions of the day in England, and on imagination, etiquette, and morality.[43] Such discussions, they admitted, would be considered tedious and archaic in a modern newspaper in England, but in the Calcutta papers they served to give the Indians a taste for "polite" literature that Englishmen were fast losing.

As a time capsule for English culture, India provided an ideal setting. The structure of Indian society, its multiple languages and multiple religions, eliminated some of the chief difficulties encountered in England in the preservation of a pure national culture. For the differentiated education that the Indian social structure encouraged—vernaculars for the lower castes and the classical languages of Arabic, Sanskrit, and Persian for the upper classes of Hindus and Muslims—minimized the possibilities of one language ever achieving the status of a common language for all the population. Linguistic stratification of classes permitted English high culture to be maintained in all its purity without the erosion that was occurring to polite literature in England. The resistance of the English language to standardization of use in England is a measure of the problematic control of linguistic and literary forms wherever English, as a living language of daily speech and communication shared by a wide public, is used and produced outside institutional controls such as, for example, formal education.

The Filtration Theory of Macaulay and John Stuart Mill, promoting a small elite group through education in English, contributed to the linguistic stratification of Indian society. The theory ostensibly had its origins in a set of practical realities: a complete education that began with a thorough study of English was within the reach of only a very small proportion of Indians. What distinguished this group of people from the masses was the amount of leisure time they possessed. Apart from the limited resources available for the wholesale education of the masses in English, the leisure time at the disposal of any group of people was a major criterion in determining who was to receive English instruction. The history of England indicates that those who studied the classical languages were men of the learned professions, men of leisure who had the time to devote themselves to a study inaccessible to the great bulk of the country. If this was true in England, it was even more so in India, which already had a class of learned men set apart from the masses. No great results were foreseen by working on the lower classes, whose circumstances did not permit them to acquire more than the basic elements of knowledge and who were in subjection to the higher classes. The cultivation of a small elite group of Indians was perceived as the foundation for a stability that "even a political revolution will not destroy and upon which after ages may erect a vast superstructure."[44]

Linguistic and social stratification constituted a necessary precondition for the preservation of a pure, frozen form of English culture, unadulterated by subsequent appropriations by other classes in any form, except perhaps in the relatively non-threatening form of translations. The English language and literature would remain confined to the class designated to receive instruction in it. The control exerted through the formal institution of education further exploited the structure of Indian society to prevent English from degenerating into sheer vulgarity as in England. Thus while the official stance was on the side of utility and modernization, the kinds of curricular decisions that were being made gave the impression that the real goal was acculturation. Consequently, it was not uncommon for failings in government institutions to be measured against the yardstick of acculturation rather than that of utility, as in the 1855 report cited earlier.

The return to a secular conception of literature, then, is not reducible to a mere repudiation of religious identity. More accurately, it is a relocation of cultural value from belief and dogma to language, experience, and history. The discriminations between English and Indian literature in their relation to Christianity and Hinduism respectively yielded a pure, almost severe understanding of English literature as intellectual and linguistic production. As a parallel process to the survival of English culture, secularization reintroduced a classical emphasis in English studies, strengthening and endorsing the legitimacy and authority of British institutions, laws, and government.

5
Lessons of History

And so they who listened with rapture to the songs of the bards overran the provinces of those who were charmed with the fairy tale.

—*Asiatic Journal* (1831), 32:142

THE ORIENTATION of literary study to the cultural heritage contained in a national past is a fairly new phenomenon, displacing an older rhetorical tradition. The inaugural lecture of A. J. Scott at University College, London, in 1848 is said to be the earliest instance of a formal academic plea for the study of literature as an expression of the culture of an age and as a reflection of society. By 1852 the historical study of English literature was firmly established in University College. In 1875 the alliance between literature and history was given institutional expression with the merging of the chair of English literature with that of history. Never very stable or clear on the point of the relationship between language and literature, English as a discipline became even more blurred and confused when a separate chair was created for English language in that same year.

The transition from the rhetorical tradition of belles lettres to the historical study of literature is explained as a displacement of Renaissance conceptions of language that "removed attention from the situation of utterance and located all significance in the logic of language, which was determined by nonlinguistic considerations."[1] With the passing of the old rhetorical traditions, the study of literary genres gradually became oriented in literary history. Present-oriented and context-bound, the formal method of disputation gave way to the authority of preexisting structures of mind and society as the prime catalyst of knowledge. The choice was *against* a kind of intellectual inquiry directed toward the present in favor of one based on the authority of established usage, historical precedent, and social convention. The object of literary training is understood as twofold: first, to develop a historical awareness of the cultural moments in which those usages, precedents, and conventions are especially strong; and second, to reclaim those moments as exemplary instances of truth, coherence, and value.

Linking "this new historical and organic awareness of society" to the Romantic reaction against the Industrial Revolution and its impoverishment of cultural life, D. J. Palmer describes the emphasis on order, continuity, sequence, and moral purpose as an internal shift within English studies, "the immediate condition alike of a revivified approach to classical studies, and of a social philosophy such as Coleridge's to bind the present with the past."[2]

Described thus, the shift within English studies appears to have an inner logic and consistency, but the description is marked by a curious reticence to account for those external conditions that produce or require any such shift from present to past, from rhetoric to history. It is not clear how exactly the "logic of language" is determined by "nonlinguistic considerations" (at best an ambiguous phrase); it is even less clear why that should cause an alliance of literature with history. To explain this development solely in terms of widened conceptions of language, with the rhetorical study of argumentation giving way to the appreciation of style as cultural expression, is to confine discussion of the development of English studies to changes merely at the level of form.

To study the institutionalization of these shifts it is impossible to evade the political context of expanding territorial control and power in which the merging of literature and history was first seriously considered and then actively urged as a principle of study and criticism. Though the influence of the Western encounter with alien cultural and literary forms on the formation of nineteenth-century English studies is not the subject of this book or this chapter, it is still necessary to signal the partial history that results from the persistent disregard of Britain's colonial involvement in producing new articulations of literary functions, unless of course such study is somehow construed to be threatening to the integrity of the British intellectual, cultural, and social tradition as a source of literary judgments.[3]

I am aware that one of the problems involved in pursuing this line of inquiry, where connections between confrontation with different cultures and societies and redefinitions of literary value are not that readily established empirically, is that of confusing the logical with the historical. That is to say, in an effort to understand the relations between English studies and colonialism there is always the danger of claiming an overriding determinism in the relation. To proceed from this assumption and draw conclusions from it is to ignore entirely that the relations may be largely historical; that is, that they occur in the form that they do, not because they are locked in a mutuality of cause-effect determination, but because the situations with which they were complicit produced such particular, detailed effects on subsequent action and policy that they render the history of English studies incomplete by itself, as is the study of colonial expansion, without reference to the mutually supportive role that each played in response to Britain's confrontation with peoples and cultures different from its own.

THE READING of literature as an expression of culture and society has an opaque, textured history in British India. It dates back to the early Anglicist-Orientalist debates out of which emerged redefinitions of truth as the discovery of error. As described in the preceding chapter, the relativization of cultures necessitated by the dialectical progression toward truth through error promoted literary study as intellectual exercise. English studies established itself in direct dialectical interplay with the Eastern tradition, taking the totality of Indian society and culture, its contradictions and anomalies, as a reference point for critical formulations that eventually fed into pedagogical practice. Given the fact that the British ruling in India were administrators and not literary critics, it is not surprising that the multiple realities of India with which they had to deal would force an expansion of the traditional framework within which literature was normally discussed to include other levels of India represented by its laws, religion, government, and social institutions.

Warren Hastings unwittingly opened the door to historical approaches to literature when he sought to popularize the translation of the *Bhagavad Gita* by Charles Wilkins, who had presented him with a copy of it in 1784, when he was governor-general of Bengal. Hastings had a difficult time reconciling the literati of the West to a poem so wholly different in structure, style, and substance from the classical models of Greece and Rome that centuries of study and imitation had consecrated. He attempted to win acceptance for the work by persuading Western literati to suspend for a while the "imperishable standards" of classical criticism:

> Might I, an unlettered man, venture to prescribe bounds to the latitude of criticism, I should exclude, in estimating the merit of such a production, all rules drawn from the ancient or modern literature of Europe, all references to such sentiments or manners as are become the standards of propriety for opinion and action in our own modes of life, and equally all appeals to our revealed tenets of religion and moral duty. I should exclude them, as by no means applicable to the language, sentiments, manners, or morality appertaining to a system of society with which we have for ages been unconnected. . . . I would exact from every reader the allowance of obscurity, absurdity, barbarous habits, and a perverted morality. Where the reverse appears, I would have him receive it as much clear gain, and allow it a merit proportioned to the disappointment of a different expectation.[4]

Though Hastings' motive was to have the *Gita* read without undue comparisons to Western literature, his argument had the effect of referring critics to that "system of society with which we have for ages been unconnected" to derive those principles empirically.

In the hands of a critic like James Mill, the derivation of standards of art by empirical methods became a devastating rationale for evaluating art not in relation to intrinsic properties, but in relation to a doctrine of utility that approached works in terms of the social and religious practice they threw open for examination.[5] To deploy his theory of historicist readings in practical criticism, Mill turned to William Jones as his foil. Jones' admiration for Indian literature and the favorable comparisons with Western literature that he made on its behalf are witheringly dismissed by Mill as naive responses made solely at the level of form. Jones had proclaimed Kalidas the Shakespeare of India and had himself undertaken the translation of *Shakuntala*. Admittedly, Mill's quarrel was not with the lyricism of the play; he even grudgingly conceded *Shakuntala* to be a perfect example of pastoral. His main objections were to Jones' belief that the features of pastoral, marked by "courtesy and urbanity, a love of poetry and eloquence, and the practice of exalted virtues,"[6] were an adequate measure of a perfect society. For Mill, this was a woefully uncritical stance, evidence that Jones had succumbed to the seductive pleasures of a literary genre that obscured consciousness of the evil social practices prevalent at the time. Using Jones as a perfect example of an ahistorical reader, Mill set out to show that only a historicist reading truly revealed the meaning of pastoral: namely, that it is a literary form produced by nations in their infancy, when individuals remained so fettered by the tyranny of despotic government that social criticism of any kind had to give way to indulgence in light romances. Mill's real message, of course, is that the more responsibility in government a people are given, the more occupied they will be with the business of state and the less prone, therefore, to pure fiction or poetry.

Mill read the lyricism and sentiment in Indian drama as a mark of a self-indulgent society and that in turn as the product of a despotic state. Developing his theory of art simultaneously with his theory of civilization, he maintained that the quality of government is largely responsible for channeling the energies of the individual to work for the common good. In the ancient despotic states, the individual primarily strove for self-gratification, which became the value by which he lived. Everything that he did and produced, even his art, was a reflection of his incapacity to perceive a higher good or duty.

The social values that *Shakuntala* celebrates—superstition, extravagant belief, and arbitrary will—appeared to prove Mill's point. He interpreted exaggeration in art as a reflection of inconsistencies in the laws and institutions of the society from which it springs and for which it is intended. A social practice that he found irreconcilable with the notions of a "refined" people is the marriage that takes place in the forest between the hero and heroine in *Shakuntala* or, in his words, "that kind of marriage which two lovers contract from the desire of amorous embraces."[7] Another custom sanctioned by Hindu society that figures in the plot of the play is the obeisance traditionally given the Brahmins. The cause of the heroine's misfortune is a Brahmin who lays a curse on her because she had neglected to receive him at the hermitage with the expected honors. Far from showing the Brahmin as an evil force whose power is to be resisted, the play merely uses his curse as a device to add a twist to the plot: "Surely no contrivance for such a purpose was ever less entitled to admiration than the curse of a Brahmen."[8] That is to say, the narrative contrivances in Sanskrit literature are not merely reflective of a childish imagination but have more sinister overtones, for they deliberately thwart reflection upon those same practices that are the source of the Indians' "degradation."

Oddly, Mill offered the kind of reading that, almost a century and a half later, Lévi-Strauss was to give in his studies of myth and culture. In much the same way that Mill interpreted the narrative structure of Indian drama as perpetuating the beliefs and practices of Hindu society, Lévi-Strauss read the structure of myth as a coded message by means of which a culture offers models of belief and action to its individual members.[9] In order to decode the message and probe the sources that give it form, the critical observer had first to break that form and recast the myth in a non-narrative mode. It is precisely in such an act that Lévi-Strauss believed the inherent contradictions of the social system are exposed.

Lévi-Strauss explains the power of myth in terms of a concept—that of mediation—that is useful in explaining the British disapproval of Indian literature on moral grounds. Essentially, mediation refers to the contrived resolution, by means of a tale or legend, of self-contradictions within a morality; for example, a society's practice of incest is mediated in the Oedipus myth by oracular prophecies and divine agencies. *Shakuntala* is replete with comparable instances of mediation, one of which is the aforementioned transformation of the Brahmin's curse from an ugly social fact to a narrative device that invokes religious mystery and awe. Other instances involve the attitude that the reader is expected to have toward King Dushyanta, who promises to send for his new bride, Shakuntala, and not only fails to do so, but rejects her when she appears at his court with his child. Were it not for yet another narrative contrivance, the lost ring, Dushyanta's callousness would have quite possibly been seen by the contemporary audience as a fairly accurate representation of the way royal personages treated women—a theme that a court dramatist like Kalidas could have pursued only with grave consequences to himself. The ring is brought into the story to offset this impression. Dushyanta is doomed by the Brahmin's curse to forget Shakuntala when it is lost. When it is found and the memory of her comes back to him, he is smitten by remorse for having rejected her. But such moments of awareness of personal guilt are not permitted to last long, and in mediating between actions and individual responsibility there is always the suggestion of external agency. The cause of her current misfortunes, Shakuntala explains to Dushyanta, is not the king or even the Brahmin who cursed her, but the sins of her past life.

The concept of mediation is also useful in explaining why the Hindu epics the *Ramayana* and the *Mahabharata* were regarded as problematic works and not readily assimilable as texts for instruction in Indian schools and colleges in British India. The contradictions in these two epics could not be explained away other than as the superimposition of Brahminical readings on what presumably originated as the heroic songs of the Kshatriyas (the second order in the caste hierarchy). A case in point is the polyandry of the heroine Draupadi in the *Mahabharata,* a practice that evidently existed in pre-Brahminical times but could not possibly have continued into the Brahminical era. British commentators explained the continuing presence of polyandry in the later versions as an attempt by the Brahmins to allegorize events in order to justify the epic as divine truth. The moral repugnance that would normally have been aroused in the reader by the literal fact of Draupadi marrying five men is mediated by a Brahminic interpretation that considers the marriage a symbolic union of the goddess Lakshmi with her consort Vishnu, of whom the five Pandavas are merely manifestations.

Ironically, it is the internal process of moralization in Indian literature —of assigning a deeper significance through allegory to a social custom that is otherwise distasteful—that struck the most discordant chords for British commentators, far more perhaps then the custom itself, for undesirable social practices, if understood as historical fact bound to a certain time and place, did not have the power to influence behavior and action in the same way that their transformation into abstract universal principles did. When allegorized, these social customs received a sanctity that prevented the reader from distinguishing a moral act from an immoral one. The Indian's insufficient sense of decency was directly attributed to the texts they read from their own tradition, which blurred distinctions between decency and indecency.[10] Morality became urgently linked to the development of a historical consciousness through which alone the reader would learn to sift fact from legend, for if it was true that "wild symbolic form and mysterious allegory formed a hieratic character in which events of the past were recorded,"[11] it was imperative to undo that form and recast it in another where the signs would be easily interpretable.

Accurate interpretation of signs therefore acquired a moral significance far surpassing any utilitarian function that might have otherwise
been assigned. A great deal of research undertaken by Europeans on the
historical basis of the two epics was motivated in large part by an urge
to demystify and de-Brahminize them. Of the historians who were
engaged in this task, J. Talboys Wheeler, who taught for some time at
Presidency College, Madras, and in 1862 became assistant secretary to
the government, most clearly and consciously aimed at separating fact
from legend in the act of reconstructing India's past from the *Ramayana*
and the *Mahabharata*. In telling the history of India from its literature,
he deliberately set out to de-allegorize and to focus attention on the
social practices themselves: "Every legend and tradition has been systematically Brahmanized for the purpose of bringing all the religious laws
and usages of the different races of India into conformity with Brahmanical ideas. When stripped of these Brahmanical grafts and overgrowth,
the legends and traditions will be found to furnish large illustrations of
old Hindu civilization."[12] The large number of histories written by
Englishmen that were part of the literature curriculum in Indian schools
and colleges no doubt performed the same function, which was essentially analytic in nature. Among the histories of India prescribed for
study were Marshman's *History of Bengal* and *History of India*, Murray's
History of India, with Readings from Mill and Other Authors, and Henry
Morris' *History of India*.[13] A point that British critics returned to with
remarkable consistency was that as long as Indian youth were without a
historical consciousness, they would remain shackled to the tyranny of
forms. The curricular juxtaposition of historical texts with native literature was part of an effort to break through those forms; as a study in
contrasting modes of explanation, the juxtaposition offered the means
to developing an analytical cast of mind required for dismantling inher-
ited structures and myths: If the genius of Sanskrit literature synthesized
and harmonized disparate elements to fit a Brahminical conception, the
whole thrust of historical instruction during the period of British rule
was to break them down and force a steady gaze on each element in
isolation. History was transformed into nothing less than the recasting
of myth in a non-literary mode by means of which the discordancies of
Hindu society were forced into the open.

Incidentally, one of the ways that nationalism sought to express itself
in the 1870s and 1880s was by restoring allegorical readings to legends
that were denounced by the British for their licentiousness. Often the

inspiration for such readings came from commentaries produced in the Orientalist period, which defiantly transformed what Anglicists attacked as sensual images in Hindu art into representations of spirit:

> Whenever I look around me, in the vast region of Hindoo mythology, I discover piety in the garb of allegory: and I see Morality, at every turn, blended with every tale; and as far as I can rely on my own judgment, it appears the most complete and ample system of Moral Allegory that the world has ever produced. . . . We satisfactorily learn from the Geeta that it is not mere images, but the invisible spirit, that they thus worship.[14]

The theosophist and nationalist leader Annie Besant, for example, took the cue from her Orientalist predecessors by reading the tale of Lord Krishna (the "philanderer-god") stealing the clothes of maidens while they were bathing as an allegory about the nakedness of the soul approaching Supreme Being.[15] Such readings were a conscious revolt against a narrow British historicism threatening to break the continuity of a popular Hindu consciousness, whose strength lay in the ability to transcend the immediate and the particular and to bring together various segments of society through an appeal to the universal and the timeless.

Gandhi, however, went a little further back than Annie Besant, to the British representations themselves, and claimed that Europeans tended to look for deeper significances in Hindu customs and practices, which were then invariably equated with the obscene:

> It has remained for our Western visitors to acquaint us with the obscenity of many practices which we have hitherto innocently indulged in. It was in a missionary book that I first learnt that Shivalingam [a Hindu phallic symbol] had any obscene significance at all and even now when I see a Shivalingam neither the shape nor the association in which I see it suggests any obscenity. It was again in a missionary book that I learnt that the temples in Orissa were disfigured with obscenities. When I went to Puri, it was not without an effort that I was able to see those things. But I do know that the thousands who flock to the temple know nothing about the obscenity surrounding these figures.[16]

An important aspect of Gandhi's observation is that in the name of separating fact from legend, British readings had introduced a literalism that was paradoxically allegorical in effect, for it assumed that every sign had to have a meaning, whereas for Hindus this was not necessarily true. Instead, a sign could easily do no more than suggest another sign, which in turn might suggest yet another, and so on. The process could continue *ad infinitum* without ever getting beyond the act of signifying, which is perfectly consistent with the Hindu belief that all phenomena are multiple manifestations of a single entity that alone has meaning but is at the same time unknowable.

But the British argument was that there was no clearer proof of the childishness of the Indian mind than its inability to pierce through the outer layers of form. If Indians failed to perceive meanings, the argument went, it was not because the signs did not contain any, but because the Indians lacked the mental capacity to see that a concrete reality lay behind these signs that was both a cause and an explanation for them. The act of forcing meanings into the open comprised an important aspect of the British ideology of literary education, owing much to critical readings of the kind produced by James Mill.

IN EVERY respect, the historical orientation to literary study reverses the assumptions and rationale of Christian instruction or, at the very least, provides a new set of terms. One such inversion is concerned with conceptions of human nature. If, according to the doctrinal basis of Christianity, man is inherently depraved and in a state of original sin, the object of an education on Christian principles is to raise individuals from the state of bestial nature in which they are born, toward the spiritual good that is their eternal promise. Whatever distinguishes man from beasts becomes the instrument of his regeneration. As Lionel Gossman points out, given the fact that there is no greater distinguishing feature than the uniquely human ability to manipulate symbolic systems, language and literature acquire an importance exceeding that of even science and technology.[17] Early British arguments for literary instruction assumed a condition of innate depravity, and the rhetoric of dualism ensuing from that assumption demarcated a "cultivated" self formed by learning, language, and literature from a "natural" self still burdened by sin, willful pride, and vileness of temperament. Clerical attacks on Utilitarian principles in education emphasized the Christian progress toward the ideal self through literature, as in the following remarks, made to the commencement audience at Cambridge in 1826 by the Rev. Hugh James Rose, later to be principal of King's College, London: "[Literature] is not partial in its cultivation of the intellect, but tends at once to correct the taste, to strengthen the judgement, *to instruct us in the wisdom of men better and wiser than ourselves,* to exercise the reasoning faculties on subjects which demand and deserve their attention, and to show them the boundaries imposed on them by Providence" (emphasis mine).[18] Rose's remark assumes a gap between the reader and the text: the reader's deficiencies are understood as the result of an innately vile and depraved nature, while the text is designated as the superior agency to lead the malformed individual to a plane of superior moral being.

It is not necessary to limit ourselves to the most obvious instances where such distinctions were routinely made, such as in the missionary curriculum in literature, to gain some sense of the widespread prevalence of such characterizations of literary functions, presupposing a dualism of man's base self and his higher nature. Significantly, much the same characterization informed Adam Smith's understanding of the uses of literature to offset the ill-effects of a crass materialism produced by laissez-faire individualism. Smith's *Theory of Moral Sentiments* (1759) remained a central text in the Indian curriculum throughout the nineteenth century, both in government and missionary institutions—the Calcutta University Commission Report of 1919, for instance, still listed it as part of the prescribed course of studies. Though it was well over a century before his proposals were implemented, Adam Smith was evidently among the earliest thinkers to propose the study of selections from the works of English prose writers as a social and moral corrective for dangers that he believed were inherent in laissez-faire capitalism, particularly dangers associated with the potential for a morally corrupted concept of individualism.[19]

In *Moral Sentiments* Adam Smith argued the need for a broad academic program that would encourage and direct a process of self-evaluation and self-enlightenment. His work can be read as a systematic argument for the education of the man of intellect who is also a man of good conduct and virtue. Smith began by noting a principle inherent in man's nature, which he called the impartial spectator, that makes him responsive to how others think and behave. Those who are able to direct our sentiments are models of intellectual virtue: the "man of taste," for instance, "who distinguishes the minute and scarce perceptible differences of beauty and deformity" or the "experienced mathematician who unravels with ease the most intricate and perplexed proportions."[20] Smith believed that through the admiration of the sentiments of these "others," these learning models, we come to realize the existence of intellectual virtues. The impartial spectator, the spectator within us, as

Smith referred to him, "enters by sympathy into the sentiments of the master" and "views the object under the same agreeable aspect."[21] The task before us, Smith claimed, if we truly wish to realize the intellectual virtues, is to cultivate the impartial spectator within us, to develop the ability to place ourselves in the context of those sentiments. The study of literature, Smith argued, provides the formative structures that will determine the development of this spectator within. Through literature, he wrote, "we endeavour to examine our own conduct as we imagine any other fair and impartial spectator would examine it. If, upon placing ourselves in his situation, we thoroughly enter into all the passions and motives which influenced it, we approve of it, by sympathy with the approbation of this supposed equitable judge. If otherwise, we enter into his disapprobation, and condemn it."[22]

Smith's concept of the impartial spectator was embedded in the rationale of literary instruction, which presupposed a divided self-consciousness. Working strictly from within the Protestant tradition, Smith had written that "when I endeavour to examine my own conduct, when I endeavour to pass sentence upon it . . . either to approve or condemn it, it is evident that, in all such cases, I divide myself as it were into two persons; and that I, the examiner and judge, represents a different character from the other I, the person whose conduct is examined and judged of."[23] The first I becomes the half he called the "spectator"; the second person is the person whose conduct, "under the character of a spectator, I was endeavouring to form some opinion [of]."[24] This concept is of instrumental value in disengaging the individual from his natural self, in order that he might observe it critically from the viewpoint of the other, the impartial I.

But the historical emphasis, which comes uncannily close to reinforcing a conception of human nature antithetical to Protestant premises, negates the dualism of nature (base)/spirit (elevated) and claims an innate goodness of Indian character that is thwarted from realizing itself by a despotic, corrupt political society. In what appears to be an abrupt reversal of the customary Western denigration of Oriental character, the basic difference between European and Oriental is claimed to be a feature not of character but of government. In an unprecedented affirmation of unity between the Eastern and the Western temperament, Indians are described in one assessment as ideally having the capacity for every virtue, having "great natural sagacity, quickness of apprehension, sound intellect, sound reasoning and eloquence of expression."[25] What prevented the Indian from realizing the potential for a common identity with Europeans, however, was the tendency toward despotic government in Oriental society, which had spread anarchy through internal administration, driving people to habits that degraded them and paralyzed "every principle intended by nature to promote the improvement of man."[26]

The ancient feudal system of Europe, on the other hand, was characterized in the same assessment as a society driven by antidespotic principles unknown in the East. "The forms of their government, the wisdom of their Statesmen, the brilliant deeds of their heroes and patriots, the effusion of their poets, and the principles of their philosophers" were purportedly built into the literary system of British schools, strengthening and stimulating the intellectual faculties to higher attainments.[27] For training in polity the youth of England had no better instructor than the history and literature of Greece and Rome, which contained enough themes to inspire them to heights of enthusiasm, heroic action, and noble passion. In contrast to the heroic fictions of the Europeans that provided an impulse to the habits and pursuits accounting for their elevated political order, the romances of the Indians, it was maintained, only encouraged indulgence and luxury. The contrast between the two strengthened the British conviction that the more dedicated to the celebration of high adventure and high exploits is an art form, the more roused the people would become to action and virtue and so to installing a form of government befitting such values. A circular definition prevailed. If strength was a prerequisite for fortification against the wild exercise of imagination, then imagination acquired a moral value when it was harnessed to the service of political organization. Unlike the inhabitants of India, the Europeans "did not convert the luxury of their imaginations into a means of weakening and effeminating their minds; but they used it as a prompter to activity and a stimulant to high enterprise."[28]

In British administrative discussions of Indian education, "right" motives for reading were vitally connected with the restructuring of society. The tradition of reading for pleasure was held responsible for preventing Oriental people from recognizing the extent to which the evils of their society were valorized in their literature, whose gorgeous texture and rich imagery were a seductive distraction from plot and theme.[29] Europeans, on the other hand, presumably read from other motives, which sprang from active engagement with the world. A mere glance at the art forms that had evolved in different societies of the West and the East was deemed sufficient to reveal the basic difference. While Eastern literature still continued to be dominated by the romance, which fed the mind on sensuous pleasure, Western literature had outgrown it, the European tradition of "restless ambition" never quite being congenial to its sustained expression. Not only did the epic spirit that was ushered in brace the mind and lift it to high thoughts, but the conflict the bards recorded provided the inspiring source of the Europeans' impulse to action and ambition and, ultimately, to conquest itself. And thus it could be said, as a writer for the *Asiatic Journal* candidly did, that "they who listened with rapture to the songs of the bards, overran the provinces of those who were charmed with the fairy tale." [30]

Such critical statements were paralleled by the judgment of those on the General Council of Public Instruction in Calcutta that the more politically enlightened a society, the more its laws could be expected to harmonize with and be reflected in literary form. One of the most forceful statements of this idea came from Charles Trevelyan, who argued that recognition of the standards of excellence in literature was one step toward establishment of "the Law" in the minds of Indians. In English literature he saw the merging of the aesthetic, the intellectual, and the moral, the means by which intellectual discernment of the rules of composition would lead the mind to an understanding and appreciation of the highest laws of the state or the moral principles that regulate and guide conduct.

The great harm done by Oriental literatures, Trevelyan implied, was that the laws represented therein were arbitrary and whimsical and the rules of composition equally so. By not allowing for prior individual reflection or understanding, they failed to give human actions a solid base and taught that man has no choice but to act arbitrarily. For Trevelyan, the cultural power of English literary study lay in its confirming that "knowledge and thought must precede action" and intellect and Christian morality act in concert in shaping man as a public being. By inducing colonial subjects to read literature as an expression of the culture of an age, the historical approach served the twin objectives of rousing Indians to a consciousness of the inconsistencies in the native system of society while simultaneously leading them to a recognition of the principles of order and justice in the Western.

In the presumed absence of comparable objects of admiration in their own history and literature, Indian youth were seen as pitiably doomed to a perpetual state of degradation. But it was a degradation that was portrayed as decidedly not intrinsic to their character but the result of despotic rule. If the Indian was made aware of the cause of his debasement, there was every likelihood that he would seek release from the bonds of a tyrannical system. As a warning lesson for Indians, C. E. Trevelyan pointed to the negative example of Arabs as a people who were so "confident in the riches of their native tongue, [they] disdained the study of any foreign idiom. If they had made themselves familiar with Greek and Roman literature, they might have suspected that their caliph was a traitor, and their prophet an impostor."[31] In the same breath, Trevelyan linked the awakening of the intellectual faculties through literary study to awareness of despotism: "The sword of the Saracens became less formidable when their youth was drawn away from the camp to the college, where the armies of the faithful presumed to read and reflect."[32] By arousing the dormant young Indian from the deep slumber of a tyrannical past to a full sense of the evils of his native political society, historical training acquired deeper, more refined, more exalted motives, reconstituting the object of instruction as the restoration of the Indian student to his original state of goodness.

The self-righteous justification for government intervention in this formulation is too obvious to require comment, but what is especially striking is the insistent reassurance that British education was not seeking to assimilate Indians to the European model by urging them to cast aside their Indian identity (and thus removing them from their native, "base" state, as Christian instruction attempted). Rather, the suggestion is that English education was designed, in a Platonist sense, to awaken the colonial subjects to a memory of their innate character, corrupted as it had become, again in a Platonist sense, through the feudalistic character of Oriental society. In this universalizing narrative, rescripted from a scenario furnished earlier by missionaries, the British government was refashioned as the ideal republic to which Indians must naturally aspire as a spontaneous expression of self, a state in which the British rulers won a figurative place as Platonic Guardians. The secular rewriting of the Christian account of sinful, fallen man identified natural self with an original, uncorrupted political order. As the British scenario envisioned it, through the catalytic agency of British intervention, specifically its laws and institutions, the educated Indian was taken *back* to a true self, not away from an (inherently corrupt) self toward an external, transcendental ideal such as implied in the missionary scheme of instruction.

By this logic, the good that England represented for India constituted the only valid content of instruction for its youth. But to perceive that good, as John Murdoch realized—with profound implications for curricular selection—Indian students required an active intellectual disposition capable of comparative distinctions. Murdoch, an official in the Madras Presidency who was commissioned to assess the importance of vernacular literature in relation to other school subjects, was baffled by the resentment to English rule by the mass of Indians he encountered. He was equally puzzled by the fact that there were no comparable records of popular hostility to earlier, more despotic governments. As he continued his project on Indian vernacular literature, he stumbled on a possible answer in an issue of the *Imperial Review* edited by William Hunter, later chairman of the Indian Education Commission. The British inability to understand native tolerance to earlier despotic rule, the article stated,

> overlooked the fact that the present generation of our Eastern subjects has not the means of instituting such a comparison. The greater part of them have had no experience of any dynasty but our own, and are not possessed of any historical information, wherewith to supply this lack of knowledge. . . . [The author then goes on to examine how British officials should respond.] All desire to falsify history or to present one-sided views is disclaimed. The amplest credit should be given to the various dynasties that have preceded us. At the same time, it seems practicable to show that, notwithstanding all our faults we have been a blessing to India. The *History of India* would be the best vehicle for such teaching, though it might also find a place, to some extent, in the general Reading Books.[33]

But as Murdoch further realized, mere comparison was not enough if it was not also accompanied by a constant reinforcement of British ideals to which Indian youth were expected to aspire. The political pitfalls of partial enlightenment are described by Murdoch in quasi-religious terms, and he concludes by urging instruction in the advantages of stable government not as an option but as public duty:

> We place in a boy's hands the histories of Greece and Rome, and hold up to his admiration the examples of those ancient patriots who have freed their country from domestic tyranny or a foreign yoke. The knowledge which we impart to him destroys the reverence which he would naturally feel for his own religion and its precepts. In its stead, we implant no other of a holier and purer kind. Can we wonder, then, at the harvest which we too frequently reap—disloyalty untempered by gratitude, a spurious and selfish patriotism, unchecked by religion and an overweening conceit of literary attainment supported by no corresponding dignity of character.[34]

The Indian Education Commission of 1882 took up the theme introduced by Murdoch of maintaining an appropriate balance between affirming British norms and preserving Indian self-respect. But it disagreed in the main with Murdoch's approbation of Morris' *History of India* as a suitable text for Indian schools and colleges, denouncing it as too overbearing and "denationalizing, the tenor of which went to magnify British power and to lower and degrade Indian men and manners."[35] Morris' *History* was replaced by William Hunter's *Indian People* as a text that was better geared to promoting loyalty to the government without coercing Indian students to believe they were only members of a great nation with certain duties toward it, thus robbing them of a sense of national character.[36]

English education, fighting to stave off the appearance of imposing an alien culture on native society, gained subtle redefinition as an instrument of authenticity. A historical consciousness was intended to bring the Indian in touch with himself, recovering his true essence and identity from the degradation to which it had become subject through native despotism. Far from alienating the Indian from his own culture, background, and traditions, English education gained the image of being an agency for restoring Indian youth to an essential self and, in turn, reinserting him into the course of Western civilization.

THE EXAMINATION questions following lessons in literature suggest a direction in British Indian classroom pedagogy closely paralleling the historical emphasis of critical readings such as those of James Mill. While the topics themselves may not seem extraordinary or innovative in the intellectual demands made on students to compare, analyze, and demonstrate with historical proof, they are quite distinctive when juxtaposed to the type of examination questions being asked in England, which tended by and large to consist of paraphrase, parsing, and direct explication. As D. J. Palmer points out in his history of English studies in England, the questions for students of an English class were constructed in the style of a catechism, consisting of four sections: History of the English Language, Principles and Practice of English Composition, Translations from Classical Authors into English, and Rhetoric. The focus on language, style, and rhetoric in the English curriculum is replicated in the examination questions. The compulsory question on Shakespeare, for example, was sometimes directed at his bad grammar:

"Derive and conjugate the irregular verb to break, and state whether there is any grammatical error in the following: 'I have broke with her father, and his good will obtained'—Shakespeare." In general, the examination questions required short, descriptive, factual answers assessing appropriateness of style and language, as for example with these questions: "Who is the first distinguished writer of English prose: Point out the characteristic features of his style, and say in what respect it differs from that of Lord Clarendon"; "When is the translation of an idiomatic expression perfect?" "Why is D a perfect letter?"[37]

By contrast, the examination questions in the Indian curriculum are less oriented toward mechanical points of grammar and less frequently ask for direct explication of specific texts. They are also less confined to single texts and appear to encompass a broader perspective on intellectual and social history, demanding an overall critical assessment of literature as an expression of culture and society. Warnings were sounded constantly about the dangers of allowing Indian examination questions to drift in the direction of essay topics in British schools and colleges mechanically testing rote recall without critical understanding. Hodgson Pratt, an Inspector of Schools, irately asked in the Bengal Public Instruction Report of 1856–1857:

> . . . why should Greeschunder Chuckerbutty be expected to know "what circumstances enabled Shakespeare to exhibit an accurate knowledge of Greek Mythology," or "in what respect the Dramatic compositions called 'Mysteries' differ from those called 'Moralities,' " and other facts of a like nature? On the other hand, it is of very great importance, that he should see clearly the dangers of living with an open sewer running under the lower floor of his house, or the cruelty of marrying his children at an immature age, or the impolicy of exhausting the soil of his fields by the disregard of important principles in Chemistry: and it is very important that his mind should comprehend the sublimity and beauty of the laws by which his own body and everything around him are governed; and that his heart should if possible, be awakened to the great facts and conclusions of Natural Theology.[38]

The comparative emphasis in the Indian curriculum is reflected in questions requiring students to commit themselves to critical judgment of the contradictory values to which their own societies adhered. In many instances the topics on which students were asked to write were worded in such a way as to predetermine the response. Missionary institutions in general posed more direct, less subtle questions than government schools did, as with the following: "On the disadvantages of Caste, and the benefits of its abolition"; "On the internal marks of Falsehood in the Hindu Shastras"; "On the Physical Errors of Hinduism"; "The best Contrast between Christianity and Hinduism, morally considered"; "Essay, illustrative of the manner in which the Law of the Hindu Caste is opposed to the Principles of Political Economy"; "The Evidences of the Antiquity of the New Testament, and the bearing of this question on the General Argument for the Truth of Christianity"; "On the Merits of Christianity, and the Demerits of Hinduism"; "On the inquiry, Whether the Savage State be the original state of Man, or not?"; "On the Exposure of the Sick on the Banks of the Ganges"; "On the Causes of Opposition to Christianity in India"; "On the History of the British Constitution"; "On the History of Bengal during the Muhammedan Period"; and "The Influence exerted on the Nations of Europe by the Maritime Discoveries of the Fifteenth Century."[39]

The questions in the government institutions shied away from direct reference to religion, but they were no less oriented toward making Indian youth conscious of the benefits of British rule, as with these topics: "The Effects upon India of the New Communication with Europe by means of Steam," "The Advantages India derives in regard to commerce, security of property, and the diffusion of knowledge, from its Connexion with England," and "The Diffusion of Knowledge through the Medium of the English Language in India."[40]

The answers that students wrote to these questions cannot be taken, of course, as indicative of their actual responses to the content of instruction. The nature of institutionalized education, with the pressure to compete for promotion and awards and prizes, is obviously too complex to permit us to read student essays categorically as personally felt, intellectually committed responses. Selections from student essays are not reproduced below as proof of either success or failure of the British ideology, but to indicate the degree of correspondence between the objectives of instruction and the internalization of what students clearly sensed as desirable responses to the content of instruction.

Rajnarain Bose, a student at Hindu College in Calcutta in 1843, was asked along with other classmates to gloss the following passage by Bacon:

> He thought also, there was found in the mind of man an affection naturally bred and fortified, and furthered by discourse and doctrine, which did pervert the true proceeding towards active and operative knowledge.

This was a false estimation, that it should be as a diminution to the mind of man to be much conversant in experiences and particulars, subject to sense, and bound in matter, and which are laborious to search, ignoble to meditate, harsh to deliver, illiberal to practise, infinite as is supposed in number, and no ways accommodated to the glory of arts.

This opinion or state of mind received much credit and strength, by the school of Plato, who, thinking that particulars rather revived the notions, or excited the faculties of the mind, than merely informed; and having mingled his philosophy with superstition, which never favoureth the sense, extolleth too much the understanding of man in the inward light thereof; and again Aristotle's school, which giveth the due to the sense in assertion, denieth it in practice much more than that of Plato.

For we see the schoolmen, Aristotle's successors, which were utterly ignorant of history, rested only upon agitation of wit; whereas Plato giveth good example of inquiry by induction and view of particulars; though in such a wandering manner as if of no force or fruit. So that he saw well that the supposition of the sufficiency of man's mind hath lost the means thereof.[41]

The passage was followed by several specific questions, including this one: "In what sense are the schoolmen here said to have been 'utterly ignorant of history'?" Though Bose's response did not specifically compare European medieval schoolmen with the classical scholars of India, the movement in his essay between specific descriptions of a historical past and generalizations with application to the present left a nebulous space where such identifications could be forged:

The schoolmen were utterly ignorant of history; i.e. the history of material nature. Men who were enamoured of theological and metaphysical inquiries, and pursued those inquiries with the greatest alacrity and application, cannot be expected to have much knowledge of natural science, and to pay much attention to its investigation. Their minds rested only upon "agitation of wit," i.e. upon wrangling and controversy on the subjects above-mentioned. Theological controversy was the chief employment of the learned in the middle ages. Any University who could puzzle and confound a rival one with their subtleties was declared victorious, and its renown was spread far and abroad. There were prizes given to the parties victorious in metaphysical disputations. These incitements had due effect upon the minds of students, and they devoted their whole attention and time to the study of theology and metaphysics, to the perusal of the huge volumes of St. Augustine, Thomas Aquinas and Duns Scotus. The sense in which the term "history" is used in this passage by Bacon, is countenanced by his division of the intellectual faculties of man and of human knowledge, in the second book of his advancement of learning. He there divides history into civil and natural history. . . . Plato saw well that if we suppose man's mind to be all-sufficient, and that it can pronounce with decision upon subjects beyond its reach, we must acknowledge on the other hand that it has not the means of doing so; for, as far as induction and view of particulars go, so far can man proceed with firm steps in his inquiries and speculation.[42]

Incidentally, Bacon was widely read in both government and missionary schools. His importance in the literary education of Indian students was so great that it was not uncommon to have students matriculating from schools possessing no knowledge other than that of Bacon's works, which were well represented in the curriculum. It was reported that James Ballantyne, a great Sanskrit scholar who had himself also translated Bacon into Sanskrit, taught English to his Brahmin students, not in the usual elementary spelling-book style followed in England, but by putting Bacon's *Novum Organon* into their hands as soon as they learned the letters of the English alphabet.[43] The selection of Bacon was particularly apt in light of the criticism that Indian literature was devoid of experimental science or natural philosophy. Condemning Hindu philosophers for being poets rather than experimental investigators with the will to submit phenomena to rigid analysis, a writer for the *Calcutta Christian Observer* dismissively characterized Hindus as half-witted mystics who "thought much and deeply, but were ever fonder of chasing the phantoms of a speculative fancy than of following the indications of nature."[44] No one was more critical of this aspect of the Hindu mind than the Indian social reformer Rammohun Roy, whose Baconian intellect rebelled against the establishment of Sanskrit seminaries "similar in character to those which existed in Europe before the time of Lord Bacon," which could only be expected to "load the minds of youth with grammatical niceties and metaphysical distinctions of little or no practical use to the possessor or to society."[45]

From the British standpoint Bacon's relevance for India lay in the command over nature exerted by philosophy to deliver substantial material benefits. Through such command, philosophy was endowed with a pragmatic dimension that enabled it to be put to the service of mankind, with the alleviation of human suffering and the increase of human happiness being as much its province as the search for truth. The application to India is self-evident in the context of critiques of the Hindu spirit of philosophy, denounced as incapable of nurturing any but "ascetic gymnosophists," mystical casuists who prevented the advancement of man's physical well-being by teaching that all matter is delusion.[46]

Fondness for Baconian ideas of material progress appears periodically in essays Indian students were assigned to write. Nobinchunder Dass, a student at Hooghly College, Calcutta, was asked to respond to the topic "The Effects upon India of the new Communication with Europe by means of Steam." His essay universalizes the myth of progress through analogies of the British presence in India and the Roman conquest of Britain. The result, a tour de force of sustained moral earnestness, is nothing short of an apology for imperialism.

Nothing tends so much to advance society, to humanize the manners, and to elevate men in the scale of civilization, as intercourse with different nations. It encourages commerce, by supplying the wants of one country with the superfluities of another; the knowledge of one people may be made the common property of all by its means, what the people of the remotest regions discover or invent, can be communicated everywhere. In short, intercourse renders the earth, separated as it is into continents, islands, &c., by vast oceans, sometimes by insurmountable mountains, into one entire whole; and all mankind, as the members of one and the same family.

It was by carrying on an intercourse with the Greeks, that the Romans were enabled to improve in the liberal and mechanic arts. It was Greek philosophy that softened and polished the rough military manners of the Romans, and soothed them when misfortune compelled them to look for the opening of a communication between Asia and Europe, the people of the latter continent who, sunk in barbarism and ignorance, were then groaning under the pressure of tyranny and oppression, received from the hands of the Asiatics, who were their superiors in civilization, the blessings of social life and happiness. But those short days of Asiatic glory and superiority are gone, the stream of civilization has taken an opposite course; before, it flowed from Asia to Europe, now, but with more than its pristine vigour and rapidity, it flows from Europe into Asia.

The blessings that Europe now showers upon us are numerous and useful. Both in ancient and modern times Europe has been the seat of philosophy and civilization, but in consequence of there being no safe intercourse in ancient times, that civilization was confined to where it grew. But now that that obstacle is removed, an entire change has taken place in the circumstances of countries; whatever is now or has been gathered in Europe or in any part of the earth, receives an universal circulation.

England which is of all the countries of Europe nearest related to India by her present position in Asia, is particularly engaged in the cause of Indian improvement. She not only carries on commerce with India, but she is ardently employed in instructing the natives in the arts and sciences, in history and political economy, and, in fact, in every thing that is calculated to elevate their understanding, meliorate their condition, and increase their resources. . . .

The English are to us what the Romans were to the English; and as the English are the children of modern times, and command more resources and power than the Romans, we derive the greater advantage. The facility afforded to communication by the use of steam has enabled the English to govern our country with great prudence and vigilance, they do not appear to be at any time at the risk of forbearing in the glorious work which they have commenced, of improving the native mind and condition, but prosecute it with honour to themselves and favour to their subjects, till they are styled the regenerators of India.[47]

This essay strikingly demonstrates the extent to which the objectives of British instruction have been internalized by this student, regardless of whether the statements themselves provide an index to personal conviction. What specifically matters is the successful transference, from ruler to subject, of the view that India will not witness progress unless channels of communication are opened with the West. And the intellectual strategy that enables it is the conjoining of commercial expansion with culture and knowledge to suggest a reciprocal, symbiotic relationship. Without commerce, without territorial expansion, without intercourse between nations, writes Nobinchunder Dass, knowledge will remain frozen. The material classification of knowledge as property, which is alternatively possessed, appropriated, received, distributed, and redistributed, further strengthens the justificatory claims of commercial expansion: ". . . whatever is now or has been gathered in Europe or in any part of the earth, receives a universal circulation."

So complete is the identification of the subject with the ruler, so precisely realigned is his divided self-consciousness, that Nobinchunder Dass can refer to his fellow Indians distantly, even contemputously, as "the natives." It is "their" understanding that must be improved; it is "their" condition and "their" resources that require remedy. In Nobinchunder Dass, Adam Smith's impartial spectator has found a congenial home: "The English are to us what the Romans were to the English." In this one sentence are redeemed years of lessons in history leading to this culminating moment of affirmation, the endorsement of the Macaulayan dream.

In yet another essay, Mahendra Lal Basak, a student at the General Assembly Institution in Calcutta, takes upon himself the Platonist project of awakening Indian youth to a memory of their innate character, corrupted by a retrograde indigenous society. His is as much of a universalizing narrative as Nobinchunder Dass':

But alas! alas! our countrymen are still asleep—still sleeping the sleep of death. Rise up, ye sons of India, arise, see the glory of the Sun of

Righteousness! Beauty is around you; life blooms before you; why, why will ye sleep the sleep of death? And shall we who have drunk in that beauty—shall we not awake our poor countrymen? Come what will, ours will be the part, the happy part of arousing the slumber of slumbering India.[48]

The British government is set up as the ideal republic to which Mahendra wants his countrymen to aspire for realization of their true selves, and it is through the catalytic agency of British intervention, specifically its laws and institutions, that Mahendra truly believes his fellow Indians *will* be returned to a true self.

In essays by students such as Mahendra Lal and Nobinchunder Dass, English education gains subtle redefinition as an instrument of authenticity. English literary instruction, with its pedagogical imperative of nurturing a historically minded youth, places the Indian reader in a position where he renews contact with himself, recovering his true essence and identity from the degradation to which it had become subject through native despotism. Far from alienating the reader from his own culture, background, and traditions, English literature, taught less as a branch of rhetoric than of history, sought to return him to an essential unity with himself and reinsert him into the course of development of civilized man. At the same time the removal of "false thinking" through English education cleared the path to a perception of the British government as a fair one promoting national prosperity and justice.[49]

6
The Failure of English

You taught me language; and my profit on't Is, I know how to curse: the red plague rid you, For learning me your language!

—*The Tempest* (1.2.426–428)

FROM THE 1820s to the mid-1850s English literary studies had a predominantly religious and moral function in the Indian curriculum. But by 1857, when the Indian university system was formally instituted on the pattern of London University, the moral motive had begun to wear thin and cultural and moral value no longer claimed a common identity or goal. Ironically, this development occurred during a period when the moral motive was slowly gaining ground in English studies in England. The discipline of English literature itself was formally instituted in British schools only as late as 1871, and the longer history of English in India may thus partly explain the lag in the pattern of studies between the two countries. But still it is worth noting that English studies in England continued to be permeated by a rhetoric of national identity and moral purpose, despite the experience of frustration associated with the Indian educational experiment for the moral elevation of Indians. The problem was not that the experiment was unsuccessful but that indeed it was *too* successful, for in combatting priestly authority and popular superstition the transmission of Western learning and culture inevitably signified the transmission of ideas of moral autonomy, self-sufficiency, and unencumbered will that caused more problems for British rule than anticipated.

The Sanskritist Monier Monier-Williams, for example, complained that English literary study unduly filled the minds of Indians with thoughts of rising above what he called their assigned position in life. He warned that in training Indians in the art of self-expression and self-scrutiny, English education had taken on a subversive role: "Those who are unsuccessful in gaining appointments will not turn to manual labour, but remain discontented members of society and enemies of our government, converting the little real education they have received into an instrument to injure us by talking treason and writing seditious articles in native journals."[1] Formerly, declared George Norton in a speech in Madras, Indian subjects obeyed their British rulers out of ignorance, because they regarded them as beings of a superior order and "crouched before us as clothed with an irresistible power."[2] But with the spread of education the tendency of familiarity was to lessen wonder, as "we have educated the people so as to enable them to judge us by a more correct standard . . . Those whom they took for gods, as the ancient Mexicans and Peruvians mistook Cortez and Pizarro, they now find to be men like themselves, their superiors, it is true, but still errant fallible men."[3] A. P. Howell in his numerous reports issued periodically over two decades from 1850 to 1870 upbraided his own government for having chosen to undertake "the direct training of whole generations above their own creed, and above that sense of relation to another world upon which they base all their moral obligations."[4] An English literary education that ostensibly set out to root Indians in a world of reciprocal obligations came to be attacked for achieving the very opposite, and Howell, along with others, strenuously argued that only a practical or non-humanistic education could successfully teach social or civic duty, hitherto associated primarily with a literary curriculum.

This chapter explores the connections between the declining importance of literary study for moral education, the renewed emphasis on English as a branch of practical study, and the rhetoric of social stratification and division of labor. The moral motive, which brought English literature into the Indian curriculum in the first place to reinforce notions of social duty, obligation, and service to the state, is disengaged from English studies as a result of British apprehensions that their Indian subjects were being encouraged to rise above their stations in the name of self-improvement and so challenge the authority of the ruling power. The humanistic idea of education as moral and intellectual elevation is drastically revised to fit a conception of education that goes as far back as Plato, which sought to confirm individuals in the social class into which they were born.

Significantly, this revision in the late 1850s (which, incidentally, coincides with the taking over of the East India Company by the British Crown and also with the Mutiny of 1857) reappropriates the secularist character of the earliest stages of the history of English in India. As discussed in earlier chapters, missionary groups, protesting what they saw as governmental arrogance in severing literary studies from the influence of religious culture, were led to suspect that the official policy of secularism in India had been instituted in a spirit of middle-class experimentation and that India was merely being used as a testing ground for secular theories of education. If secularism in British India eventually faced the kind of opposition it experienced in England, it was largely due to the fierce resistance put up by missionaries like Alexander Duff who unequivocally denounced it as an expression of British middle-class, laissez-faire interests. The missionaries' relative success in educational matters is gauged by the fact that for nearly three decades, from the mid-1820s to the mid-1850s, English studies derived its main rationale from the impulse to Christianize. This was true even in the so-called non-denominational schools like the Hindu College in Calcutta, which was set up by a small group of Bengali upper-caste men and later received substantial funding from the British government. English education was so closely associated with Christian instruction in the institutions receiving government patronage that at least one native convert was known to have said that "the best Missionary institutions are the Government schools."[5]

But even as early as 1835, with Macaulay's minute, the religious motive showed signs of stress. It is worth noting that despite Macaulay's outrage over British patronage of Oriental literature and his advocacy of the inclusion of English literature in the Indian curriculum, at no point did he urge the study of English on purely humanistic or moral grounds. For Macaulay the separation between the cultural and the moral was a matter of no great difficulty, and it was possible for him to plead for the cultural value of English literature without necessarily having to base his appeal on moral or religious grounds. Macaulay was widely read in the writers of antiquity, but he came away from the reading with the conviction that their worth had to be measured in terms of what they had to offer by way of "useful results," which to him amounted to very little.[6] On the whole, Macaulay's interest did not lie in the deeper moral reflections of the ancient writers. Reluctant to consider moral arguments apart from their political implications, he was drawn to Bacon precisely because of Bacon's lack of concern with the grounds of moral obligation. Bacon's appeal for Macaulay lay in the fact that in raising only the kinds of questions that led to useful results, Bacon dispensed with insurmountable metaphysical questions. In the tradition of Bacon and the Utilitarians, Macaulay acknowledged that societies and laws existed only for the purpose of increasing the sum of private happiness. It might be expected that, as a Whig, he would hold liberty as a supreme end, yet he consistently and emphatically held that liberty was no more than a useful means of promoting the security of persons and property.

The blending of political and moral considerations, with the inevitable subordination of the moral argument, is evident in Macaulay's justifications for reforms. He supported parliamentary reform less for its own sake than because of the dangers inherent in withholding it. Liberty had greater meaning for him as a stabilizing force on government: free expression revealed discontents, which could then be dealt with in an appropriate manner and by timely concessions. *Morality* and *policy* were for Macaulay identical and interchangeable terms. In a distinct shift of emphasis from the Whig tradition, he emphasized what was useful rather than what was good in the course of defending policies. Without abandoning the traditional Whig rationale for toleration and liberty, Macaulay, as a spokesman for a new generation of Whigs, added a more amoral, functional tone. As a result, he exposed himself to charges of Philistinism and of reducing pure intellectualism to insignificance.[7]

Macaulay's minute paved the way for the transition from religious to secular motives in English education. By mid-century a pedagogy of Christian morality gradually yielded to a pedagogy of worldly knowledge geared to the various occupations of life. Secularization freed the British government in India to pursue an educational policy that actually confirmed, not altered, the patterns of stratification already indigenous to Indian society. It introduced new relationships whose tendency was to transform society from a basis of status to one of contract. To give one example, the Law Commission in 1862 made law a civil institution and separated its professional study from religion—any religion—in order to break the priestly monopoly in legal studies. But though this decision was characterized as a move to make law "a fit object of pursuit not limited to a small priestly order but open to all interested persons regardless of caste or creed,"[8] the recruitment of students to the study of law still followed traditional caste patterns. Perhaps this is because the more "objective" criteria of admission that were added, such as certificates of character, marks of distinction, and fixed qualifications established by the Sadr Diwani Adalat, still depended on a system of evaluation drawn from a religious hierarchy. But the new system did not have the looseness or fluidity of the older one, which tacitly acknowledged indefinable qualities such as self-cultivation and self-discipline as criteria for inclusion. The importance of paper qualifications in a secularized society marks the growth of a contractual principle of social relationships, often described as the basis of a class concept in social development.

The hostility to a moral emphasis in education coincided with new legislation aimed at stratification of classes. The direction was set in the 1854 dispatch issued by Sir Charles Wood, also known as Lord Halifax. The dispatch can only be described as functionalist in character: the rhetoric of morality gave way to the demands of political economy, from which evolved a scheme of education that set out to create a middle class serving as an agency of imperialist economy and administration and, through it, to initiate social change through a process of differentiation. Though the dispatch acknowledged a need to ensure the probity of Indian bureaucrats by instruction in English principles, the main emphasis fell on the expediency of creating a class that might emulate Europeans in the development of India's resources and increase demand for the consumption of British goods, for the advancement of European knowledge and European culture

> will teach the natives of India the marvellous results of the employment of labour and capital, rouse them to emulate us in the development of the vast resources of their country, guide them in their efforts, and gradually, but certainly, confer upon them all the advantages which accompany the healthy increase of wealth and commerce; and, at the same time, secure to us a large and more certain supply of many articles necessary for our manufactures and extensively consumed by all classes of our population, as well as an almost inexhaustible demand for the product of British labour.[9]

With the extended use of English as the language of commerce was brought into existence a much larger class of Indians willing to cooperate with the British in the exploitation of India's resources. On the theory that division of labor was the key to England's economic prosperity, the dispatch proposed, through education, to achieve a comparable system of stratification in India. Education for the masses was limited to "useful and practical knowledge."[10] In addition to the mechanical arts and skills of agriculture, such knowledge included basic skills of literacy geared to specific regional needs, such as, for example, land measurement and land registration. The revenue settlement in the Northwest Provinces and the registration of land that was required thereafter provided a new stimulus for acquiring practical language skills, purportedly to "enable each man to look after his own rights."[11]

While meting out a fare of useful and practical skills to the lower orders of society, the dispatch simultaneously promoted the growth of a small but influential intellectual class through scholarships to the proposed universities of Bombay, Calcutta, and Madras. This class, which was largely drawn from the indigenous learned classes, was targeted for eventual induction into government service. The bias toward selective higher education is apparent in the fact that while scholarships were increased for those seeking admission to universities, government funds were withdrawn from lower schools and the practice of charging fees introduced. The government abolished stipends in these schools and replaced them with grants in aid, with the added proviso that these grants were to be given only to those schools already charging fees. This condition, which runs contrary to the avowed intention to expand educational opportunities, was justified on the grounds that an entirely gratuitous education was not valued and the practice of charging fees would at once promote more regular attendance and increase the value of education; grants in aid ceased to function as responses to need and were reduced to the status of rewards for complying with government requirements. The missionary Alexander Duff accidentally stumbled upon this piece of wisdom through the sad experience in his own school when he realized that it was the anticipation of free books rather than the attractions of Christianity that drove the poor to them. Huge numbers of Indian children were known to flock to new schools and, once the free books were distributed, run away with them and never turn up again. As Duff sadly concluded, book pages found their way not into the minds and hearts of "benighted" peoples, but into bazaars and marketplaces as wastepaper for retailers.

The universities were set up primarily as a way of eliminating the cumbersome lists the government had hitherto relied on to recruit meritorious students for public employment. Till 1857 the practice was for government colleges to draw up lists of the students who had distinguished themselves in literary attainments and these lists were then made available to the government. But because of bureaucratic inefficiency, the lists were never submitted systematically, with the result that many educated Indians never came to the notice of the government. The returns of 1852, for example, showed that only two gazetted officers had come from the government colleges, and as for the others listed in the *Bengal Gazette,* it could only be assumed that their educational qualifications were not of the high level that the government would have preferred its recruits to have.[12] With the establishment of the universities these lists were dispensed with, for under a centralized system that submitted all students to a common examination the acquisition of a university degree and university distinctions automatically brought the most capable young men to the government's notice.

The move to establish a centralized university system linked with public employment came out of the need to demonstrate that an arts curriculum had tangible material rewards.[13] The discouragingly small number of educated Indians going into public service was explained by the fact that young men who had passed an arduous examination in philosophy and literature were disinclined to accept the subordinate jobs (chiefly of a clerical nature) open to them in government service. In 1825 Rammohun Roy wrote an indignant letter to the governor-general-in-council deploring the exclusion of Indians from the political privileges he claimed they had enjoyed under Muslim rule:

> In former times Native fathers were anxious to educate their children according to the usages of those days, to qualify them for such offices under government . . . and young men had the most powerful motives for sedulously cultivating their minds in laudable ambition of rising by their merits to an honourable rank in society; but under the present system, so trifling are the rewards held out to Native talent that hardly any stimulus to intellectual improvement remains.[14]

This was a liability of English education that William Adam, author of the comprehensive report on education in Bengal, had warned of as early as 1835 when he wrote: "[The Indians] have been raised out of one class of society without having a recognized place in any other class."[15] The highest position that educated young men could aspire to was the meager-paying one of copying clerk, a position that required the mechanical copying of English without understanding. Without honor or reward, these meager employment prospects were adversely affecting the traditional Indian reverence for education and the self-esteem that usually accompanied it. The elevation of circumstances that English instruction had promised was slowly being eroded, as the 1882 Education Commission reported, by "the narrow circle of [the Indian's] life; the absence of facile ties for travel, whereby his sympathies and experience might be enlarged; the strong temptation to lay aside his studies . . . all help to dwarf the moral and intellectual growth, and to foster those faults."[16]

The Indian university system evolved from a theory of culture often referred to as the Filtration Theory, which was first enunciated by Macaulay and later refined by John Stuart Mill in his dispatches from the office of the East India Company. The theory ostensibly had its origins in a set of practical realities: because of the extraordinary costs in training and recruiting teachers of English, a complete education that began with a thorough study of English was within the reach of only a very small proportion of Indians. But even though only this class would receive an English education, their more important function would be to act as teachers and translators of useful books, through which they would communicate to the native literature and to the native community "that improved spirit" they had imbibed from the influence of European ideas and sentiments. The theory required the few to teach the many.

A unified culture was not only thought possible in a differentiated society, but in fact deemed essential to it. John Stuart Mill envisioned culture as at once an agency of unification and division between social classes, declaring in one of his dispatches that "the character which may be given to the classes possessed of leisure and natural influence, ultimately determines that of the whole people."[17] The theory operated on the principle that only those who had the time and the leisure to acquire knowledge of the English language and English literature in the classical manner should be encouraged to do so. In the meantime, the rest of the population was consigned to studying their own languages but receiving Western ideas through them at the same time. In employing the criterion of leisure to distinguish the few from the many, Mill evoked the formulation of his father, who had earlier asked the question:

What is the sort of education required for the different classes of society, and what should be the difference in the training provided for each? There are certain qualities, the possession of which is desirable in all classes. There are certain qualities, the possession of which is desirable in some, not in others. As far as those qualities extend which ought to be common to all, there ought to be a correspondent training for all. It is only in respect to those qualities which are not desirable in all, that a difference in the mode of training is required.[18]

James Mill goes on to explain that the three qualities desirable in all men are intelligence, temperance, and benevolence. He has no difficulty in seeing how the last two could be practically instilled in all the different classes of society. But when it comes to intelligence, his enthusiasm is noticeably qualified:

As we strive for an equal degree of justice, an equal degree of temperance, an equal degree of veracity, in the poor as in the rich, so ought we to strive for an equal degree of intelligence, if there were not a preventing cause. It is absolutely necessary for the existence of the human race, that labour should be performed, that food should be produced, and other things provided, which human welfare requires. A large proportion of mankind is required for this labour. Now, then, in regard to all this portion of mankind, that labours, only such a portion of time can by them be given to the acquisition of intelligence, as can be abstracted from labour. The difference between intelligence and the other qualities desirable in the mind of man, is this: . . . Time must be exclusively devoted to the acquisition of it; and there are degrees of command over knowledge to which the whole period of human life is not more than sufficient. There are degrees, therefore, of intelligence, which must be reserved to those who are not obliged to labour.[19]

James Mill's hesitation in providing for the training of the mind across all classes undercut the concept of a unified culture that he simultaneously sought to promote. The conflict in Mill is that ideally he wants to see all classes receive intellectual training but he cannot accept the disruption to the existing social divisions that it implied. For, though logically it might be difficult to argue with the statement that one must be released from other occupations to devote oneself to the serious pursuit of knowledge, the treachery of using that argument as a justification for dispensing with the education of the laboring classes was sensed even by Charles Wood in his educational dispatch. Indeed, he was farsighted enough to recognize the dangerous implications of a theory of education that pretended to unite while keeping separate. What distinctly set Wood's dispatch apart from the earlier dispatches of

Macaulay and James and John Stuart Mill was a revision of the priorities in what was to be achieved by the theory of downward filtration and there was less talk now of high culture and more of useful education. The dispatch conceded the success of the Filtration Theory insofar as it had ensured a new generation of Indians trained to a high level of excellence in the study of English literature, but it lamented that these high attainments remained confined only to a small number of persons. It insisted that European knowledge would never filter downward to a larger base unless it was of a "less high order, but of such a character as may be practically useful to the people of India in their different spheres of life."[20] There was an implicit recognition in the dispatch that the British government now had to contend with the consequences of an educational policy based on the Filtration Theory as conceived by Macaulay and the two Mills, for instead of a monolithic society linked by a single set of ideas emanating from the West, as originally intended, it had produced a stratified society in which boundaries between the select few educated in English and the masses had grown so sharp as to thwart the percolation of European ideas down to the latter in any form, even through translations.

Ironically Orientalism, which ostensibly aimed to protect the native culture from total oblivion, sharpened the lines of stratification. Wherever there flourished institutions of Oriental learning (such as the one at Tirhoot, for instance) there happened also to be the highest illiteracy and the fewest number of vernacular schools, as recorded by British officials.[21] The effects of Orientalist policy are visible in the history of Sanskrit College, which was established in 1823 after the founding of Hindu College. Intended to teach primarily the English language and literature, Hindu College was open to boys of all classes and castes on the payment of five rupees per month, whereas Sanskrit College, which was established for the exclusive cultivation of Sanskrit literature, was open only to Brahmins, who got a monthly stipend to study grammar, general literature, rhetoric and prosody, law, arithmetic, and theology.[22]

Though from its earliest involvement in Indian education the British objective was the abolition of caste feeling, the actual practice suggests otherwise. In the very manner that students were recruited and institutions of learning established it is clear that there was a capitulation to caste sentiments aimed at conciliating the Brahmins, whose position in Hindu society had been eroded with British rule. For example, the only way the upper ranks could be enticed to the government schools was by preventing a mixture of castes and the lower castes were either placed in separate classes or siphoned off to the missionary schools, which became associated in the public mind with lower-caste education. Sensing economic opportunities, the upper castes were lured to an education in English language and literature that was offered in the government schools in the anticipation that it "will raise them among their countrymen [and] they will become again objects of respect and admiration, and attain an influence upon grounds on which it is not only safe, but desirable they should possess it."[23] The presence of two separate institutions, the government and the missionary schools, tended to reinforce caste distinctions and gave the impression that there were two castes in education, with the Brahmins attending the regular orthodox colleges of the government and the lower castes the missionary institutions.[24] The whole concept of education favoring the highest caste was denounced by some missionaries as an abdication of the government's Christian duty to ameliorate the condition of the downtrodden.[25] Nor were they convinced by government claims about the positive effects of English studies in altering attitudes to caste. As the Serampore missionary John Marshman sardonically remarked, "I am not certain that a man's being able to read Milton and Shakespeare, or understand Dr. Johnson, would make him less susceptible of the honour of being a Brahmin."[26]

But at the same time, the missionaries were not above soliciting the patronage of the upper castes. If English literature marked the boundary between classes, missionaries resolutely tried to cross it by offering English literary instruction in their institutions as well, even though their commitment was supposedly to education of the masses in the vernaculars. The missionaries' bid to lure members of other castes into their schools through a course of studies in English literature also showed that they took seriously the warnings sounded in certain quarters about the danger of offering special encouragement to the lowest castes, for, as the "most despised and least numerous of society," there was the distinct possibility that "if our system of education took root among them, it would never spread farther, and in that case we might find ourselves at the head of a new class superior to the rest in useful knowledge, but hated and despised by the castes to whom these new attainments would always induce us to prefer them."[27]

The divisions between Hindus and Muslims grew even wider with state education in 1854, which put the finishing stroke to the influence of the Muslims as the former ruling group in India. British accounts observed that Hindus tended to seize opportunities offered by state education more than Muslims did. By 1871 only 92 Muslims to 681 Hindus held gazetted appointments in Lower Bengal, a province that a hundred years earlier had been officered by a few Englishmen, a sprinkling of Hindus, and a multitude of Muslims. A similar change occurred in the only secular profession then considered open to well-born Muslims: law. With the organization of state education in 1854, different tests of fitness were prescribed and a new breed of professional men came to the fore. Out of 240 native pleaders admitted from 1852 to 1868, no fewer than 239 were Hindus; only one Muslim was in the High Court of Calcutta.[28] In the next higher grade of attorneys there were twenty-seven Hindus and not a single Muslim. Among articled clerks, there were twenty-six Hindus and again not a single Muslim. William Hunter, who presided over the Indian Education Commission of 1882, was sternly critical of the role of state education in creating these occupational patterns along religious and caste lines: "Alike therefore in higher official employments, and in the higher practice of law, Muhammedans had fallen out of the race in Bengal before the end of the first fifteen years of State Education on lines laid down in 1854."[29]

WOOD'S DISPATCH despaired of ever achieving a unified culture, and the more the prospect of its attainment receded, the greater grew the conviction that once a secular policy in education had been adopted, there was no choice but to accept differentiation as a principle of social and cultural organization. This position was spelled out most sharply by Holt Mackenzie, secretary to the Bengal government, in his communications to the governor-general on the education question.[30] Though he made an attempt to appeal to higher motives for the creation of a truly enlightened system of education in India, in the end he admitted that the only alternative open to the government was to attend to the instruction of the educated and the influential classes. Conceding that it was impossible to educate the masses in English or even in European thought through vernacular translations, he argued that the limitation lay not only in the enormous numbers to be instructed, in contrast to the number of qualified teachers available. Rather, Britain was also hobbled by its commitment to observing religious neutrality in India, which could only be ensured by a differentiated education. The situation in England, Mackenzie argued, was more conducive to a unified culture in that its parish schools, which had mostly carried on the work of general education, were identified closely enough with the religion of the country to assist the state in imparting a common education:

> Take from the peasant his Bible, and (if it be possible) the knowledge and sentiments that have flowed from that sacred source, and how worthless will be his lowly literature. The education indeed of the great body of the people can never, I think, be expected to extend beyond what is necessary for the business of life; and it is only therefore through religious exercises, which form a great part of the business of life, that the labourer will turn his thoughts on things above the common drudgery, by which he earns his subsistence. Hence it is under the Christian scheme alone, that I should expect to find the labouring classes really educated: and their station in the scale of instructed and humanized beings will, I imagine, be pretty closely proportioned to their piety.[31]

In contrast, secularism committed the British in India to the worldly motive of teaching the Indians "the business of life," for which purpose a differentiated education was the most efficient political and economic solution.

But the dispatch did not abandon the Filtration Theory altogether and instead modified its cultural objectives by identifying the true diffusion of European knowledge with its adaptation to the native culture. The real value of the Filtration Theory, it emphasized, did not in any event lie in the strengthening of English culture but in the potential enrichment of the vernacular literatures, through translations of European books or the "original compositions of men whose minds have been imbued with the spirit of European advancement."[32] Deviating from the Macaulayan emphasis on the filtering down of a pure form of English thought, the dispatch referred to an earlier recommendation made by William Adam in his 1835 *Reports on Education in Bengal and Bihar* that the British goal should be "not to translate European works into the words and idioms of the native languages but so to combine the substance of European knowledge with native forms of thought and sentiment."

The dispatch also hinted at what the Indian Education Commission of 1882 later confirmed: that having created a complex society through a policy favoring differentiated education, British administrators had now to reconsider the adequacy of a purely literary culture to do the work of sustaining an increasingly specialized society. This may possibly explain the halfhearted interest shown by Wood's dispatch in high European culture as the continuing basis of modern Indian education. The problematical question was whether the task of preparing the Indians to take up their various "stations in life" was compatible with the larger goal of elevating them above the general condition of the people, as implied by a scheme of literary education.

The Indian Education Commission hedged on this question. Both in its minutes of evidence and in its final report it vacillated between commitment to the cultural premises of the Filtration Theory (that invigoration of the native society could best be achieved by the spread of European ideas) and promotion of a scheme for educating Indian youth in their traditional callings. On the one hand, it noted that one favorable outcome of the Filtration Theory was that there was an increase in the number of occupations requiring "culture" and recommended that there should be a corresponding amount of culture in those preparing for them.[33] But on the other, it recommended that literary studies—the fountain of European culture—should not be required of youth if they lacked a literary bent of mind and that these students should instead be encouraged to go into a non-literary or commercial stream. But what this virtually amounted to was endorsement of stratification within the ranks of public service, for those educated in the practical division of the high school, intended to fit students for commercial or non-literary pursuits, were eligible only for "subordinate" public appointments and not for "those offices of responsibility and emolument in which a high degree of intelligence is required, and for which a liberal education has been commonly thought necessary."[34] By "offices" were meant the Revenue and Judicial departments, the branches of government that employed the most numbers of Indians.

The Commission desperately tried to mediate between these two positions and sought to find a middle ground where literary and "practical" education could meet: "The extension of this [practical] knowledge should be along those lines where it will be grasped and incorporated by the interests and teachings of active life. Still it should be education, aimed at making the mind robust and flexible, rather than at shabbily decking it with some rags of 'business information' of low technical skill."[35] In its own ambiguous way the Commission made feeble attempts to resolve the seeming incompatibility of the two goals. But it was at best an evasive reply that did nothing to address the real problem at hand.[36]

Those who harangued most loudly against education for social mobility also expressed an open dislike and suspicion of literary education. The Utilitarian writer Monier Monier-Williams was among the most vocal critics to raise serious questions about the desirability of diffusing European culture to the lower ranks of society. To his mind this was an impossible, if not dangerous, task. In dismissing the possibility of any reconciliation between literary and practical education, he gave a solid stamp of approval to the ideological premises of stratification. He was inflexible on the point that the sons of persons of low social status not be given an education above the rank of their fathers and that any training they received should be suited to their position and prospects in life. The aim, he contended, should be to educate them in their stations rather than above them, to make the son of a potter a better potter, the son of a mechanic a better mechanic, and so forth.[37]

A similar implacability can be seen in Henry Sumner Maine's views on literature, the study of which assumed a mind that was capable of being driven by reason, an assumption that Maine felt was entirely inappropriate in the Indian context. Maine, who was Legal Member of the Supreme Council of India and one of the great legal minds of his time, had little faith in the perfectability of human beings; human nature remained for him fickle, variable, and totally intractable. To work upon it as if it were otherwise was simply to engage in a futile and wasteful endeavor. However, in a secular pedagogy of impersonal law he found a more stable and constant alternative. Not unlike Lord Cornwallis, the steely, uncompromising governor-general who preceded him by almost a century, Maine steadfastly insisted that a good government was held together not by moral criteria or by men of character and integrity but by political principles and laws and in these alone rested absolute authority. Any form of education that trained for critical thinking, self-development, or moral reasoning was useless unless it clearly and openly aimed at the affirmation of these principles and laws.

In Maine's view, liberal education gave Indians the illusion that they could be better than they actually were and that they were being empowered to change their personal destiny and affect the course of things. This, he maintained, would have the most disastrous effect on the running of government, which he conceived of as a pure and efficient machine functioning independently of the character or dispositions of men. Maine represented a later voice in English education, the voice of constitutional liberalism, which foresaw that literary study advanced for purely moral reasons would only add new weapons to error, that "the permanent conquest of falsehood will never come from the discovery of moral truths."[38] Deploring what he called the "tenderness of the Eastern imagination," he argued that while classical education could be favored over empirical study in England because there the imagination never overruled reason, in India the same course would be catastrophic, for the native mind required (as he put it) "stricter criteria of truth":

> We may teach our students to cultivate language, and we only add strength to sophistry; we teach them to cultivate their imagination, and it only gives grace and colour to delusion; we teach them to cultivate their reasoning powers, and they find a thousand resources in allegory, in analogy, and in mysticism, for evading and discrediting truth.[39]

An uncompromising Utilitarian, Maine was highly alarmed about the possible consequences of the Indians' receiving an overly literary education, one of which was to allow them to believe that their history and belief were capable of coexisting with modern knowledge. Already one effect of exposure to imaginative literature was that the Indians had caught from Europeans "the modern trick of constructing by means of fiction an imaginary past out of the present, taking from the past its externals but building in the susceptibilities of the present."[40] Though Maine lets the point pass and makes no further references, it is worth noting that the literary efforts of early Indian nationalists were precisely in this direction. Nationalist writers like the Bengali novelist Bankim Chandra Chatterjee, who were schooled in the best Western literary establishments in Bengal, turned their attention to reviving myths and tales of the past to stir up longings in the people for the return of a golden age. Maine's allusion to the spirit of reconstruction of a Romantic past strongly suggests that he saw as potentially insurrectionary the literary model of German Romanticism. The fact that educated Indians were reading Goethe in translation caused infinitely greater concern in British administrative circles than their reading the works of political liberals like Locke or Hume, whose appeal to reason and constitutionalism rather than the imagination presumably posed fewer dangers of shaping a unified nationalist sentiment.

With Maine the severing of the moral impulse from English education is complete. In upholding a secular vision, Maine gave Utilitarianism in India a sterner cast, investing more faith in physical rather than moral laws. Typically, he refused to concede that the pattern of studies evolving in England had any applicability to India. He based his claim on the view that the characters of the two nations were so totally different as to warrant an entirely different educational emphasis. To his mind education grounded in a theory of morality only gave the Indians more leeway to continue with their erroneous ways of thinking and the British administration was only deluding itself when it believed that the Indian character would be strengthened by a moral pedagogy.

Curiously, while the moral imperative shaped and gave an identity to English studies in India, only to blend with and eventually be superseded by the practical and the scientific, in England, where the institutionalization of English took much longer (English literature became a class subject there only as late as 1872, following Matthew Arnold's complaints against its exclusion), the moral motive gained rather than lost in importance. As D. J. Palmer points out, the second half of nineteenth-century England saw a transition in the attitude toward English as a practical field of study to a "profound conception of the moral power of great literature, a belief in its humanizing influence, counteracting malignant forces in a rapidly changing society."[41] But for Maine and other Utilitarians in India like Monier Monier-Williams, who joined their voices with Maine's, this conception of an education in literature and the arts had little meaning in India. On the contrary, they found that the humanizing motive was in fact an evasion of responsibility toward equipping the Indian with the knowledge required for making him useful to society. Clearly, for both men the starting point of educational reform had to be the redirection of mind to a full recognition of economic and political order and not some vague abstraction called moral character.

Once the creation of a specialized work force was agreed on as the primary objective, reports were commissioned to determine possible obstacles to its realization. Intriguingly, the single greatest threat was believed to come from Indian folklore, which, in the opinion of at least one commentator, cultivated the myth of upward mobility:

> With regard to the lower orders excluded from all participation in the honour or profits of our government, they cannot feel as interested in it as in a government in which the lowest individual might hope to rise to rank and power by his personal exertions. Their common sayings, their tales, their aphorisms, are full of allusions to those vicissitudes of human life, by which the humble and obscure are so often elevated.[42]

The theme of mobility was a dimension of Indian literature and culture that the author of this statement, Thomas Macan, found peculiarly difficult to understand. It was especially so because it was irreconcilable with the cherished notion of caste as a system based on ascribed status, which the author seems genuinely to have believed would readily accommodate the British policy of differentiated education. Other reports made similar observations, adding that in England there was nothing in the folklore to suggest that the poor could rise through labor, integrity, and ability or that the British social system was obliged to respond in any way to the "demands of an eternal justice."[43] Rather, youths were taught to be content with their callings in life: "In England such youths would with satisfaction to themselves and benefit to the community look forward to an honest life of handicraft work, to be bakers, carpenters, tailors, labourers, and workers in some shape or the other; here they wish to live by their wits. It is a simple impossibility."[44]

SIMULTANEOUSLY, THERE was increasing resentment against Utilitarianism as a philosophy that had polluted literary study, thwarting it from fulfilling moral functions. In the name of utility, literary education had become merely a mechanical acquisition of knowledge that neither required nor encouraged any of the finer qualities of literary culture (style, good judgment, taste) or moral discrimination. The study of English literature had merely succeeded in creating a class of Babus (perhaps the Indian equivalent of the English Philistines of whom Matthew Arnold wrote so scathingly) who were intellectually hollow and insufficiently equipped with the desirable amount of knowledge and culture. English education came to be criticized for its imitativeness and superficiality and for having produced an uprooted elite who were at once apostates to their own national tradition and imperfect imitators of the West. English education had failed to make "good English scholars, good Christians, or good subjects of the Queen," in that order.[45] Lord Curzon, who was quick to fault his countrymen for misguided educational policies, also lamented the unfulfilled promises of English literary education: "Everywhere it was words that were studied, not ideas. The grain was being spilled and squandered, while the husks were being devoured. . . . But of real living, the life of the intellect, the character of the soul, I fear that the glimpses that were obtainable were rare and dim."[46]

To make matters worse, English-educated Indians were equally complicit with the project of annihilating the literature and language of the masses. As a disenchanted writer for the *Calcutta Review* wrote:

We admire their taste for English literature, their boldness in writing against their countrymen's defects,—but where is their patriotism or love of the masses or their countrymen, when, instead of lending a helping hand to improve the literature of their country, they stand aloof, boxing themselves up with Shakespeare,—when for the convenience of the stranger they would have English in the courts, a language entirely unknown to the peasantry,—when like the Moslem conquerors, they would debar all useful knowledge from thirty-seven million, unless they obtain it through the portals of a difficult foreign language, which requires an eight-years' study, thus closing the temple of knowledge to the millions. . . . These men, in consequence of despising the vernaculars, are falling into the errors of the men of the middle ages, a proneness to dialecticism, a renunciation of useful tracks of thought—they are in fact, becoming a sort of schoolmen, following a slavish imitation of foreign models, extinguishing fertility of thought, and all the generous impulses bound up with the speech of our father-land."[47]

But paradoxically, while Christian moralists attacked Utilitarianism for its neglect of the spiritual life, Utilitarian educational practice was criticized as strongly in India for not being utilitarian enough, for not steering the native mind away from mundane and useless preoccupations. Even the institutions that had matured with the spread of English education—the literary societies, public lectures, and debating clubs— had become empty forums. While some Englishmen lauded the imitation of the structure of societies in England and regarded the Indians' ability to quote from Hume, Gibbon, Reid, Bolingbroke, Voltaire, Shakespeare, and Milton as a measure of their "mental improvement,"[48] a large majority of Englishmen felt that the rising young talents of India were wasting their energy and time on purposeless disquisitions on abstract questions. (One such topic, debated with great vigor and energy at Hindu College's Literary Society, was "whether posthumous fame be a rational principle of human action or not."[49])

Mediocrity became the route to fame, and even the best writers fell into the trap of repeating the greatest number of truisms in order to acquire renown. Not much better were the interminable literary disquisitions in which, as one report sardonically put it, "young Babus undertake to reveal to the admiring world beauties in Milton which Macaulay never perceived, and archaisms in Shakespeare which Halliwell never detected."[50] Most alarmingly, talented young minds were being diverted by fruitless and trivial literary pursuits from dealing with more pressing social problems. The literary mania was particularly acute in Calcutta where, out of any seventeen essays written for these societies (which were designed as a forum for exchange of ideas of general intellectual interest), ten would have been on the merits of Pope, two on Milton's *Paradise Lost* ("Young Bengal has no idea of *Comus*"), two on Shakespeare's tragedies, and one on Kalidas.[51]

But explanations for the limited and partial influence of the literary societies in India were not hard to find, and as on other occasions, Indian deficiencies of character bore the brunt. No literary society in India, after all, could be expected to assume the position of literary societies in England, "where elaborate papers are read to men with minds of a high calibre." In imitating the structure of the English literary societies, the Indian version had forgotten that its object was "to train, to discipline, to lead out the dormant faculties of passive Hindoos and not to appeal to them as having minds already developed and educated."[52]

The kinds of publications that were coming out of these societies were denounced no less severely. One such book by G. Lewis that appeared as a critical commentary for reading Shakespeare seemed to verify a growing suspicion that "the spirit of pedantry [had] fled from Britain to India." Far from offering a richer education in literary excellence, such books helped to do nothing more than complement the mechanical literary instruction given in the government colleges:

> The useless, even for disciplining the faculties of the mind, the showy, the bombastic, the ridiculous, these have been too much its characters hitherto, as though the Hindoos, in common with all oriental nations, were not sufficiently addicted to these, without having them scientifically taught in a systematic course of education.[53]

It is impossible not to detect a certain ambivalence on the part of the British toward giving an education to Indians that would be wholly on the side of the practical and the useful. While on the one hand colonial administrators charged their subjects with being too speculative, on the other they admitted that one virtue of having a contemplative, dreamy-eyed set of subjects was that it kept them from pursuits of gain.[54] A minute issued by Francis Warden claimed that the "present depressed state of trade is peculiarly favourable to the conversion of a commercial spirit into a literary one."[55] If Indians were given a desire for reading, he suggested hopefully, they could be lured away from their traditional commercial ventures, allowing the British to step into that field.

The same motive would surely appear to be behind the staunch

Anglicist Charles Trevelyan's abrupt volte-face in the parliamentary sessions when he urged that the British encourage Indian art as a compensation for the material losses the Indians had suffered as a result of the heavy import duty on manufactures.[56] The equation that is made here between art and material wealth is absurd enough to indict it as an offensive solution. But in the context of the numerous governmental reports that attributed the "sorry state" of Indian culture to the "gradual but general impoverishment of the country"[57] and charged Britain with "shutting up all the sources from which the magnificence of the country was derived," while not themselves constructing a single work,[58] and with importing English literature into India in the same manner that English cottons were,[59] Trevelyan's solution would not have appeared at all outrageous, for it suggested giving to the Indians something they valued but which had no value for the British whatsoever. The British, in other words, had nothing to lose and the Indians everything to gain. Converting loss into gain runs parallel to converting the commercial spirit into the literary, both power moves aiming to render the Indian politically weak but at the same time contented with his situation.

Quite possibly, one may attribute the discrepancy between stated goals and actual practice to the existence of widely differing schools of opinion among administrators and divergent views on the nature of British rule and the conditions of Indian society. But on the whole, as David Lelyveld observes, British administrators tended to diagnose failures of an English-style education in terms of Indian culture, not of British policy.[60] In the voluminous *Calcutta University Commission Report 1917–19*, the general consensus of those who submitted evidence was that despite the attempt to introduce a useful education, the Indians somehow managed to convert even the practical into the impractical and the useless, so much so that "the present B.A. would be more intelligible to Shakespeare's contemporaries than to the moderns."[61] The Indian predilection for "useless" literature was hardly new, or so one must believe from letters written to the editor of the *Calcutta Gazette* as early as 1816. Curious to see what books were bought at a public auction, one writer was dismayed to find that there was no demand for the histories of Greece, Rome or anything "of serious or national nature." On the contrary, Indians had bought up all the copies of *Sorrows of Werther, Life of Rochester*, Byron's *Works*, Scott's *Poetical Works, Spirit of English Wit*, and *Spirit of Irish Wit*. "Is it not a disgrace, Mr. Editor, that such trash as I have mentioned should be sought after with so much avidity in India?"[62]

BUT NO explanation of the diminished value of literary studies in preparing for a specialized society can ignore the most basic reality of all: the failure of the British government to supply enough jobs for the numbers receiving liberal education. This is, of course, not a unique problem limited to British India, but what sets the Indian situation apart from others is the narrow limits within which literary education was defined (that is, as moral education), initially for reasons of social and political control but eventually posing serious political threats as well. Assessing the failure of British educational policy, James Johnstone observed:

> In Europe, the higher education is part of the equipment for the life of a gentleman, as well as a qualification for professional employment. To the Indian, this European culture is almost exclusively a preparation for professional and still more for official life, and disappointed of these, this education has only excited wants and raised expectations which leave the unsuccessful aspirant a discontented and dangerous man.[63]

Cut off from a social context where literature was assimilated into daily life, literary education in India became narrowly restricted and depended almost exclusively on material incentives in order to retain its authoritative hold. But where material rewards were not forthcoming, the social control that literature as moral study was able to exert in England collapsed in India. John Murdoch, surveying the effects of English education on Indian youth, wrote: "Educated young men of the present day betray a want of gentleman-like bearing in their social intercourse with their superiors and elders, whether European or Native, and that evil is a growing one, and seems coincident with the general spread of education throughout the country."[64] The growing insubordination of Indian youth was blamed on the British policy of promoting literary training for entry into the professions, to the neglect of the making of gentlemen through which respect for authority could be enjoined. In one of the most severe condemnations of English education, Murdoch concluded: "Our young men do not know or care to know how to respect their superiors. This may appear strange, for the Natives of India are known to be fastidiously polite. English education has made them self-sufficient, and infused into their minds a kind of false independence which knows of no distinction between high or low, old or young."[65]

The key phrase is "false independence," for it could not be said in

India as it was in England, where the attractions of learning were supposedly more diffuse, that

> the primary motive with any father of a family which induces him to give his children the best education his means allow is not that they shall be brought up to love literature for its own sake in a dilettante or nobler spirit, not even is it primarily his aim to make good citizens and good members of society; but to put within their reach by a sound education the means of acquiring if not distinctions and wealth, at least an honest honourable independence."[66]

Educated Indians living under foreign rule were deprived of access to precisely this "honest honourable independence." The tension between the upward mobility promised by modern studies and the limited opportunities open to the colonized for advancement exposed the fundamental paradox of British imperialism: economic exploitation required the sanction of higher motives, but once colonial intervention took on a moral justification—that is, the improvement of a benighted people—the pressure to sustain the expectations of the people by an equalization of educational opportunities created new internal stresses. Nothing less than the most extraordinary political agility was called for in reconciling the democratic promise with the division of labor required for a capitalist system of production to flourish. The price of failure of course was the exposure of the moral pretensions of British colonialism. At one level, education as part of the state is complicit with the reproduction of an economic and cultural order. But because education is also expected to provide opportunities for advancement, it becomes an arena of social conflict, and this tension ultimately reduced the British administration to a position of acute vulnerability and paralysis.

For after all, state intervention in Indian education came about as a demonstration of justice and moral concern in an inherently unjust and immoral system of colonial domination. British education was dedicated to the elevation of a so-called effete population by making available to them the advanced knowledge of the West, with its promise of removal of caste and religious barriers, increased social mobility, and enlightened participation in the administration of their own country. At the same time, official statements like Wood's dispatch clearly articulated the material interests of a capitalist society and endorsed an educational system whose role was to reproduce division of labor directly and caste structure and social inequalities indirectly. This conflict between producing greater equality through the diffusion of Western culture and Western knowledge and reproducing inequality through the occupational structure is inherent in the very institution of modern Indian education, as indeed it can be said to inhere in most institutions structured according to class, race, and gender within a society in conflict.

But at the same time, in that tension are the beginnings of resistance to a dependency role. Again paradoxically, the space for such resistance is provided by the modern secular capitalist state requiring the sanction of moral principles for its program of economic or territorial expansion. The East India Company was by and large indifferent to the education of Indians and long considered it an enterprise outside the purview of its strictly commercial interests. Its conflict with the British Parliament over trading rights had led to increasing parliamentary involvement in Indian affairs, and for the first time education of Indians was taken up as a serious moral responsibility, albeit initially to fortify the native subjects against the excesses of rapacious Company men. When the East India Company was taken over by the British Crown in 1858, the state incorporated the two roles of amelioration and economic expansion as legacies of the long-standing conflict between the English Parliament and the East India Company on one side and between the Company and the missionaries on the other. Between the 1820s and the 1850s, competing hegemonies kept the clash between moral and economic motives as an open, visible conflict and criticism of colonialism was privileged by those who ruled rather than by those who were ruled.

But with the takeover by the British Crown the incorporation of the moral and the economic as a single imperative of colonial rule produced a different sort of conflict, less overt perhaps but more prone to internal contradictions arising out of the state as at once reproducer of relations of production and division of labor and guarantor of opportunity and advancement. The colonial subject's resistance to British rule occurs in the ideological space created by this contradiction, transforming education in its dual aspects of social control and social advancement into the supreme paradox of British power.

7
Conclusion: Empire and
the Western Canon

The genius of literature . . . clearly sees . . . that she has found the men who are to
extend her empire to the ends of the earth, and give her throne a stability that will
be lasting as the sun.
—*Madras Christian Instructor and Missionary Record* (1844), 2(4):185.

FINALLY, THE emergence of the discipline of English in colonial India,
its rootedness in strategies of sociopolitical control, opens up fresh
inquiry into possible implications of empire for current debates on
curriculum in general. When, in our own times, students and faculty
clamor for a broadening of curriculum to include submerged texts of
minority and third world cultures, the knowledge that the discipline of
English developed in colonial times would appear likely to strengthen
their claims and force their opponents to reconsider the premises of the
traditional Eurocentric curriculum. And to an extent a major objective
of this book has been to point the direction to reconceptualizations of
curriculum along these lines, for it should be amply clear by now that
the Eurocentric literary curriculum of the nineteenth century was less a
statement of the superiority of the Western tradition than a vital, active

instrument of Western hegemony in concert with commercial expansionism and military action.

It goes without saying that the degree to which knowledge of imperialism's shaping hand in the formation of English studies affects the concept of canon formation depends on our own willingness to historicize any given curriculum. Of the many possible positions on the curriculum, two modern positions correspond roughly, in their extremity, to the ideological standpoints of the Anglicists and Orientalists of nineteenth-century British India. Celebrating the dominant culture as the arbiter of standards, morals, and religious values, the first position insists on the universality of a single set of works, primarily those of its own culture, in an effort to assimilate individuals to a single identity. The other position, which is more relativistic in intent, claims to broaden the curriculum to include the literature of other cultures. But the relative tolerance of the latter position does not negate the possibility that even the most inclusionary curriculum can itself be part of the processes of control. As the history of Orientalist education demonstrates, a curriculum may incorporate the systems of learning of a subordinate population and still be an instrument of hegemonic activity. Indeed the point of departure of this book is its argument that both the Anglicist and the Orientalist factions were equally complicit with the project of domination, British Indian education having been conceived in India as part and parcel of the act of securing and consolidating power. The acceptance or rejection of other cultures becomes a moot point in the face of the more encompassing motives of discipline and management.

. The role of empire in the history of English studies demonstrates conclusively that the main issues in curriculum will remain unaddressed as long as the debate continues to be engaged by appeals to either universalist or relativist value, religious identity or secular pluralism. Until curriculum is studied less as a receptacle of texts than as activity, that is to say, as a vehicle of acquiring and exercising power, descriptions of curricular content in terms of their expression of universal values on the one hand or pluralistic, secular identities on the other are insufficient signifiers of their historical realities. The nineteenth-century Anglicist curriculum of British India is not reducible simply to an expression of cultural power; rather, it served to confer power as well as to fortify British rule against real or imagined threats from a potentially rebellious subject population.

With few exceptions, wherever the Eurocentric curriculum is described in the scholarly literature in terms of Western cultural superiority, there is an underlying assumption that superiority is a measure of dominance. But it is incorrect to assume that the canon is necessarily expressive of the unquestioned political supremacy of a group, for if we refer to the history of conflict between various groups in India—the East India Company and the missionaries, the Parliament and the East India Company, the Anglicists and the Orientalists—we perceive that the Western literary canon evolved out of a position of vulnerability, not of strength. Only through historicization is it possible to determine the degree to which a culturally homogeneous curriculum is the result of the relative strength or weakness of a governing class; to assess the extent to which educational measures are either an assertion of uncontested authority or a mediated response to situational imperatives, camouflaging acute vulnerability to assaults upon the intention to rule.

In these pages I have attempted to document British educational enterprise in nineteenth-century India as an activity, the stratified conferring of cultural power on a dominated society designed to transmute even the faintest traces of mobilized, unified sentiment against British rule into internal schisms. The attendant limitations of such maneuvers are visible in the incessant pressure on the British to unsettle the objectives of English instruction at regular intervals and modulate the tone of Indian education to achieve an ideal balance between secular and religious policy which, being unattainable in the long run or a least promising only very limited duration, opened the way for native interrogation of British ideology. The checkered history of English studies in India points to the inherent contradictions of the British sociocultural project that allowed it to fail in its own (heterogeneous) terms.

A consideration of English studies in decolonized India is regrettably beyond the scope of this book and I will not presume to offer substantive comment on the current status of English in these concluding pages. But the fact that English continues to be taught and studied in today's India obliges me to sound a final, cautionary note against reading the history of nineteenth-century English studies as continuous with contemporary educational practice in India. The danger of reading the history of modern English studies as uninterrupted narrative is so obvious that I fear I may be insulting the intelligence of my readers by warning against certain possible inferences, the two most treacherous being that assaults on the Western canon are virtually precluded in the land where the discipline of English was shaped and that an unquestioning acceptance of Western literary values is now firmly institutionalized there. This book would have been written to very little purpose if such conclusions were drawn. Conceptions of the British literary curriculum as unmediated assertion of cultural power, which I have argued against throughout, are partly responsible for promoting the illusion of historical continuity in that they systematically ignore the continual modifications of British educational goals and the strategic maneuvering that produced English studies in India.

The relation between past and present Indian education is no more straightforward than the one between educational developments in nineteenth-century England and India or, for that matter, between the British empire and the practice of the humanities today. This is not to say that there is no connection at all—of course there is—but that connection is no more readily understood through cause-effect explanations than by a global theory that presumes to account for the features of one in terms of the other. There are no simple lessons to be derived from this history, least of all the lesson that imperialism can be swiftly undone merely by hurling away the texts it institutionalized. Though T. S. Eliot's moving statement, "after such knowledge, what forgiveness?" has understandable appeal, I am not advocating that today's students must close their English books without further ado because those works were instrumental in holding others in subjugation or, if that is too extreme, that at least Shakespeare and Milton must be dropped from the English curriculum because their texts were used at one time to supply religious values that could be introduced into the British control of India in no other way.

What I am suggesting, however, is that we can no longer afford to regard the uses to which literary works were put in the service of British imperialism as extraneous to the way these texts are to be read. The involvement of colonialism with literary culture is too deep, too pervasive for the disciplinary development of English literary pedagogy to be studied with Britain as its only or primary focus. Large areas of discussion have yet to be fully mapped out, but I am hopeful that with sustained cross-referencing between the histories of England and its colonies the relations between Western culture and imperialism will be progressively illuminated.

Notes

INTRODUCTION

1. Antonio Gramsci, *Selections from the Prison Notebooks of Antonio Gramsci,* Quintin Hoare and Geoffrey Nowell Smith, eds. (London: Lawrence and Wishart, 1971), p. 57.

2. Minute by J. Farish dated August 28, 1838, quoted in B. K. Boman-Behram, *Educational Controversies of India,* p. 239.

3. See D. J. Palmer, *The Rise of English Studies;* Terry Eagleton, *Literary Theory;* Chris Baldick, *The Social Mission of English Criticism;* Peter Widdowson, eds., *Re-Reading English;* Janet Batsleer et al., *Re-writing English: Cultural Politics of Gender and Class;* and Colin McCabe, "Towards a Modern Trivium—English Studies Today."

4. See also Richard Altick, *The English Common Reader,* p. 161. As a result of the pressure exerted by Matthew Arnold, new sets of textbooks were produced and adapted for the new Mundella's Code of 1883 empowering inspectors to hear children in standards five, six, and seven read from books of extracts from standard authors. The new subject of "English literature" was introduced in 1871, and it consisted of memorizing of passages of poetry and testing knowledge of meaning and allusions. By 1880, according to Altick, "English literature" had become the most popular subject in schools. The Taunton Com-

mission found that very few schools gave lessons in English literature even as late as the mid-1860s.

  5. Richard Poirier, "What is English Studies, and If You Know What That Is, What Is English Literature?," in Gregory T. Polleta, ed., *Issues in Contemporary Literary Theory,* (Boston: Little, Brown, 1973), p. 558.

  6. Terry Eagleton, *Criticism and Ideology,* p. 57.

  7. Culling through nineteenth-century periodicals like the *Asiatic Journal* and the *Oriental Herald,* one will be struck by the number of articles on the Oriental tale, that species of literature imported into England for consumption in fashionable literary salons and polite circles. The Oriental tale ranged from direct translations of works like the *Arabian Nights* to complete adaptations to Western themes, such as Addison's *Vision of Mirza,* Johnson's *Rasselas,* Southey's *Curse of Kehama,* and Thomas Moore's *Lalla Rookh.* While some articles in these periodicals deplored the extravagance of imagery in Oriental literature as unbefitting the more sober strains of classical Western literature, a surprisingly large majority found morality of sentiment in the tales, as well as charm and elegance and inventiveness of expression in them. Cf. "Every Oriental tale has generally for its aim the illustration of some point in morality: sometimes destiny, sometimes conduct and virtue." "Excellence of Oriental Tales," *Oriental Herald* (1824), 1:422.

  8. One of the later criticisms of British educational policy made by British administrators themselves was its inattention to amusement as a legitimate motive for reading. The Indian Education Commission Report of 1882 pleaded the need of Indian students for the kind of extensive reading that English boys were accustomed to. "An English boy at the same stage of instruction will find in the Waverly Novels, in voyages and travels, and in tales of danger and daring, an unending source of delight for his leisure hours. To the native relaxation of this kind is denied." Further, added the report, the Indian's familiarity with English was never so great that he could read books in that language for the sake of amusement. *Report of the Indian Education Commission,* February 3, 1882, p. 231.

  9. Great Britain, *Parliamentary Papers, 1852–53,* Evidence of Charles Trevelyan, 32:198.

  10. Great Britain, *Parliamentary Papers, 1852–53,* Evidence of the Rev. J. Tucker, 32:349.

  11. "On the Inefficacy of the Means Now in Use for the Propagation of Christianity in India," *Oriental Herald,* (1825), p. 587.

  12. Alexander Duff, *India and India Missions,* p. 429.

  13. For a discussion of comparable developments in the administrative structures of Britain and India in the early nineteenth century see Eric Stokes, "Bureaucracy and Ideology in the 19th Century," pp. 131–156. Stokes argues that financial stringency and the need for centralized control joined the histories of Britain and India in a common ideological purpose. Specifically, Stokes considers the reformist period of Bentinck (1828–1835) to have had the greatest mirroring effect on British institutions.

  14. Raymond Williams, "Base and Superstructure in Marxist Cultural Analysis," p. 7.

  15. Benita Parry, "Problems in Current Theories of Colonial Discourse," p. 34.

  16. Edward W. Said, *Orientalism,* pp. 58–59.

  17. *Parliamentary Papers, 1852–53,* Evidence of W. Keane, 32:203.

  18. David Kopf, *British Orientalism and the Bengal Renaissance,* p. 275.

  19. Thomas B. Macaulay, "Speech in the House of Commons, dated 2 February, 1835," in G. W. Young, ed., *Speeches* (Oxford: Oxford University Press, 1935), pp. 153–54. This speech should not be confused with the better known minute of July 1835, though its significance in shaping British official opinion toward India was in no way less.

  20. Pierre Bourdieu, "Systems of Education and Systems of Thought," in Michael F. D. Young, ed., *Knowledge and Control,* p. 194.

  21. See William Spanos, "The Apollonian Investment of Modern Humanist Educa-

tion: The Examples of Matthew Arnold, Irving Babbit, and I. A. Richards," *Cultural Critique* (Fall 1985), 1(1):7–72.

22. Matthew Arnold, *Culture and Anarchy*, John Dover Wilson, ed. (Cambridge: Cambridge University Press, 1971), pp. 44–54.

23. Matthew Arnold, *Essays Literary and Critical*, G. K. Chesterton, ed. (London and New York: Everyman Library, 1906), p. 71.

24. C. E. Trevelyan, *On the Education of the People of India*, p. 176.

25. Edward W. Said, *Beginnings*, p. 12.

I. THE BEGINNINGS OF ENGLISH LITERARY STUDY

1. Great Britain, *Parliamentary Debates, 1813*, 26:562.
2. Great Britain, *Parliamentary Debates, 1813*, 26:830.
3. Great Britain, *Parliamentary Debates, 1813*, 26:830.
4. See P. J. Cain and A. G. Hopkins, "Gentlemanly Capitalism and British Expansion Overseas: 1. The Old Colonial System, 1688–1850," pp. 501–525, for an elaboration of the argument that "gentleman capitalists" were more important than industrialization in shaping British imperialism after 1700.
5. Great Britain, *Parliamentary Papers, 1831–1832*, General Appendix, "Observations on the State of Society among our Asiatic Subjects," 8:10. Henceforth abbreviated as "Observations."
6. "Observations," p. 17.
7. "Observations," p. 20.
8. "Observations," p. 80.
9. "Observations," p. 80.
10. Ninth Report of Select Committee on the Affairs of India, 1783, quoted in Eric Stokes, *The English Utilitarians and India*, p. 2.
11. *Adam's Reports on Vernacular Education in Bengal and Bihar in 1835 and 1838*, p. 340.
12. Letter of Hastings to Nathaniel Smith, October 4, 1784, quoted in David Kopf, *British Orientalism and the Bengal Renaissance*, p. 18.
13. Percival Spear, *Oxford History of Modern India 1740–1975* (Oxford: Oxford University Press, 1965), p. 89.
14. Eric Stokes, *The English Utilitarians and India*, p. 16.
15. Cf. "To allure the natives of India to the study of European science and literature, we must, I think, engraft this study upon their own established methods of scientific and literary institutions; and particularly in all the public colleges or schools maintained or encouraged by government, good translations of the most useful European compositions on the subjects taught in them, may, I conceive, be introduced with the greatest advantage." Paper by J. H. Harington, June 19, 1814, quoted in *Adam's Reports on Vernacular Education in Bengal and Bihar*, p. 310.
16. Great Britain, *Parliamentary Papers, 1831–32*, appendix I, Minute of James Mill, 9:408.
17. Great Britain, *Parliamentary Papers, 1831–32*, 9:489.
18. C. H. Philips, *The East India Company 1784–1834* (Manchester: Manchester University Press, 1940; rev. ed., 1961), p. 8. See also William D. Grampp, "How Britain Turned to Free Trade," pp. 86–112, for a discussion of the influence of Hume and Adam Smith on gaining unanimous support for free trade as a means of raising England's real income.
19. Great Britain, *Parliamentary Debates, 1813*, 26:1027.
20. Great Britain, *Parliamentary Papers, 1831–32*, Appendix I, Extract of Letter in the

Public Department, from the Court of Directors to the Governor-General-in-Council, dated September 6, 1813, 9:486.

21. Thomas B. Macaulay, *Speeches*, p. 345.

22. Great Britain, *Parliamentary Papers, 1831–32*, appendix 1, Extract of Letter in the Public Department, from the Court of Directors to the Governor-General in Council of Bengal, dated September 5, 1827, 9:488.

23. Great Britain, *Parliamentary Papers, 1831–32*, appendix 1, 9:488.

24. Great Britain, *Parliamentary Papers, 1831–32*, appendix 1, 9:488.

25. Eric Stokes, *The English Utilitarians and India*, p. 58.

26. Great Britain, *Parliamentary Papers, 1852–53*, Evidence of Horace Wilson, 29:7.

27. Great Britain, *Parliamentary Papers, 1852–53*, Evidence of Horace Wilson, 29:19.

28. *Calcutta Review*, (1845), 3(6):229–230.

29. "Of Government Education in Bengal," *Calcutta Review* (1845) 3; 259.

30. Great Britain, *Parliamentary Papers, 1852–53*, Appendix K, 32:484.

31. The direct influence of Macaulay's minute on this act is by no means an accepted historical fact. Percival Spear sees both Macaulay and Bentinck as merely agents and not initiators of a new educational policy already decided upon by the Company's Court of Directors. "Bentinck and Education," 78–101. K. A. Ballhatchet, on the other hand, argues that Bentinck's position favoring English was forged in India, with little influence coming from the home government. "The Home Government and Bentinck's Educational Policy," 224–229.

32. Horace Wilson, "Education of the Natives of India," *Asiatic Journal* (1836), 29:14.

33. "General Progress of Education, and Obstacles to Its Introduction in British India," *Oriental Herald* (November 1825), 7(3):491.

34. Alexander Duff, *New Era of the English Language and English Literature in India*, p. 22.

35. Duff, *New Era of the English Language and English Literature in India*, p. 30.

36. Great Britain, *Parliamentary Papers, 1852–53*, Evidence of William Wilberforce Bird, 32:237.

37. Great Britain, *Parliamentary Papers, 1852–53*, Appendix E, The English Education Act of Lord William Bentinck, 32:408.

38. Great Britain, *Parliamentary Papers, 1852–53*, Evidence of Thomas A. Wise, 32:222.

2. PRAEPARATIO EVANGELICA

1. *Atheneum* (1839), p. 108.

2. "The Evils of Poetry," *Asiatic Journal* (1825), 19:772.

3. "Review of *Nalodaya* by Kalidasa," *Calcutta Review* (1845), 3:33.

4. Great Britain, *Parliamentary Papers, 1831–32*, appendix 1, Report of A. D. Campbell, August 17, 1823, 32:503.

5. *Parliamentary Papers, 1852–53*, Evidence of Horace Wilson, 32:264.

6. George Smith, *The Life of Alexander Duff, D.D., LL.D* (New York: A. C. Armstrong, 1879), 2:291.

7. A. M. C. Waterman in "The Ideological Alliance of Political Economy to Christian Theology, 1798–1833," pp. 231–244, draws attention to Thomas Chalmers' kinship with Malthus, William Paley, Edward Copleston, Richard Whately, and J. B. Sumner, all of whose works maintain a belief in the reciprocity of Christian theology and political economy, that is, the inseparability of moral virtue from material realities such as private property, population, and wealth.

8. George Smith, *Life of Alexander Duff*, p. 78.

9. George Smith, *The Story of Dr. Duff* (London and Madras: Christian Literature Society for India, 1898), p. 18.

10. Great Britain, *Parliamentary Papers, 1852–53*, Evidence of Edward Thornton, 32:36.

11. Alexander Duff, *The Indian Rebellion*, pp. 99–106.

12. Alexander Duff, *India and India Missions*, p. 430.

13. Alexander Duff, *India and India Missions*, p. 587.

14. Alexander Duff, *Letters to Lord Auckland*, p. 58.

15. Great Britain, *Parliamentary Papers, 1852–53*, Appendix D, General Report of Public Instruction in the North-Western Provinces of the Bengal Presidency, 1843–4, by J. Muir, 32:450–451.

16. Great Britain, *Parliamentary Papers, 1852–53*, Appendix N, 32:491–572. The information about Macaulay is provided on page 148 of the same volume.

17. See Amy Cruse, *The Victorians and Their Books*, p. 16.

18. "The Power of Moral Painting," *Madras Missionary Register* (February 1836), 2(1):36.

19. *Calcutta Christian Observer* (1833), 2:87.

20. David Newsome, *Godliness and Good Learning*, p. 6.

21. Fred Clarke, *Education and Social Change*, p. 25.

22. T. W. Bamford, "Thomas Arnold and the Victorian Idea of a Public School," in Brian Simon and Ian Bradley, ed., *The Victorian Public School* (Dublin: Gill and Macmillan, 1975), p. 63.

23. Ellen McDonald, "English Education and Social Reform in Late Nineteenth Century Bombay," pp. 466–467.

24. Lal Behari Day, *Recollections of Alexander Duff, D.D., LL.D.*, p. 46.

25. Lal Behari Day, *Recollections of Alexander Duff, D.D., LL.D.*, p. 51.

26. Alexander Duff, *India and India Missions*, p. 545.

27. *Missionary Register*, November 1825, quoted in "Missionary Efforts in India," *Asiatic Journal* (1826), 21:450.

28. Alexander Duff, *India and India Missions*, p. 427.

29. Alexander Duff, *A Vindication of the Church of Scotland's India Missions: An Address before the General Assembly of the Church, May 24, 1837* (Edinburgh: John Johnstone, 1837), p. 32.

30. Duff, *India and India Missions*, p. 563.

31. Duff, *India and India Missions*, p. 507.

32. Duff, *Vindication*, p. 33.

33. Duff, *India and India Missions*, p. 429.

34. T. W. Bamford, *Thomas Arnold* (London: Cresset Press, 1960), p. 122.

3. "ONE POWER, ONE MIND"

1. Michalina Vaughan and Margaret Archer, *Social Conflict and Educational Change in England and France 1789–1848* (Cambridge: Cambridge University Press, 1971), p. 10.

2. Quoted in M. G. Jones, *The Charity School Movement* (Cambridge: Cambridge University Press, 1938), p. 74.

3. M. G. Jones, *The Charity School Movement*, pp. 373–375.

4. Great Britain, *Parliamentary Papers, 1852–53*, Minute of the Marquess of Tweeddale on Education, July 1846, 29:190.

5. Great Britain, *Parliamentary Papers, 1831–32*, General Appendix, "Observations on

the State of Society among Our Asiatic Subjects," 8:80. Henceforth abbreviated "Observations."

    6. "Observations," p. 34.

    7. "Observations," p. 82.

    8. "Observations," p. 83.

    9. "Observations," p. 81.

    10. "Observations," p. 10.

    11. Both Grant and Wilberforce quote rather extensively from the reports of police commissions in India, which address the problem of crime in quasi-religious terms. Cf. "If we would apply a lasting remedy to the evil, we must adopt means of instruction for the different classes of the community, by which they may be restrained, not only from the commission of public crimes, but also from acts of immorality, by a dread of the punishments denounced both in this world and in a future state." Great Britain, *Parliamentary Debates, 1813,* "The Propagation of Christianity," 26:841.

    12. "Observations," p. 51.

    13. "Observations," p. 80.

    14. Great Britain, *Parliamentary Papers, 1852–53,* Evidence of the Rev. W. Keane, 32:301.

    15. Great Britain, *Parliamentary Papers, 1852–53,* Evidence of the Rev. W. Keane, 32:313.

    16. Great Britain, *Parliamentary Papers, 1852–53,* Evidence of Major F. Rowlandson, 29:155.

    17. "Observations," p. 75.

    18. *Reports and Documents on the Indian Mission,* p. 115.

    19. "A Sketch of the Origin, Rise, and Progress of Hindoo College," *Calcutta Christian Observer* (June–December 1832), 1:124.

    20. *Papers Referring to the Educational Operations of the Church Missionary Society in North India,* p. 5.

    21. "Literary Fruits of Missionary Labours," *Calcutta Review* (1845), 3:44.

    22. "Progress of Education in British India," *Asiatic Journal* (1826), 21:322.

    23. Great Britain, *Parliamentary Papers, 1852–53,* Evidence of J. C. Marshman, 29:26.

    24. Great Britain, *Parliamentary Papers, 1852–53,* Minute by M. Elphinstone, December 13, 1823, 29:519.

    25. "The Hindu Character," *Asiatic Journal* (1828), 26:692.

    26. Great Britain, *Parliamentary Papers, 1852–53,* Evidence of Thomas Wise, 32:233.

    27. Great Britain, *Parliamentary Papers, 1852–53,* Evidence of W. Keane, 32:303.

    28. *Calcutta Review,* 19:131–132.

    29. *Madras Christian Instructor and Missionary Record* (September 1844), 11(4):195.

    30. *Parliamentary Papers, 1852–53,* Evidence of the Rev. W. Keane, 32:202.

    31. Great Britain, *Parliamentary Papers, 1852–53,* Evidence of the Rev. J. Kennedy, 29:171.

    32. *Calcutta Review* (1853), 9:127.

    33. *Madras Christian Instructor and Missionary Record* (September 1844), 1(4):185.

    34. "Evils of Poetry," *Asiatic Journal* (1825), 19:774.

    35. "Evils of Poetry," p. 774.

    36. The gradual shift from the early Utilitarian and Evangelical attitude to poetry as error and deception to a greater acceptance of its elevating properties began to be felt some time between 1820 and 1830 and was vitally linked with the attempt to restore poetry to its original union with religion. The shift coincided with an increasing recognition that English literature and Christianity shared a common fate and that if one was in decline, the other was too, for "what was true of the long prevailing literature of Europe, appeared substantially true of its long established religion." *Papers on Baptist Missions: Minutes and*

Reports of a Conference of the Baptist Missions of the Northwest Provinces, 1855 (Calcutta: Baptist Mission Press, 1856), p. 28.

37. *Papers on Baptist Missions,* p. 13.

38. *Reports and Documents on the Indian Mission,* p. 16.

39. "Prospectus of London Missionaries at Madras," *Oriental Herald* (October 1828), 19:493.

40. *Reports and Documents on the Indian Mission,* p. 82.

41. Alexander Duff, *India and India Missions,* p. 288.

42. *Reports and Documents on the Indian Mission,* p. 248.

43. "Facts Illustrative of the Character and Condition of the People of India," *Oriental Herald* (October 1828), 19:491.

44. "Facts Illustrative of the Character and Condition of the People of India," p. 493.

45. *Asiatic Journal,* 8:285.

46. *Papers on Baptist Missions: Minutes and Reports of a Conference of the Baptist Missions of the Northwest Provinces, 1855* (Calcutta: Baptist Mission Press, 1856), p. 28.

47. "Letter of Duff, Trevelyan, and W. H. Pearce to Friends of Education in India," *Calcutta Christian Observer* (January–December 1834), 3:350.

48. *Calcutta Christian Observer* (1834), 3:359.

49. Charles E. Trevelyan, *On the Education of the People of India,* p. 74.

50. *Madras Christian Instructor and Missionary Record* (January 1844), 1(8):46.

51. Great Britain, *Parliamentary Papers,* Evidence of Thomas Wise, 32:29.

52. William Ward, *A View of the History, Literature, and Mythology of the Hindoos,* 2d ed. (Serampore: Mission Press, 1818), p. 598.

53. Eustace Carey, ed., *Memoirs of William Carey, D.D.,* p. 151.

54. Great Britain, *Parliamentary Papers, 1852–53,* Evidence of F. J. Halliday, 29:56.

55. "General Progress of Education, and Obstacles to Its Introduction in British India," *Oriental Herald* (November 1825), 7(23):491.

56. Great Britain, *Parliamentary Papers, 1831–32,* Minute by Francis Warden, December 29, 1823, 9:520.

57. Great Britain, *Parliamentary Papers, 1852–53,* 32:32.

58. John Murdoch, *Education in India,* p. 91. Murdoch, who was with the Christian Vernacular Society of Madras and organized supplies of vernacular and English literature for native schools, did an intensive analysis of Hindu texts in order to determine their suitability for rearing trustworthy servants of the Empire. He submitted examples to Lord Napier and Lord Ripon to urge stronger government control of reading materials.

59. "System of Education Adapted to India," *Oriental Herald and Colonial Review,* (January–April 1824), 1:261. Cf. the testimony of a Roman Catholic bishop in the Indian Education Commission: "Education has for its object to direct the children of the people towards the same end towards which the law and the government of the land direct their parents," the object of all law and government being "to guide the people towards happiness." Education Commission, *Report by the Bombay Provincial Committee,* p. 378.

60. Great Britain, *Parliamentary Papers, 1831–32,* Evidence of James Mill, February 21, 1832, 9:46.

61. Great Britain, *Parliamentary Papers, 1831–32,* Evidence of James Mill, February 21, 1832, 9:56.

62. Great Britain, *Parliamentary Papers, 1831–32,* Evidence of James Mill, February 21, 1832, 9:57.

63. Great Britain, *Parliamentary Papers, 1831–32,* Evidence of James Mill, February 21, 1832, 9:57.

64. Great Britain, *Parliamentary Papers, 1831–53,* Evidence of Trevelyan, 32:164.

65. Great Britain, *Parliamentary Papers, 1831–32*, Appendix J, 9:413.
66. *Report of the Indian Education Commission*, p. 308.
67. Great Britain, *Parliamentary Papers, 1854*, 47:2.
68. Great Britain, *Parliamentary Papers, 1854*, 47:14.
69. Chief Justice Sir Charles Turner's address to the University of Madras, quoted in *Report of the Indian Education Commission*, p. 302.

4. REWRITING ENGLISH

1. Great Britain, *Parliamentary Papers, 1852–53*, Evidence of Charles Trevelyan. 32:185.
2. Great Britain, *Parliamentary Papers, 1852–53*, Evidence of Charles Cameron, 32:287.
3. Great Britain, *Parliamentary Papers, 1852–53*, Evidence of Charles Cameron, 32:287.
4. Homi K. Bhabha, "Signs Taken for Wonders, p. 153.
5. Eustace Carey, ed., *Memoirs of William Carey, D.D.*, p. 151.
6. "Literary Fruits of Missionary Labours," *Calcutta Review* (1845), 3:49.
7. See S. Cromwell Crawford, *Ram Mohan Roy*, pp. 64–88, for a discussion of the influence of Unitarianism, especially American Unitarianism, on Bengali intellectuals. Unitarianism's deemphasis of doctrinal points, its adherence to the belief drawn from the Bible that the "unity of God accompanied by its appropriate expression in moral conduct is the only prerequisite for finding favor with God," had huge appeal for young Indians.
8. *The English Works of Raja Rammohun Roy*, quoted in S. Cromwell Crawford, *Ram Mohan Roy*, p. 67.
9. For an exhaustive study of Halhed's career as a Sanskritist, see Rosane Rocher, *Orientalism, Poetry, and the Millennium*, 1983.
10. Great Britain, *Parliamentary Debates, 1813*, "The Propagation of Christianity, 26:840.
11. The signatures on the dispatch, dated August 18, 1824, from the General Committee of Public Instruction to the governor-general include those of J. H. Harington, J. P. Larkins, W. W. Martin, J. C. C. Sutherland, Henry Shakespear, Holt Mackenzie, Horace Wilson, A. Stirling, and W. B. Bayley. Henry Sharp, ed., *Selections from Educational Records, Part I (1781–1839)* (Calcutta: National Archives of India, 1920), p. 98.
12. Henry Sharp, ed., *Selections from Educational Records*, p. 96.
13. "Letter of John Tytler to T. B. Macaulay, Calcutta, January 26, 1835," quoted in Gerald and Natalie Sirkin, "The Battle of Indian Education," p. 425.
14. Kenneth Ingham, *Reformers in India 1793–1833*.
15. *Calcutta Review* (1845), 3:35.
16. Northampton MS., William Carey to Andrew Fuller, April 23, 1796, cited in M. A. Laird, *Missionaries and Education in Bengal 1793–1837*, p. 56.
17. "Missionary Efforts in India," *Asiatic Journal* (1826), 21:447.
18. Great Britain, *Parliamentary Papers, 1852–53*, Appendix B, Report of Warden, President of the Board of Education at Bombay, April 1853, 32:377.
19. Great Britain, *Parliamentary Papers, 1852–53*, Evidence of J. C. Marshman, 29:26.
20. Significantly, the British anxiety about being mistrusted by their subjects also formed the basis of British interpretations of Indian texts. The view that Indian teachings encouraged lying and deception was extended to explain the "treachery" of Nana Sahib at Kanpur in 1857. John Murdoch, commissioned to conduct a detailed investigation into ancient Indian texts to determine the level of morality in them, wrote of the permission the laws of Manu granted to the breaking of those oaths that were made in the utmost solemnity. The evidence he cites is the Brahmin prime minister Maha-Kalinga telling Dhriti, "In seeking reconciliation with a foe, lull his suspicions with the most solemn oaths

and slay him. The holiest of saint-preceptors declares that there is no harm in in this."
John Murdoch, *Education in India*, p. 90.

21. Great Britain, *Parliamentary Papers, 1852–53*, Evidence of Cameron, 32:287.

22. "Of Government Education in Bengal," *Calcutta Review*, (1845), 3:230. Of course, if one were to pursue Martin Green's line of thought in *Dreams of Adventure, Deeds of Empire*, the most obvious rebuttal would be that Milton's description of Satan deliberately evokes the context of Oriental literature and reinforces the association of Satan with the monstrous and the seductive. The association is further strengthened by the fact that the Milton passage is believed to derive from Sir Thomas Roe's description of the Mughal emperor Jahangir, to whom he was sent as ambassador (p. 40).

23. Great Britain, *Parliamentary Papers, 1852–53*, Evidence of Alexander Duff, 32:412. Partha Mitter, an art historian, points out that in nineteenth-century European discussions of Indian art the crucial issue was the uses to which the imagination was put. In terms similar to Duff's, Ruskin made a distinction between the legitimate use of grotesque motifs in a high form of art like the Christian and in a superstitious artistic tradition like the Hindu. Although he felt that the grotesque in Venetian architecture went against all bounds of reason and natural order, its existence was justified on the grounds that its conception was self-consciously extravagant. When the appeal is purely to the imagination, as Milton's description of Satan in Hell can claim to be, the reader is in less danger of being misguided or led astray, for "the imagination which is thoroughly under the command of the intelligent will, has a dominion indiscernible by science, and illimitable by law." Quoted in Partha Mitter, *Much Maligned Monsters*, p. 242.

24. James Mill, *History of British India*, p. 49.

25. James Mill, *History of British India*, p. 47; G. W. F. Hegel, *Lectures on the Philosophy of History*, J. Sibree, ed. (New York: Dover Books, 1956), p. 162.

26. "Review of *Annals and Antiquities of Rajasthan*," *Quarterly Review* (1832), 48:1

27. "Review of *Nalodaya* by Kalidasa," *Calcutta Review*, (1845), 3:12.

28. "Facts Illustrative of the Character and Condition of the People of India," *Oriental Herald* (1828), 19:102.

29. H. M. Elliott and John Dowson, *The History of India as Told by Its Own Historians*, p. xx.

30. Horace Wilson, "On the Education of the Natives of India," *Asiatic Journal* (1836), p. 14.

31. Great Britain, *Parliamentary Papers, 1852–53*, Evidence of Horace Wilson, 32:262.

32. Great Britain, *Parliamentary Papers, 1852–53*, Evidence of Charles Cameron, 32:280.

33. Edward Said draws attention to a similar tendency in modern Orientalism to separate literature from language. Though he has Oriental studies in the West in mind, his contention that the Western idea of the Orient is more readily disseminated when there is no literature to challenge it with its depiction of a "living reality" has obvious resonances in Cameron's proposal. See *Orientalism*, p. 291.

34. "Selections from the Records of Government, North West Provinces," part 20, *Calcutta Review* (1855), 24:xx.

35. F. W. Farrar, ed., *Essays on a Liberal Education*, p. 88.

36. *Parliamentary Papers, 1831–32*, Extract Minute by Mountstuart Elphinstone, Governor of Bombay, December 13, 1823, 9:515.

37. See J. E. Chamberlin, "An Anatomy of Cultural Melancholy," pp. 691–705, for an effective discussion of midnineteenth-century perceptions of culture in general as "degenerate." The critique of culture ranged from attacks on institutional decay to "shoddy habits of language." According to Chamberlin, the processes of degeneracy were explained by analogies drawn from the sciences, especially biology; the corresponding cure was also described in metaphors of biology, such as grafting.

38. Richard D. Altick, *The English Common Reader,* p. 183.

39. Cf. *Quarterly Review,* 107:418: "Much more is it a thing to wonder at and be ashamed of, that, with such a literature as ours, the English lesson is still a desideratum in nearly all our great places of education, and that the future gentry of the country are left to pick up their mother tongue from the periodical works of fiction which are the bane of our youth, and the dread of every conscientious schoolmaster."

40. Great Britain, *Parliamentary Papers, 1831–32,* 9:445.

41. "On the Intellectual Character of the Hindus," *Asiatic Journal* (1828), 25:718.

42. Great Britain, *Parliamentary Papers, 1852–53,* Evidence of Charles Trevelyan, 32:48.

43. *Selections from the Calcutta Gazette,* October 24, 1816, p. 148.

44. *Asiatic Journal* (1826), p. 450.

5. LESSONS OF HISTORY

1. Colin McCabe, "Towards a Modern Trivium," p. 70.

2. D. J. Palmer, *The Rise of English Studies,* p. 42.

3. An intriguing discussion of the effect of the colonial encounter on redefinitions of literary forms is provided by Judith Wilt in "The Imperial Mouth," 618–628. Wilt argues that Western incursions into the unknown in Africa, India, and the Middle East produced a neurosis in the Victorian imagination about how the future would appear. That anxiety is reflected in works like H. G. Wells' *War of the Worlds* (1898), Bram Stoker's *Dracula* (1897), and Joseph Conrad's *Heart of Darkness* (1899), science fiction works that Wilt reads as mutations of Victorian gothic, the colonial encounter being the catalytic agent for such transformation.

4. "Warren Hastings' letter to Nathaniel Smith, Esq., of the Court of Directors, October 4, 1784," preface to *The Bhagvat Geeta, or Dialogues of Kreeshna and Arjoon,* trans. Charles Wilkins (London: C. Nourse, 1784), p. 7.

5. History for Mill was not a recital but a "methodical description of social phenomena and the laws which regulate them." Elie Halévy writes that "far from using the empirical knowledge which he obtained from the history of British India to determine inductively the necessary movement of progress from the barbarous state to civilization, he rather writes conjectural history and, in most cases, he takes as a point of departure a definition of progress based on the constant facts of human nature and deduces from that what, in fact, the progress of Hindu society must have been." *The Growth of Philosophical Radicalism,* Mary Morris, trans. (London: Faber and Faber, 1928; reprint, 1952), p. 274.

6. William Jones, *Asiatic Researches,* 2:3; quoted by James Mill in *History of British India,* vol. 2, book 2, p. 111.

7. James Mill, *History of British India,* p. 37.

8. James Mill, *History of British India,* p. 39.

9. See Claude Lévi-Strauss, *Structural Anthropology,* translated from the French by Claire Jacobsen and Brooke Grundfest Shoepf (New York: Basic Books, 1963), particularly the essay "The Structural Study of Myth."

10. Great Britain, *Parliamentary Papers, 1852–53,* Evidence of J. Tucker, 32:349.

11. *Quarterly Review* (1832), 48:4.

12. J. Talboys Wheeler, *The History of India from the Earliest Ages,* p. 6.

13. Great Britain, *Parliamentary Papers, 1852–53,* 32, Appendix D.

14. Colonel "Hindoo" Stewart, *Vindication of the Hindoos, by a Bengal Officer* (London, 1808), p. 97, quoted in David Kopf, *British Orientalism and the Bengal Renaissance,* p. 141.

15. "Avataras: Four Lectures Delivered at the Theosophical Society, Madras 1899," in Ainslee T. Embree, ed., *The Hindu Tradition* (New York: Modern Library, 1965), pp. 322–324.

16. "Drain Inspector's Report," in *Collected Works of Mahatma Gandhi* (Ahmedabad: Navajivan Press, 1969), 34:546.

17. Lionel Gossman, "Literature and Education," *New Literary History* (Winter 1982), pp. 344–45. Gossman writes that "underpinning the central place of language and literature in the eighteenth-century college curriculum were certain ideas about the nature of man and of culture. One of these was that, as Herder put it, following Descartes over a century earlier, it is language—the ability to manipulate symbolic systems—that distinguishes man from the beasts (and not science or technology as we might tend to think). To learn to speak and write well was to be humanized. Protestants, especially, valued literacy and—more cautiously—literature as the instrument by which man might enter into the immediate presence of the Word of God in Holy Scripture and thus be freed from narrow, traditional, and—as they saw it—corrupt doctrines and practices. . . . The acquisition and use of correct literary models of expression was seen by Christians and *philosophes* alike as a defense against the constant threat of regression into the bestiality of our original condition . . . [and] the teaching of language and literature as a means of weaning young men from their natural beastliness. Seventeenth- and eighteenth-century teachers thus saw in polished language and literature an essential instrument for removing their pupils from natural origins, releasing them from the narrowness of an oral, largely peasant culture, presumed to be shut in on itself and enslaved to routine and superstitition, and for introducing them to the larger view of a universal, human culture, spanning the ages and the nations."

18. Hugh James Rose, *The Tendency of Prevalent Opinions about Knowledge Considered* (Cambridge: Deighton, and London: Rivington, 1826), p. 11, quoted in Alan Bacon, "English Literature Becomes a University Subject," p. 594.

19. For this insight I am indebted to Franklin Court's article, "Adam Smith and the Teaching of English Literature," pp. 325–341.

20. Adam Smith, *Theory of Moral Sentiments*, p. 214.

21. Adam Smith, *Theory of Moral Sentiments*, pp. 257–258.

22. Adam Smith, *Theory of Moral Sentiments*, p. 162.

23. Adam Smith, *Theory of Moral Sentiments*, p. 164.

24. Adam Smith, *Theory of Moral Sentiments*, p. 165.

25. "Facts Illustrative of the Character and Condition of the People of India," *Oriental Herald* (October 1828), 19:129.

26. "Facts Illustrative of the Character and Condition of the People of India," p. 127.

27. "Facts Illustrative of the Character and Condition of the People of India," p. 101.

28. "Philosophy of Fiction," p. 142.

29. "Philosophy of Fiction," p. 141. Oriental people were deemed to have "unfurnished, uncultivated, unreflecting, and unobservant minds," as a result of which their fictional characters were completely without interest.

30. "Philosophy of Fiction," *Asiatic Journal*, p. 142. The Asiatic tale on the other hand "lets the mind sit on a couch of luxury and indolence. . . . [The Asiatic tales of adventure] indicate a sympathy with fate, rather than a sympathy with an energy that defies fate and contends against destiny."

31. Charles Trevelyan, *On the Education of the People of India*, p. 192.

32. Charles Trevelyan, *On the Education of the People of India*, p. 192. Recorded accounts by English-educated Indians confirmed Trevelyan's assessment, as in the following statement by one recipient of English education, Chander Nath Bose: "English education tells

us that we live under tyrannies more numerous and more radically mischievous than those, which produced the great revolution of '89. It tells us that, here in India, we have a social tyranny, a domestic tyranny, a tyranny of caste, a tyranny of custom, a religious tyranny, a clerical tyranny, a tyranny of thought over thought, of sentiment over sentiment. And it not only tells us of all these tyrannies, but makes us feel them with terrific intensity." "High Education in India: An Essay Read at the Bethune Society on the 25th April, 1878," quoted in Bruce McCully, *English Education and the Origins of Indian Nationalism*, p. 221.

33. John Murdoch, *Education in India*, pp. 104–105.

34. John Murdoch, *Education in India*, p. 17.

35. Education Commission, *Report by the Bombay Provincial Committee* (Calcutta: Superintendent of Government Printing, 1884), p. 235.

36. John Murdoch, *Education in India*, p. 111. The selection of Hunter's text is understandable in light of the fact that the Commission that recommended it was headed by Hunter himself.

37. D. J. Palmer, *Rise of English Studies*, p. 22.

38. *Bengal Public Instruction Report for 1856-7*, Appendix A, p. 213, quoted in John Murdoch, *Education in India*, p. 44. There were numerous complaints that subjects like health, thrift, extravagance in marriage and funerals, and the role of women were not taught adequately by professors of English literature, who had "neither knowledge of the people nor sympathy with them." Consequently selections of readings to communicate informed attitudes to these issues were considered absolutely essential.

39. Great Britain, *Parliamentary Papers, 1852-53*, Appendix G, Statement of the Progress and Success of the General Assembly (now Free Church) Institution at Calcutta, 32:452–453.

40. Great Britain, *Parliamentary Papers, 1852-53*, Appendix N, General Report on Public Instruction in the Lower Provinces of the Bengal Presidency for 1843–1844, pp. 491–617.

41. Great Britain, *Parliamentary Papers, 1852-53*, Appendix N, Scholarship Examination Questions 1843: Literature, 32:573.

42. Great Britain, *Parliamentary Papers, 1853-53*, Appendix N, Hindoo College Answers, 32:587.

43. Great Britain, *Parliamentary Papers, 1852-53*, Evidence of Alexander Duff, 32:47.

44. *Calcutta Review* (1845), 3:13.

45. "Letter to His Excellency the Right Hon'ble William Pitt, Lord Amherst, 11 December 1823," in *Selected Works of Raja Rammohun Roy*, p. 301.

46. "Baconian Philosophy Applicable to the Mental Regeneration of India," *Calcutta Christian Observer* (January–December 1838), 7:124.

47. Great Britain, *Parliamentary Papers, 1852-53*, Appendix N, Hooghly College Essays, 32:594–595.

48. Great Britain, *Parliamentary Papers, 1852-53*, Extract from Mahendra Lal Basak's essay "The Influence of Sound General Knowledge on Hinduism," 32:450.

49. Great Britain, *Parliamentary Papers, 1852-53*, Evidence of George Norton, 32:105.

6. THE FAILURE OF ENGLISH

1. Monier Monier-Williams, *Modern India and the Indians*, p. 161.

2. *Speech of Mr. George Norton*, p. 20.

3. *Speech of Mr. George Norton*, p. 21.

4. *Selections from Educational Records*, Vol. 1, *1859-1871*, p. 168.

5. "Minute by the Hon'ble Mr. Bethune, dated 23rd January 1851," *Selections from Educational Records*, vol. 1 *1840–1859*, J. A. Richey, ed. (Calcutta: Superintendent of Government Printing, 1922), p. 29.

6. Thomas B. Macaulay, "Thoughts on the Advancement of Academical Education in England," *Edinburgh Review* (1826), 43:334.

7. Joseph Hamburger, *Macaulay and the Whig Tradition*, p. 17.

8. B. B. Misra, *The Indian Middle Classes*, p. 174.

9. Great Britain, *Parliamentary Papers, 1854*, vol. 47. For an effective discussion of the economics of imperialism see Lance E. Davis and Robert A. Huttenback, *Mammon and the Pursuit of Empire*, in particular chapters 1, 8, and 9.

10. Middle-class Bengalis were often suspicious of the meaning of "practical knowledge" and occasionally interpreted it as a cover for British wiliness. George Campbell, seeking to promote land surveying in Bengal, decided that the Bengali physique first required improvement for the task, to which end he encouraged a regimen of gymnastic exercises. The *Murshedabad Patrika*, reporting on it, immediately saw a deep-laid, crafty design: "All the pupils at Berhampore College spend the afternoon in wrestling and other gymnastic exercises. They then return to their homes and eat a little, then lie down and sleep like dead people until morning, when they wake up with stiff limbs. The time for reading is wasted in this way. Chota Srijudto (Lieutenant-Governor) is not wanting in artfulness. He has devised many methods to 'eat the head' of the higher Bengali learning; though this may not be his design, this is the fruit which will result." *Indian Mirror*, May 1, 1873, quoted in John Murdoch, *Education in India*, p. 108.

11. Great Britain, *Parliamentary Papers, 1854*, 47:171.

12. Great Britain, *Parliamentary Papers, 1854*, 47:14.

13. Wood's dispatch confirmed the need for closer ties between education and government service, maintaining that "admission to places of instruction, which are maintained by the State, for the purpose of educating persons for special employments under government, might be made the rewards of industry and ability, and thus a practical encouragement to general education."

14. *Oriental Herald*, May 5, 1825, p. 512. Thomas Munro said in 1822: "Besides the necessity for having good native advisers in governing natives, it is necessary that we should pave the way for the introduction of the natives to some share in the government of their own country. It may be half a century before we are obliged to do so; but the system of government and of education which we have already established must some time or other work such a change on the people of this country, that it will be impossible to confine them to subordinate employments." Quoted in H. R. James, *Education and Statesmanship in India 1797–1910*, p. 143. Munro attached little value to the education of Indians unless they were given a greater share in the honors and emoluments of office. "Our present system of government by excluding all natives from power and trust and emolument is much more efficacious in depressing them than all our laws and school books can do in elevating their character. We are working against our own designs, and we can expect to make no progress while we work with a feeble instrument to improve and a powerful instrument to deteriorate. The improvement of the character of a people and the keeping them at the same time in the lowest state of dependency on foreign rulers to which they can be reduced by conquest, are matters quite incompatible with each other."

15. *Adam's Reports of the State of Education in Bengal and Bihar in 1833 and 1838*, p. 159.

16. *Report of the Indian Education Commission*, February 3, 1882, p. 298.

17. Great Britain, *Parliamentary Papers, 1831–32*, 9:393. For an analysis of Mill's writings about India in relation to his political theory, describing the contradictions in Mill's

theoretical and pragmatic positions, see R. J. Moore, "John Stuart Mill at the East India House," pp. 497–519. Also see Eileen P. Sullivan, "Liberalism and Imperialism", pp. 599–617 for an extended discussion of Mill's role in culture and empire building. Mill, argues Sullivan, anticipates the theories of J. A. Hobson decades later in the view that imperialism offered the means by which England would retain its economic world dominance. For other discussions of Mill and empire see also Jeane Clare Blaney, "Savages and Civilization," and Lynn Zastoupil, "John Stuart Mill and the British Empire."

18. James Mill, "On Education," pp. 58–59.

19. James Mill, "On Education," pp. 61–62.

20. Great Britain, *Parliamentary Papers, 1854*, 47:12.

21. "Of Government Education in Bengal," *Calcutta Review* (1845), 3:259.

22. "A Sketch of the Origin, Rise, and Progress of Hindoo College," *Calcutta Christian Observer* (June–December 1832), 1:118.

23. Great Britain, *Parliamentary Papers, 1831–32*, Minute of Sir John Malcolm, Governor of Bombay, 1828, 9:526.

24. Great Britain, *Parliamentary Papers, 1852–53*, 29:32.

25. "Oppression of Zemindars," *Calcutta Christian Observer* (1833), 2:213.

26. Great Britain, *Parliamentary Papers, 1852–53*, Evidence of J. C. Marshman, 32:119.

27. Great Britain, *Parliamentary Papers, 1831–32*, Minute by M. Elphinstone, December 13, 1823, 9:519.

28. William W. Hunter et al., *State Education for the People*, p. 8.

29. William W. Hunter et al., *State Education for the People*, p. 8. The deep despondency that spread among Muslims in the Lower Provinces enhanced the disaffection toward British rule. The government officer in charge of the chief Wahabi prosecution (continuing from 1865 to 1870) came to a conclusion supporting Hunter's: "I attribute the great hold which Wahabi doctrines have on the mass of the Muhammedan peasantry to our neglect of their education" (p. 8).

30. Educated at Haileybury, Mackenzie was sent out to India in 1808 as a member of the East India Company's Civil Service. In 1817 he became secretary to the government in the Territorial Department. In 1820 he was a member of the Supreme Council and in 1825 became president of the Council of the College of Fort William. He is best remembered for his work as a settlement officer, particularly for his association with the great Settlement Regulation VII of 1822.

31. Note, dated July 17, 1823, by Holt Mackenzie (Territorial Department, Revenue Consultations, dated July 17, 1823, no. 1), in Henry Sharp, ed., *Selections from Educational Records*, Part I, *1781–1839* (Calcutta: Superintendent of Government Printing, 1920), p. 59.

32. Great Britain, *Parliamentary Papers, 1854*, 47:12.

33. *Report of the Indian Education Commission*, p. 471.

34. *Report of the Indian Education Commission*, p. 222.

35. *Report of the Indian Education Commission*, p. 220.

36. Fred Clarke in *Education and Social Change*, p. 25, notes a parallel development in British education: "[The state] will have culture, but it will also have competence and power to discharge a skilled task responsibly. There is strength in such a position, Philistine enough to be a little contemptuous of a pure culture that can do nothing in particular, and cultivated enough to have a healthy distaste for mere efficiency without style or grace of action."

37. Monier Monier-Williams, *Modern India and the Indians*, p. 151. Monier Williams pointed out the vast gap in perceptions of British rule by the educated elite and the masses. "I have found all intelligent Natives generally satisfied with our rule. It is useless, however, to conceal from ourselves the existence of much discontent, chiefly among the men who have been educated above their stations" (p. 361).

38. Henry Sumner Maine, *Village Communities of the East and West*, p. 276.

39. Henry Sumner Maine, *Village Communities of the East and West*, p. 270. Similar complaints were made elsewhere in Indian newspapers. One article in the *Indian Mirror*, dated September 3, 1873, observed that rationalism had one meaning in England and other "civilized" countries and a totally different one in countries that had not reached the same level of intellectual development. "In India it denotes both intellectual infidelity and moral degradation. . . . It is not difficult to understand how in a state of society governed by a healthy public opinion and surrounded by a moral atmosphere surcharged with Christian influences men may apostasize intellectually without ruining their character. Though they do not acknowledge any moral or religious control and even audaciously and scoffingly ignore everything sacred, they are compelled to bow before the tribunal of human society, and submit to its decrees and injunctions which are all evidently based upon religion. Western civilization has been in a large measure moulded by Christianity; its discipline must therefore, be of an essentially moral character. . . . Such is not the case in our country [India]. Those who renounce Hinduism and become unbelievers wildly run away beyond the reach of all moral discipline and fall into unbridled vicious indulgence. We have hardly anything like educated public opinion outside the pale of Hindu society. Heterodoxy has no code of morals, no system of discipline. . . . Where there is no fear of social or religious discipline, the heart naturally runs into vicious excesses. Our unbelieving countrymen defy both God and their parents and also the opinion of their neighbours, and think that their infidelity is a sufficient plea for all their immoralities."

40. Henry Sumner Maine, *Village Communities of the East and West*, p. 290.

41. D. J. Palmer, *The Rise of English Studies*, p. 15.

42. Great Britain, *Parliamentary Papers, 1831–32*, Evidence of Captain T. Macan, 9:160.

43. *Speech of Mr. George Norton*, p. 10.

44. John Murdoch, *Letter to the Right Hon'ble Baron Napier*, p. 108.

45. Monier Monier-Williams, *Modern India and the Indians*, p. 154.

46. "Educational Conference, Simla," in *Lord Curzon in India: Being a Selection from His Speeches as Viceroy and Governor-General of India 1898–1905*, Sir Thomas Raleigh, ed. (London: Macmillan, 1906), p. 352.

47. "Vernacular Education for Bengal," *Calcutta Review*, (1854), 22:300.

48. *Athenaeum* (1835), p. 351.

49. Great Britain, *Parliamentary Papers, 1831–32*, Evidence of Charles Lushington, March 3, 1832, 29:111.

50. "Third Report of the Students' Literary and Scientific Society, Bombay 1852," *Calcutta Review* (1852), 18:vii.

51. One of the best known societies, the Bethune Society, was created in order to excite a "greater desire for intellectual pursuits among hitherto apathetic natives, of carrying on that education which an itching for speedily earning rupees causes to be so stinted at the public schools or colleges, and of giving ideas of literary excellence, mental power, and even national duties beyond what had hitherto existed." "Selections from the Bethune Society's Papers," *Calcutta Review*, (1855), 24:1.

52. "Selections from the Bethune Society's Papers," p. ii.

53. "Selections from the Bethune Society's Papers," p. iii.

54. "Baconian Philosophy Applicable to the Mental Regeneration of India," *Calcutta Christian Observer*, p. 125.

55. Great Britain, *Parliamentary Papers, 1831–32*, Minute of Francis Warden, 9:522.

56. Great Britain, *Parliamentary Papers, 1852–53*, Evidence of Charles Trevelyan, 32:156.

57. Great Britain, *Parliamentary Papers, 1831–32*, Report of A. D. Campbell, 1823, 9:503.

58. Great Britain, *Parliamentary Papers, 1831–32*, Minute by Mountstuart Elphinstone, December 13, 1823, 9:518.

59. Bureau of Education, India, *Selections from Educational Records,* Part 2, Minute of Colonel Jervis, February 24, 1847, p. 13.

60. David Lelyveld, *Aligarh's First Generation,* p. 84.

61. *Calcutta University Commission 1917–19: Evidence and Documents* (Calcutta: Superintendent of Government Printing, India, 1919), p. 392.

62. *Calcutta Gazette,* August 22, 1816. Many of the books sold in public auctions originally belonged to East India Company officials, who brought them to India as part of their cultural baggage. When they left India, they either auctioned them off or donated them to libraries. The pages of the *Calcutta Gazette* are full of their advertisements and are a good source for studying the development of reading interests in India.

63. James Johnstone, *On the Educational Policy in India,* p. 47. Morever, as Monier Monier-Williams pointed out, for the educated unemployed in England the colonies always provided a convenient outlet, whereas educated Indians obviously had no such alternative. *Modern India and the Indians,* p. 154.

64. John Murdoch, *Letter to the Right Hon'ble Baron Napier,* p. 13.

65. John Murdoch, *Letter to the Right Hon'ble Baron Napier,* p. 13.

66. *Speech of Mr. George Norton,* p. 9.

Select Bibliography

GOVERNMENT PRINTED SOURCES

Adam's Reports of the State of Education in Bengal and Bihar in 1835 and 1838. A. N. Basu, ed. Calcutta: University of Calcutta Press, 1941.

Bureau of Education. *Selections from Educational Records.* Part I: *1781–1839.* Henry Sharp, ed. Calcutta: Superintendent of Government Printing, 1920.

———. *Selections from Educational Records.* Part II: *1840–1859.* J. A. Richie, ed. Calcutta: Superintendent of Government Printing, 1922.

Calcutta University Commission. *Evidence and Documents, 1917–19.* Calcutta: Superintendent of Government Printing, 1919.

Education Commission. *Report by the Bengal Provincial Committee.* Calcutta: Superintendent of Government Printing, 1884.

———. *Report by the Bombay Provincial Committee,* vol 2. Calcutta: Superintendent of Government Printing, 1884.

———. *Report by the Central Provinces Provincial Committee.* Calcutta: Superintendent of Government Printing, 1884.

————. *Report by the Madras Provincial Committee.* Calcutta: Superintendent of Government Printing, 1884.
————. *Report by the North Western Provinces and Oudh Provincial Committee.* Calcutta: Superintendent of Government Printing, 1884.
Great Britain. *Parliamentary Debates.* Vol. 26: *1813.*
————. *Parliamentary Papers: Accounts and Papers,* Vol. 47: *1854.*
————. *Parliamentary Papers.* Vol. 8: *1831–32.*
————. *Parliamentary Papers (Reports from Committees): East India Company's Affairs.* Vol. 9: *1831–32.*
————. *Parliamentary Papers (Reports from Committees): East India Sixth Report.* Vol. 29: *1852–53.*
————. *Parliamentary Papers: Second Report from the Select Committee of the House of Lords, Together with the Minutes of Evidence.* Vol. 32: *1852–53.*
Report of the Indian Education Commission: February 3, 1882. Calcutta: Superintendent of Government Printing, 1883.
Selections from Educational Records of the Government of India. Vol. 1: *1859–1871,* with the reports of A. P. Howell. Delhi: National Archives of India, 1960.
Selections from Educational Records of the Government of India (New series). Vol. 1, part 1: *Development of Educational Service, 1859–1879.* J. P. Naik and Suresh Chandra Ghosh, eds. New Delhi: Zakir Husain Centre for Educational Studies, JNU, 1976.
Selections from the Records of the Government of Bombay: Education. Part 1: *1819–52.* R. V. Parulekar, ed. Bombay: Asia Publishing House, 1953.
Selections from Educational Records of the Government of Bombay, Part 2: *1815–40.* R. V. Parulekar, ed. Bombay: Asia Publishing House, 1955.
Selections from Educational Records of the Government of Bombay, Part 3: *1826–40.* R. V. Parulekar and C. L. Bakshi, eds. Bombay: Asia Publishing House, 1957.
Survey of Indigenous Education in the Province of Bombay, 1820–1830. R. V. Parulekar, ed. Bombay: Asia Publishing House, 1945.

CONTEMPORARY PERIODICALS AND NEWSPAPERS

Asiatic Journal.
Athenaeum.
Calcutta Christian Observer.
Calcutta Gazette.
Calcutta Monthly Journal.
Calcutta Review.
Edinburgh Review.
Madras Christian Instructor and Missionary Record.
Madras Missionary Register.
Oriental Herald.
Quarterly Review.
Westminster Review.

PAMPHLETS, TRACTS, AND OTHER PRIMARY SOURCES

Brief Narrative of the Baptist Mission in India, Including an Account of the Sacred Scriptures into Various Languages of the East. London: E. W. Morris, 1813.

Carey, Eustace, ed. *Memoirs of William Carey, D.D.* Boston: Gould, Kendall, and Lincoln, 1836.

Day, Lal Behari. *Recollections of Alexander Duff, D.D. and the Mission College Founded in Calcutta.* London: T. Nelsen, 1879.

Duff, Alexander. *A Vindication of the Church of Scotland's India Missions: An Address Before the General Assembly of the Church, May 24, 1837.* Edinburgh: John Johnstone, 1837.

Duff, Alexander. *India and India Missions.* Edinburgh: John Johnstone, 1839.

Duff, Alexander. *Letters to Lord Auckland on the Subject of Native Education.* Calcutta: Baptist Mission Press, 1841.

Duff, Alexander. *New Era of the English Language and English Literature in India.* Edinburgh: John Johnstone, 1837.

Duff, Alexander. *The Indian Rebellion: Its Causes and Results.* London: James Nisbet, 1858.

Elliott, H. M. and John Dowson. *The History of India as Told by Its Own Historians.* 8 vols. 1867–77. Reprint. Allahabad: Kitab Mahal, 1964.

Elphinstone, Mountstuart. *The History of India: The Hindu and Mahometan Periods.* London: John Murray, 1841.

Farrar, F. W., ed. *Essays on a Liberal Education.* London: Macmillan, 1867.

Gogerly, George. *The Pioneer: A Narrative of the Early Christian Bengal Missions (Chiefly Relating to the Operations of the London Missionary Society).* London: John Snow, 1871.

Holland, Henry S., ed. *The Call of Empire and Other Papers.* Westminster: Society for the Propagation of the Gospel, 1917.

Hossein, Syed Ameer. *Mohammedan Education in Bengal.* Calcutta: G. C. Bose, 1880.

Hunter, William W. *Address to the Convocation of Calcutta University.* Calcutta: Superintendent of Government Printing, 1887.

Hunter, William W. *The Indian Empire: Its Peoples, History, and Products,* 2d ed., London: Trübner, 1886; 3d ed., New York: AMS Press, 1966.

Hunter, William W. et al. *State Education for the People.* London: George Routledge, 1890.

James, H. R. *Education and Statesmanship in India 1797–1910.* London: Longmans, Green, 1917.

Johnstone, James. *Abstract and Analysis of the Report of the Indian Education Commission.* London: Hamilton, Adams, 1884.

Macaulay, Thomas Babington. *Speeches, with the Minute on Indian Education.* G. M. Young, ed. London: Oxford University Press, 1935.

Macleod, Norman. *Address on Christian Missions to India.* Madras: Scottish Press, 1868.

Maine, Henry Sumner. *Village Communities of the East and West, and Other Lectures, Addresses, and Essays.* New York: Holt, 1880.

Mayhew, Arthur. *Christianity and the Government of India.* London: Faber and Gwyer, 1927.

Mayhew, Arthur. *Education of India.* London: Faber and Gwyer, 1926.

Mill, James. *History of British India.* With Notes by Horace Hayman Wilson. 6 vols. 1817. Reprint. London: Piper, Stephinson and Spence, 1858.

Mill, James. "On Education." In *James Mill on Education.* W. H. Burston, ed. Cambridge: Cambridge University Press, 1969.

Miller, William. *Indian Missions, and How to View Them.* Edinburgh: James Thin, 1878.

Monier-Williams, Monier. *Modern India and the Indians.* London: Trubner, 1878.

Muir, Ramsay. *The Making of British India 1756–1858.* Manchester: University Press, 1923.

Murdoch, John. *Education in India: Letter to His Excellency the Most Honourable Marquis of Ripon, Viceroy and Governor-General of India.* Mardras: S.C.K.S. Press, Vepery, 1881.

190   Select Bibliography

Murdoch, John. *Letter to the Right Hon'ble Baron Napier on Government and University Education in India*. Madras: Caleb Foster, 1872.

Opinions of the Hon. Mountstuart Elphinstone upon Some of the Leading Questions Connected with the Government of India Examined and Compared with Those of the Late Sir T. Munro and Sir John Malcolm. London: Farbury, Allen, 1831.

Papers Referring to the Educational Operations of the Church Missionary Society in North India. London: Church Missionary House, 1864.

Raleigh, Thomas, ed. *Lord Curzon in India: Being a Selection from His Speeches as Viceroy and Governor-General of India 1898–1905*. London: Macmillan, 1906.

Reports and Documents on the Indian Mission: Prepared for the Use of the Committee of the Baptist Missionary Society. London: Baptist Mission House, 1872.

Satthianadhan, S. *History of Education in the Madras Presidency*. Madras: Srinivasa, Varadachari, 1894.

Selected Works of Raja Rammohun Roy. Delhi: Publications Division, Government of India, 1977.

Selections from the Calcutta Gazettes, vol. 2. 1789. Reprint. Calcutta: Military Orphan Press, 1865.

Smith, Adam. *The Theory of Moral Sentiments: An Essay Towards an Analysis of the Principles by Which Men Naturally Judge Concerning the Conduct and Character, First of Their Neighbours, and Afterwards of Themselves*, 1759. Reprint. London: Henry G. Bohn, 1853.

Speech of Mr. George Norton at the 14th Anniversary Meeting of the Patcheapah Moodelliar's Institution in Madras, Thursday, April 23, 1857. London: James Ridgway, 1857.

Strachey, John. *India: Its Administration and Progress*. London: Macmillan, 1903.

The Bible in India. Ext. 40th Report of the Calcutta Auxiliary Bible Society. London: W. H. Dalton, 1853.

Thornton, Edward. *India: Its State and Prospects*. London: Parbury, Allen, 1835.

Trevelyan, Charles E. *Letters of Indophilus to "The Times."* 3d ed. London: Longman, Brown, Green, Longmans and Roberts, 1858.

Trevelyan, Charles E. *On the Education of the People of India*. London: Longman, Orme, Brown, Green and Longmans, 1838.

Underhill, B. *Papers on Baptist Missions: Minutes and Reports of a Conference of the Baptist Missions of the Northwest Provinces, 1855*. Calcutta: Baptist Mission Press, 1856.

Wheeler, J. Talboys. *The History of India from the Earliest Ages*. London: Trübner, 1869. Reprint. Delhi: Cosmo Publications, 1922.

SECONDARY WORKS

Altbach, Philip and Gail Kelly, eds. *Education and the Colonial Experience*. 2d rev. ed. New Brunswick, N.J.: Transaction Books, 1984.

Altick, Richard. *The English Common Reader: A Social History of the Mass Reading Public 1800–1900*. Chicago: University of Chicago Press, 1957.

Appadurai, Arjun. *Worship and Conflict Under Colonial Rule: A South Indian Case*. Cambridge: Cambridge University Press, 1981.

Apple, Michael. *Ideology and Curriculum*. London: Routledge and Kegan Paul, 1979.

Bacon, Alan. "Attempts to Introduce a School of English Literature at Oxford: The National Debate of 1886 and 1887." *History of Education* (1980), 9:303–313.

Bacon, Alan. "English Literature Becomes a University Subject: King's College, London, as Pioneer." *Victorian Studies* (1986), 29(4):591–612.

Baldick, Chris. *The Social Mission of English Criticism 1848-1932*. Oxford: Clarendon Press, 1983.

Ballhatchet, Kenneth A. "The Home Government and Bentinck's Educational Policy." *Cambridge Historical Journal* (1951), 10(2):224-229.

Ballhatchet, Kenneth. "Missionaries, Empire, and Society: The Jesuit Mission in Calcutta 1834-46." *Journal of Imperial and Commonwealth History* (1978), 7(1):18-34.

Ballhatchet, Kenneth. *Race, Sex, and Class under the Raj: Imperial Attitudes and Policies and Their Critics, 1793-1905*. New York: St. Martin's Press, 1980.

Barker, Francis, Peter Hulme, Margaret Iversen, and Diana Loxley. *Literature, Politics and Theory: Papers from the Essex Conference 1976-84*. London: Methuen, 1986.

Basu, Aparna. *The Growth of Education and Political Development in India 1898-1920*. Delhi: Oxford University Press, 1974.

Basu, B. D. *History of Education under the Rule of the East India Company*. Calcutta: Modern Review Office, 1922.

Batsleer, Janet, Tony Davies, Rebecca O'Rourke, and Chris Weedon, eds. *Rewriting English: Cultural Politics of Gender and Class*. London: Methuen, 1985.

Bearce, George. *British Attitudes to India 1784-1858*. Oxford: Oxford University Press, 1924.

Bhabha, Homi K. "Signs Taken for Wonders: Questions of Ambivalence and Authority under a Tree Outside Delhi, May 1817." *Critical Inquiry* (1985), 12(1):144-165.

Bhattacharya, K. S. "Social and Political Thinking of Young Bengal." *Journal of Indian History* (1979), 57(1):129-161.

Blaney, Jeanne Clare. "Savages and Civilization: References to Non-Western Societies in the Theories of John Locke and John Stuart Mill." Ph.D. dissertation, Princeton University, 1983.

Bolgar, R. R. "From Humanism to the Humanities." *Twentieth Century Studies* (1973), 9:8-21.

Boman-Behram, B. K. *Educational Controversies of India: The Cultural Conquest of India under British Imperialism*. Bombay: Taraporevala, 1946.

Bourdieu, Pierre. *Distinction: A Social Critique of the Judgement of Taste*. Cambridge, Mass.: Harvard University Press, 1984.

Bourdieu, Pierre and Jean-Claude Passeron. *Reproduction in Education, Culture and Society*. Richard Nice, trans. Beverly Hills: Sage Publications, 1977.

Brantlinger, Patrick. *Rule of Darkness: British Literature and Imperialism, 1830-1914*. Ithaca: Cornell University Press, 1988.

Bryant, G. J. "Scots in India in the 18th Century." *Scottish Historical Review* (1985), 64(1):22-41.

Bryant, Gerald. "Officers of the East India's Army in the Days of Clive and Hastings." *Journal of Imperial and Commonwealth History* (1978), 6(3):203-227.

Burrow, J. W. "The English Tradition of Liberal Education." *History of Education Quarterly* (1980), 20(2):247-253.

Cain, P. J. and A. G. Hopkins. "Gentlemanly Capitalism and British Expansion Overseas: 1. The Old Colonial System, 1688-1850." *Economic History Review* (1986), 39(4):501-525.

Carnoy, Martin. *Education as Cultural Imperialism*. New York: David McKay, 1974.

Carnoy, Martin. "The Dialectic of Education: An Alternative Approach to Education and Social Change in Developing Countries." In E. B. Gumbert, ed., *Expressions of Power in Education*. Stanford: Stanford University Press, 1984.

Carrol, Lucy. "Colonial Perceptions of Indian Society and the Emergence of Caste(s) Associations." *Journal of Asian Studies* (1978) 37(2):233-250.

Chamberlin, J. E. "An Anatomy of Cultural Melancholy." *Journal of the History of Ideas* (1981), 42(4):691–705.

Chatterjee, Kalyan. *English Education: Issues and Opinions.* Delhi: Macmillan, 1976.

Chatterjee, Partha. *Nationalist Thought and the Colonial World: A Derivative Discourse.* Delhi: Oxford University Press, 1986.

Chowdhury, Kabir. "Foreign Literatures: Their Influence on a National Literature." *Dhaka University Studies,* part A. (1980), 32:115–23.

Clarke, Fred. *Education and Social Change: An English Interpretation.* London: Sheldon Press, 1940.

Collini, Stefan. "The Idea of 'Character' in Victorian Political Thought." *Transactions of the Royal Historical Society* (1985), 35:29–50.

Conant, Martha. *The Oriental Tale in England in the Eighteenth Century.* New York: Columbia University Press, 1908.

Conrad, Peter. "The Englishness of English Literature." *Daedalus* (1983), 112(1):157–173.

Court, Franklin. "Adam Smith and the Teaching of English Literature." *History of Education Quarterly* (1985), 25(3):325–340.

Court, Franklin. "The Social and Historical Significance of the First English Literature Professorship in England." *Publications of the Modern Language Association of America* (October 1988), 103(5):796–807.

Crangle, John N. "English Nationalism and British Imperialism in the Age of Gladstone and Disraeli, 1868–1880." *Quarterly Review of Historical Studies* (1981–1982), 21(4):4–12.

Crawford, S. Cromwell. *Ram Mohun Roy: Social, Political and Religious Reform in 19th Century India.* New York: Paragon House Publishers, 1987.

Cross, Charles Wallace, Jr. "Selection and Training of the Candidates for the Indian Civil Service: 1870–80." Ph.D. dissertation, Vanderbilt University, 1983.

Cruse, Amy. *The Victorians and Their Books.* London: George Allen and Unwin, 1935.

Davis, Lance E. and Robert A. Huttenback. *Mammon and the Pursuit of Empire: The Political Economy of British Imperialism 1860–1912.* New York: Cambridge University Press, 1987.

De Schweinitz, Karl, Jr. *The Rise and Fall of British India: Imperialism as Inequality.* London: Methuen, 1983.

Eagleton, Terry. *Criticism and Ideology.* London: Verso Editions, 1978.

Eagleton, Terry. *Literary Theory: An Introduction.* Minneapolis: University of Minnesota Press, 1983.

Embree, Ainslie T. *Charles Grant and British Rule in India.* New York: Columbia University Press, 1962.

Fanon, Frantz. *Black Skin, White Masks.* Charles Lam Markmann, trans. New York: Grove Press, 1967.

Fanon, Frantz. *The Wretched of the Earth.* Constance Farrington, trans. New York: Grove Press, 1968.

Foreman, H. "Some 17th Century Baptist Educational Textbooks." *Baptist Quarterly* (1983), 30(3):112–124.

Freire, Paolo. *Education for Critical Consciousness.* Translation of Educção como pratica da liberdade and of Extensión y communicación. New York: Herder and Herder, 1973.

Freire, Paolo. *Pedagogy of the Oppressed.* Myra Bergman Ramos, trans. New York: Seabury Press, 1970.

Frykenberg, Robert E. "Elite Groups in a South Indian District:1788–1858." *Indo-British Review* (1983), 10(1):42–57.

Frykenberg, Robert Eric. "Modern Education in South India, 1784–1854: Its Roots and

Its Role as a Vehicle of Integration under Company Raj." *American Historical Review* (1986), 91 (1):37–65.

Gabriel, Ruth. "Learned Communities and British Educational Experiments in North India 1780–1830." Ph. D. diss., University of Virginia, 1979.

Glucklich, Ariel. "Conservative Hindu Response to Social Legislation in Nineteenth Century India." *Journal of Asian History* (1986), 20(1):33–53.

Golant, W. "Imperialism and India." *History* (1981), 66(216):61–68.

Gooneratne, M. Y. *English Literature in Ceylon 1815–1878.* Dehiwala, Ceylon: Tisara Press, 1968.

Gossman, Lionel. "Literature and Education." *New Literary History* (Winter 1982), 13(2):341–71.

Grafton, Anthony and Lisa Jardine. *From Humanism to the Humanities: Education and the Liberal Arts in 15th and 16th Century Europe.* Cambridge, Mass.: Harvard University Press, 1986.

Grampp, William D. "How Britain Turned to Free Trade." *Business History Review* (1987), 61(1):86–112.

Graff, Gerald. *Professing Literature: An Institutional History.* Chicago: University of Chicago Press, 1987.

Green, Martin. *Dreams of Adventure, Deeds of Empire.* New York: Basic Books, 1979.

Hagen, James Ray. "Indigenous Society, the Political Economy, and Colonial Education in Patna District: A History of Social Change from 1811 to 1951 in Gangetic North India." Ph.D. dissertation, University of Virginia. 1981.

Halstead, John P. *The Second British Empire: Trade, Philanthropy, and Good Government 1820–90.* Contributions in Comparative Colonial Studies, no. 14. Westport, Conn.: Greenwood, 1983.

Hamburger, Joseph. *Macaulay and the Whig Tradition.* Chicago: University of Chicago Press, 1976.

Hobsbawm, Eric and Terence O. Ranger, eds. *The Invention of Tradition.* Past and Present Publications. New York: Cambridge University Press, 1983.

Hussain, Mohammed Delwar. "The Role of Providence and the Writing of History: John Clark Marshman (1794–1877): A Case Study." *Dhaka University Studies* part A (1984), (41):64–69.

Hutchins, Francis. *Illusion of Permanence: British Imperialism in India.* Princeton: Princeton University Press, 1967.

Ingham, Kenneth. *Reformers in India 1793–1833.* Cambridge: Cambridge University Press, 1956.

Iyer, Raghavan. "Utilitarianism and Empire in India." In Thomas Metcalf, ed., *Modern India: An Interpretive Anthology.* London: Macmillan, 1971.

Jeffrey, Keith. "The Eastern Arc of Empire: A Strategic View, 1850–1950." *Journal of Strategic Studies* (1982), 5(4):531–545.

Johnson, Richard. "Educational Policy and Social Control in Early Victorian England." *Past and Present* (1970), 49:96–119.

Johnson, W. Ross. *Great Britain, Great Empire: An Evaluation of the British Imperial Experience.* New York: University of Queensland Press, 1981.

Jones, Gareth Stedman. "Class Expression versus Social Control." In Stanley Cohen and Andrew Scull, eds., *Social Control and the State.* New York: St. Martin's Press, 1983.

Kopf, David. *British Orientalism and the Bengal Renaissance: The Dynamics of Indian Modernization 1773–1835.* Berkeley: University of California Press, 1969.

Laird, M. A. *Missionaries and Education in Bengal 1793–1837.* Oxford: Clarendon Press, 1972.

Law, N. N. *Promotion of Learning in India by Early European Settlers.* London: Longmans, Green, 1915.

Lelyveld, David. *Aligarh's First Generation: Muslim Solidarity in British India.* Princeton: Princeton University Press, 1978.

Lewis, Donald M. *Lighten Their Darkness: The Evangelical Mission to Working-Class London, 1828–1860.* Contributions to the Study of Religion, no. 19. Westport, Conn.: Greenwood Press, 1986.

Lukes, Steven, ed. *Power.* New York: New York University Press, 1986.

Malik, Yogendra, ed. *South Asian Intellectuals and Social Change: The Role of Vernacular-Speaking Intelligentsia.* New Delhi: New Heritage Publishers, 1982.

Manickam, Sundaraj. "Missionary Attitudes Towards Observance of Caste in the Churches of Tamil Nad, 1606–1850." *Quarterly Review of Historical Studies.* (1983), 22(4):53–66.

Manickam, S. "Hindu Reaction of the Methodist Missionary Actives in the Negapatam and Trichopoly District, 1870–1920." *Journal of Indian History* (1981), 59(1–3):315–333.

Marsh, Peter, ed. *The Conscience of the Victorian State.* Syracuse: Syracuse University Press, 1979.

McCabe, Colin. "Towards a Modern Trivium—English Studies Today." *Critical Quarterly* (1984), 26(1–2):69–82.

McCully, Bruce. *English Education and the Origins of Indian Nationalism.* New York: Columbia University Press, 1942.

McDonald, Ellen. "English Education and Social Reform in Late Nineteenth Century Bombay: A Case Study of the Transmission of a Cultural Ideal." *Journal of Asian Studies* (1965–1966), 5:453–470.

McGuire, John. *The Making of a Colonial Mind: A Quantitative Study of the Bhadralok in Calcutta, 1857–1885.* Canberra: Australian National University Press, 1983.

McMinn, Ney, J. R. Hainds, and James McNab McCrimmon, eds. *Bibliography of the Published Writings of John Stuart Mill.* Evanston, Ill.: Northwestern University Press, 1945.

Memmi, Albert. *The Colonizer and the Colonized.* Howard Greenfield, trans. Boston: Beacon Press, 1967.

Mendilow, Jonathan. "Past, Future, and Present Perfect: Three Tenses of the British Idea of Empire." *Australian Journal of Politics and History* (1984), 30(2):209–223.

Metcalf, Thomas. "The Indian Empire: 1858–1900: Its Structures and Processes under the British." *Indo-British Review* (1983), 10 (1):37–41.

Misra, B. B. *The Central Administration of the East India Company 1773–1834.* Manchester: Manchester University Press, 1959.

Misra, B. B. *The Indian Middle Classes: Their Growth in Modern Times.* London: Oxford University Press, 1961.

Mitter, Partha. *Much Maligned Monsters: A History of European Reactions to Indian Art.* Oxford: Oxford University Press, 1978.

Moore, R. J. "John Stuart Mill at the East India House." *Historical Studies* (1983), 20(81):497–519.

Morgan, I. "Theories of Imperialism: A Bibliographical Sketch." *Journal of Area Studies* (1982), (6):18–22.

Mukherjee, S. N. *Sir William Jones: A Study in Eighteenth-Century British Attitudes to India.* Cambridge: Cambridge University Press,

Nagarajan, S. and S. Viswanathan, eds. *Shakespeare in India.* Delhi: Oxford University Press, 1987.

Naik, J. V. "An Early Appraisal of British Colonial Policy." *Journal of the University of Bombay* (1975–1976), 44–45 (80-¥81):243–270.

Nandy, Ashis. *The Intimate Enemy: Loss and Recovery of Self under Colonialism.* Delhi: Oxford University Press, 1983.

Newsome, David. *Godliness and Good Learning: Four Studies of a Victorian Ideal.* London: John Murray, 1961.

Nijjar, Bakshish Singh. "Education and Literature in the Punjab during the 18th Century." *Journal of Indian History* (1980), 58 (1–3):121–137.

Nurullah, Syed and J. P. Naik. *A History of Education in India during the British Period.* 2d ed., revised, Bombay: Macmillan, 1951.

Palit, Chittrabrata. "Young Bengal: The Quest for an Identity (1830–1876)." *Quarterly Review of Historical Studies* (1983), 22(4):23–29.

Palmer, D. J. *The Rise of English Studies.* London: Oxford University Press, 1965.

Parry, Benita. "Problems in Current Theories of Colonial Discourse." *Oxford Literary Review* (1987), 9(1–2):27–58

Qaisar, Ahsan Jan. *The Indian Response to European Technology and Culture (1498–1707).* New York: Oxford University Press, 1982.

Raychaudhuri, Tapan. *Europe Reconsidered: Perceptions of the West in Nineteenth-Century Bengal.* Oxford: Oxford University Press, 1988.

Ridley, Hugh. *Images of Imperial Rule.* New York: St. Martin's Press, 1983.

Robb, Peter. "British Rule and Indian 'Improvement.' " *Economic Historical Review* (1981), 34(4):507–523.

Rocher, Rosane. *Orientalism, Poetry, and the Millennium: The Checkerd Life of Nathaniel Brassey Halhed, 1751–1830.* Columbia, Mo.: South Asian Books, 1983.

Ross, Robert, ed. *Racism and Colonialism: Essays on Ideology and Social Structure.* Comparative Studies in Overseas History, no. 4. The Hague: Leiden University Press, 1982.

Rosselli, John. "The Self-Image of Effeteness: Physical Education and Nationalism in 19th Century Bengal." *Past and Present* (1980), 86:121–148.

Said, Edward W. *Beginnings: Intention and Method.* 1975; rpt. New York: Columbia University Press, 1985.

Said, Edward W. *Orientalism.* New York: Pantheon Books, 1978.

Said, Edward W. *The World, the Text, and the Critic.* Cambridge, Mass.: Harvard University Press, 1983.

Shahidullah, Kazi. "Missionaries and the Beginnings of the New Education in Early 19th Century Bengal." *Dhaka University Studies,* Part A. (1984), 41:70–76.

Sinha, B. K. "The Growth of Primary Education in Bihar during the Second Half of the Nineteenth Century." *Quarterly Review of Historical Studies* (1984), 24(1):41–48.

Sinha, D. P. *The Educational Policy of the East India Company in Bengal to 1854.* Calcutta: Punthi Pustak, 1964.

Sirkin, Gerald and Natalie Robinson Sirkin. "The Battle of Indian Education: Macaulay's Opening Salvo Newly Discovered." *Victorian Studies* (1971), 14(4):407–428.

Spear, Percival. "Bentinck and Education." *Cambridge Historical Journal* (1938), 6(1):78–101.

Stieg, Margaret F. "Indian Romances: Tracts for the Times." *Journal of Popular Culture* (1985), 18(14):2–15.

Stokes, Eric S. "Bureaucracy and Ideology: Britain and India in the 19th Century." *Transactions of the Royal Historical Society* (1980), (30):131–156.

Stokes, Eric. *The English Utilitarians and India.* Oxford: Oxford University Press, 1959.

Sullivan, Eileen P. "Liberalism and Imperialism: John Stuart Mill's Defense of the British Empire." *Journal of the History of Ideas* (1983), 44(4):599–617.

Symonds, Richard. *Oxford and Empire: The Last Lost Cause?* London: Macmillan, 1986.

Vashishta, G. S. "Apprehension of Anti-British Combination in North India in 1824–25." *Quarterly Review of Historical Studies* (1978–1979), 18(1):43–48.

Vasudevan, C. P. A. "The Nature of the European Expansion," part 3. *Journal of Indian History* (1978), 56(1):119–128.

Walsh, Judith. *Growing Up in British India: Indian Autobiographies on Childhood and Education under the Raj.* New York: Holmes and Meier, 1983.

Waterman, A. M. C. "The Ideological Alliance of Political Economy and Christian Theology, 1798–1833." *Journal of Ecclesiastical History* (1983), 34(2):231–244.

Watson, I. Bruce. "Fortifications and the Idea of Force in Early English East India Company Relations with India." *Past and Present* (1980), (88):70–87.

Wickwire, Franklin, and Mary Wickwire. *Cornwallis: The Imperial Years.* Chapel Hill: University of North Carolina Press, 1980.

Widdowson, Peter, ed. *Re-reading English.* London: Methuen, 1982.

Williams, C. P. " 'Not Quite Gentlemen': An Examination of 'Middling Class' Protestant Missionaries from Britain c. 1850–1900." *Journal of Ecclesiastical History* (1980), 31(3):301–315.

Williams, Raymond. "Base and Superstructure in Marxist Cultural Analysis." *New Left Review* (1973), 82:3–16.

Williams, Raymond. *Culture and Society 1780–1950.* 1958; rpt. New York: Columbia University Press, 1983.

Williams, Raymond. *The Long Revolution.* New York: Columbia University Press, 1961.

Wilt, Judith. "The Imperial Mouth: Imperialism, the Gothic and Science Fiction." *Journal of Popular Culture* (1981), 14(4):618–628.

Wurgaft, Lewis D. "Another Look at Prospero and Caliban: Magic and Magical Thinking in British India." *Psychohistory Review* (1977), 6(1):2–26.

———. "History as Mythology: The 'Punjab Style' in British India." *Psychohistory Review* (1978), 6(4):33–44.

———. *The Imperial Imagination: Magic and Myth in Kipling's India.* Middletown, Conn.: Wesleyan University Press, 1983.

Young, Michael F. D., ed. *Knowledge and Control: Essays in the Sociology of Education.* London: Collier-Macmillan, 1971.

Zastoupil, Lynn Barry. "John Stuart Mill and the British Empire: An Intellectual Biography." Ph.D. diss., University of Minnesota, 1985.

Index